现代实用商务英语丛书
Modern Practical Business English

丛书主编 \ 张立玉

国际贸易结算

International Trade Payment

第三版

主 编 何康民 易 静 于 建
副主编 杨 静 严 慧 樊金琪

WUHAN UNIVERSITY PRESS
武汉大学出版社

图书在版编目（CIP）数据

国际贸易结算 = International Trade Payment/何康民,易静,于建主编. —3 版.
—武汉：武汉大学出版社,2017.1
现代实用商务英语丛书
ISBN 978-7-307-19198-3

Ⅰ.国… Ⅱ.①何… ②易… ③于… Ⅲ.国际贸易—国际结算—英
语 Ⅳ.F830.73

中国版本图书馆 CIP 数据核字（2016）第 326900 号

责任编辑:谢群英 责任校对:李孟潇 版式设计:韩闻锦

出版发行:**武汉大学出版社** （430072 武昌 珞珈山）
（电子邮件:cbs22@whu.edu.cn 网址:www.wdp.com.cn）
印刷:湖北金海印务有限公司
开本:787×1092 1/16 印张:15.25 字数:363 千字 插页:1
版次:2004 年 2 月第 1 版 2010 年 9 月第 2 版
2017 年 1 月第 3 版 2017 年 1 月第 3 版第 1 次印刷
ISBN 978-7-307-19198-3 定价:30.00 元

前　　言

自中国加入 WTO 以来，"遵守国际游戏规则，按国际惯例办事"已成为各级政府和工商企业的共识。特别是近几年来，国外著名跨国集团公司、金融机构、工商企业纷纷抢滩中国市场，在中国设立分支机构、分公司及合资企业，引发了新一轮对高素质复合型外经贸人才的需求：要求他们具备良好的英语听、说、读、写、译及对外交流、沟通能力，同时熟知外经贸专业知识及国际贸易惯例。所有这些对高等院校在人才培养方面提出了新的挑战，如何充分利用现有教育资源，培养大批社会急需的复合型跨境电商人才是我们所面临的重大研究课题。

为了实现高等教育培养目标，大力推行专业课程双语教学法，培养高素质复合型跨境电商专业人才，我们在《国际贸易结算》第二版的基础上，重新编写了《国际贸易结算（第三版）》。本书重点介绍有关国际贸易结算方面的基本理论、基本知识和基本技能，以及相关的国际贸易惯例和规则。在引进消化国外原版教材的基础上，进行了本土化移植，使之既保留了相关专业内容的原汁原味，又符合中国的具体国情，并力争做到专业语言与国际接轨。

由于国际贸易结算是一门实践性、操作性极强的应用性课程，本书在编写过程中，一方面力争使语言精练、通俗易懂，体系完整，知识系统全面，另一方面尽可能用图示方法辅以文字说明来准确阐明国际贸易结算的操作程序，以加深和巩固学习者的理解及记忆。

因编写人员能力有限，难免在编写中出现一些疏漏或错讹之处，欢迎读者予以批评指正。

编者

武汉晴川学院

2016 年 12 月于武汉

Table of Contents

Chapter 1 — Overview of International Settlement

This chapter mainly introduces the concept of International Trade Payment and key issues in international trade payment. According to the information mentioned below, it is self-evident that without bank's participation, modern international trade payment system would not exist any more.

1. Definition and Implications of International Trade Payment

International Trade Payment refers to studying the system of effectively identifying or supervising performance of both the buyer and the seller with best possible low payment transaction costs and their practice.

From the definition mentioned above, it is obvious that the objects researched here is concerned with both the buyer and the seller.

In the process of international trade, at the heart of every business transaction is the buyer and the seller. Both parties have one thing in common; to profit from the transaction and to expose themselves to the least risk possible. All transactions, no matter how innocent, expose buyers and sellers to risk.

Fundamentally, the concern of the buyer and the seller are at the same in both domestic and international trade. The buyer wishes to get the goods ordered and paid for, and the seller wishes to get paid for the goods shipped. International trade, however, add a layer of uncertainty and risk for the buyer and the seller that does not exist in purely domestic trade because the buyer and the seller are separated by long distances, differences in culture and business tradition, different government and economic systems, different currencies, and different banking and legal systems.

The essence of both the buyer and the seller's concerns is whether the counterpart fulfills the contract. The motivation for the seller to supply and ship the goods is to obtain money. Meanwhile, the buyer must exchange money for the goods he orders. It is obvious that the concern of both sides is eventually about money. Therefore, payment becomes the touchstone for checking performance sincerity of the two parties.

If one party of international trade insists that the counterpart's fulfilling of the contract be the prerequisite of his performance, the transaction would be aborted. A cautious buyer would not give all the money to the seller, whom he never met, before shipment. The buyer most likely exits from the transaction if the seller refuses to conclude a contract without such condition. Hence, from the beginning of trade negotiation and in the process of dividing trade surplus, they constantly have contest of strength and balance interest of each other. On a win-win basis, firstly, effective methods to supervise and even force counterpart to fulfill his obligation have to be defined. Secondly, one among the methods with the lowest supervision cost should be found out. According to the modern supply chain concept, both parties in the transaction will care the supervision costs, they have common interest within a supply chain. If the supervision cost is so high as or even higher than the trade surplus, the supervision method would be seldom used or not used.

The two parties must weigh and balance the effectiveness and costs of supervision, so as to smoothly obtain relative benefit from international trade. Therefore, payment, as the most important stage in international trade seems to be a funds transfer, a clearance of debit and credit, actually it is to seek the methods being able to supervise the performance of both sides not only effectively but also efficiently.

In international trade practice, due to the involvement of banks for a long time, people have created many effective methods which have been feasible to examine fulfillment of the two parties. Commonly used payment systems in today's international society, namely, payment in advance, collections, letter of credit, and open account. Factoring as well as Forfaiting are widely used in international trade practice. Under each payment system, effectiveness and efficiency in respect of supervising or impelling counterpart's performance have been researched. As a practice, the common usage of each system, particularly in China, is well-known by everyone. Therefore, international trade payment is not only a theory, but a practice as well.

1. 1　Key Issues in International Payment

There are several broad issues that affect what payment method will ultimately be used in a specific international trade. Every participant in the transaction must carefully consider these issues, though they will affect each differently and to a different degree.

Even after these broader issues are resolved, questions will continue to be raised throughout the transaction. Therefore, careful consideration of these issues can make a transaction go smoother, keep costs to a minimum, and ensure timely and efficient delivery and distribution of goods.

1. 1. 1　Who Bears the Credit Risk?

In almost all business transactions the buyer would prefer to obtain easy, extended, and inexpensive credit terms. Credit gives the commercial buyer the opportunity to resell the goods before having to pay for them. In many instances, the buyer will have a market for goods but not possess sufficient working capital to make an outright purchase and payment prior to their resale. Credit makes many such transactions possible.

At the same time, the seller has a different set of priorities. Having paid for product development, raw materials, components parts, labor, and overhead, the seller needs to get his investment back. The seller may not know the buyer or may not trust that the buyer is financially stable enough to make payment at a future date. International transactions are not as stable, secure, transparent, or reliable as domestic transactions and many things can happen between the time of the sales and the expected time of payment. For these and other reasons, the seller will always prefer to be paid immediately; either at delivery or even prior to delivery. In a word, the buyer or importer prefers that the seller bear the credit risk and wants to make certain that the receives the goods once he has paid, while the seller or exporter prefers that the buyer bear the credit risk and wants to make certain he receives payment for goods shipped.

1.1.2　What Will Be the Transaction Costs of Payment?

What do the transactions costs of payment mean? First, the costs do not contain the expenses in respect of production, transportation and insurance. Second, the costs must be associated with the choice of payment methods. For example, using one method probably brings about increase of one party's financial cost or increase of banking charges, and so on. Actually, payment transaction costs mean total costs by using a certain payment method, including financial cost, fund transfer expense, default risk of counterpart and exit risk of counterpart. The explanations of above mentioned costs are as follows.

(1) Financial cost means extra financial expenses for fulfilling the contract do to different payment timing, or the opportunity cost of using their own working capital. If timing of payment is to be classified as date of conclusion, date of shipment, date of unloading and date of clearance, financial cost borne by the importer is decreased in above order, while it is increased to the exporter.

(2) Fund transfer expense means the expense used to transfer the proceeds from importer to exporter. For example, in Middle Ages, the expense to make payment could be the freight for transporting gold. In modern economic society, funds transfer are mostly handled by banks and banks will charge for it. But the expense charged differs from one payment method to the others, because banks undertake varying obligation and responsibility therefore. Comparatively, banks expense is increased by the order of remittance, collections, letter of credit, letters of guarantee, Factoring and Forfaiting.

(3) Default risk of counterpart means the possibility of default of the other side after performance of one side, in other words, it means the space for the counterpart to be in breach of contract under certain payment method. Reasons of the counterpart's default could be

commercial, could be also non-commercial. Commercial default refers to that the counterpart fails to perform the contract due to the business in a worse off situation, or due to market changed, or because he does not have good faith to do business at all. Non-commercial reason means that the environment of politics, economy, law and policy of related country changed unexpectedly. For example, after the exporter delivered the goods to the importer's country, the possibility for the importer refuse to pay and pick up the goods under collections is much higher than under letter of credit. That is because the importer will not suffer from losses or punishment from a third party if he do so with various excuses.

(4) Exit risk of counterpart means the possibility for the counterpart to exit from the transaction due to un-favorite conditions under certain payment method. Maximizing his interest in a transaction is rational behavior of international trader. The maximum benefit for the importer is not higher than to receive the goods desired without paying, while for the exporter is to obtain proceeds without shipping products. There is, however, good exit mechanism in actual market economy, that is to say, if the transaction is not win-win, one part would exit and there is no benefit to the other side at all, nor does he will get maximum benefit. Thus, the prerequisite of using a particular payment method is that both sides are willing to accept it, at least in certain extent. For example, total amount payment in advance is favorable for the exporter, but the importer perhaps exits from the transaction because of the high risk he will bear. In other words, the exporter will be confronted with higher exit risk of counterpart in this case.

1.1.3　What Will Be the Supervision Mechanism of Performance?

How do both sides "know" or "supervise" whether the counterpart fulfills the contract? If one party has no sincerity to fulfill contract at all, the counterpart is hard to avoid being cheated even though he has made strict supervision measures. In fact, fulfillment of contract rests on the participant's willingness. In reality, in most cases of default, the party concerned did so unintentionally. Because, from long term point of view, fulfilling contracts benefits the businessmen much more than defaulting.

Many things motivate the participants to fulfill contract. In traditional society, within a relatively small business circle, deals are made between acquaintances. Following morality standard, maintaining and elevating self-reputation enable the businessmen do business with more people and earn more money. That is the main motivation for the businessman's performance. The credit chain between seller and buyer in the circle of acquaintance is effective. That is to say, the public praise makes the participants fulfill the contract willingly and therefore could be one kind of supervision method. And this method is also efficient, i.e. with lower costs, because without supervision of the third party and law judgments there are no extra expenses certainly.

In modern business living, the business circle could reach the whole world, "acquaintance" and "reputation" do no long motivate people to fulfill the contract, in other words, the power of morality is not so strong as to maintain the credit any more, and it has been replaced by agreement, contract and law. In contract, the obligation of parties is stipulated clearly, so as to avoid the punishment of social impartiality — court, which is one of the possible motivations of participant's performance. However, it is not very difficult for a party to find out chance to maximize his benefit, which attracts him rushing into danger. In such cases, although the sufferer could be compensated by law, it could be time — consuming or even lose is more than gain. In one word, the cost is too high. If there is a third party, who has good reputation, is familiar with the two parties, or even capable of threatening the party who is possible of defaulting, to take the role of witness, supervisor and the guarantor to both sides, there must be a strong force for two parties to fulfill the agreement. The most qualified third party is banking.

Banking has vast penetrating power in modern economic society, and owns the reputation of blood vessel of national economy. They are indispensable partners to enterprises. The relationship between enterprises and banks is something like "acquaintance" in traditional society, they maintain their long-term relationship by credit. Credit chain (see Figure 1.1) between one party (Buyer) and his bank (Bank A) can be connected to the credit chain between the other party (Seller) and his bank (Bank B) through worldwide banking network. The indirect credit chain between buyer and seller through bankers is much stronger than the direct credit chain between them, even though it is longer. Among "shorter" and "stronger", businessmen would prefer to choose the stronger one instead of the shorter one. The complete credit chain is composed by the direct chain between buyer and seller as well as the indirect chain through banks.

Figure 1-1: Credit Chain in Payment Transaction

As shown in Figure 1-1, the indirect credit chain between buyer and seller through bankers is longer than the direct chain between them. To "rent" the "credit" from the third parties, the "rental" must be paid, which would increase transaction cost. Although it is effective from the transaction to be succeeded, it is inefficient or non-economic.

Even in modern business world, is there any direct, economic credit chain between two parties from different countries, which is strong enough for promoting them to fulfill the contract actively? Actually, that direct credit chain is existed in three cases. First, thanks to high reputation, both sides sincerely believe that the counterpart do fulfill the contract. Second, the buyer and the seller have established long-term business relationship or even strategic cooperative partnership, in view of long-term benefit both sides are motivated to fulfill the contract. Third, although the two parties are from different countries, they belongs to one economic entity — transnational company, the responsibility or obligation of two parties — paying and delivering in time — are coordinated or assumed by the headquarter.

To sum up, there are four reasons for the participants to fulfill contract actively. Firstly, defaults damage one's reputation among acquaintances. Secondly, defaults will likely be punished according to laws. Thirdly, defaults would result in economic sanctions by banks. Finally, defaults would do harm to the long-term cooperative relationships. In a word, the essential motivation of doing performance is fearing of benefits losses.

1. 1. 4 What Are the Roles of Banking in the International Trade Payment?

1. 1. 4. 1 Facilitating Funds Transfer

Banking is engine of today's economic society; its roles in international trade payment can be summarized as follows:

In modern business world, without banks, we can not imagine how to make international trade payment with vast amount of money, not to conduct it efficiently. In current business environment, through worldwide network banks could easily transfer money from the buyers to the sellers. Considering the whole world as one unit, cost of transferring fund could be saved greatly through banking systems.

Suppose that the buyers make payment without banks, it must be a real physical procedure, that is to say, a certain amount of money is transferred by hand to hand, which will suffer from safety risk, and expenses of transportation. If a couple of businessmen make payment in this way are acceptable, how much money will spend if thousands of businessmen clear their debits by this method? However, banks have different way to transfer funds; funds given by the buyer will be paid to the seller by their oversea institutes. Banks are capable of handling all international payment. And through a clearing mechanism between banks, physical flow of funds between countries is greatly decreased, so as to reduce transaction cost and improve economic efficiency.

1. 1. 4. 2 Promoting Conclusion of International Trade

Banking's role in international trade is much more than only facilitating funds transfer. As an intermediary with good reputation, they act as, at the same time, counterparts of both sides (i. e. the seller and the buyer), and are capable of supervising both sides, so as to promote the business to succeed. The best example is letter of credit. Under letter of credit, banks guarantee in their own name that they will make payment definitely provided the exporter presents documents in line with the credit, meanwhile, they engage that the importer do obtain documents after his effecting payment or promising payment. With the promise of bank, exporters are willing to prepare and ship goods prior to obtaining money. Exporter will not worry about that the importer would refuse to pay, for bank is the primary obligor under a letter of credit. Just with the participation of banks, many international trades, which seems too hard to come to conclusion, become to be feasible.

1. 1. 4. 3 Extending Loans for International Trade

Banks take another important role in international trade, that is extending loans for every side, which is an important function that no sophisticated traders would neglect. Banks could facilitate finance for both the buyer and the seller. From the position of exporters, banks can extend an unsecured loan against order; or a packing credit against an original letter of credit; or a loan against shipping documents or negotiating documents presented. From the position of importers, bank can grant credit line for opening letter of credit, by which the importer is allowed not to pay cash collateral, issuing shipping guarantee which enables the buyer to pick up the goods before paying, so as to put them into production or market as soon as possible. Additionally, bank can also accept bills of exchange made by the buyer for discounting in money market and paying for the goods contracted.

Another important thing having to be mentioned here is that banks take a vital role in hedging foreign exchange risk, which is faced by both sides. Banks could manage, reduce, and even eliminate foreign exchange exposures by means of foreign exchange forward, future, options and so on, for themselves and for enterprises.

In conclusion, in international trade payment, banks take four roles: first, to facilitate fund transfer efficiently world wide; second, to promote transactions because of their easily supervising both sides; third, to provide loans to international traders, so as to make them capable of fulfilling the contracts; fourth, to help the foreign trade company to manage or reduce foreign exchange exposures. After Second World War, world trade has been growing faster than ever, annual growth rate about 6% averagely, higher than that of world GDP of about 4%. It can be asserted that such development partially owns to the active involvement of banking.

1. 2 The Purpose of Learning This Course

The objectives of learning this course are that (1) It tries to provide some information on fundamental principles and theories which are closely associated with the international trade payment; (2) It tries to offer the experiences and skills about how to deal with the safe exchange between the proceeds and goods in international trade; (3) It tries to make the readers or learners familiarize with the customs and practice in international trade payment.

Hopefully, this book may play an important role in combining the theory with practice, which can facilitate learners' absorption, digestion and accumulation of knowledge and skills about international trade payment.

2. Prospect of International Trade Payment

As an ancient international business, international trade payment has been adjusting its best trade-off point between ensuring performance and lowering transaction costs in the wake of change of the global economy and development of science and technology. Relative stability of international economic and financial system after the Second World War, and globalization of world economy make international trade settlement be developed more and more towards lowering its transaction costs. In view of competition between supply chains in today's world, both the buyer and the seller in an international deal are no longer competitors, but cooperative partner for seeking long-term and common interest. Ever-improved E-commerce technology is promoting international trade settlement to develop itself towards a non-paper, automatically handled transaction.

2. 1　Usage of Documentary Credits

Documentary letters of credit carry a big weight in China's foreign trade, approximately accounting for 70% of volume of export and import business. Reasons of letters of credit being very popular in China are as follows: First, there are only about over 20 years since China has been opening its door to the outside world, Chinese business not yet to a great extent established relationship of a long-term strategic partnership with the foreign colleagues. It takes time to gain trust of each other. In spite of high bank fees, letter of credit can motivate both sides to fulfill the contract. Promoting performance, after all, is more important than low bank fees.

Second, China has a vast territory, averagely all countries are long distance from China, even the closest ones. Thus both sides are hard to know each other about operating way, financial standing, etc. in other words, credit chain between them are pretty weak, so being forced rend bank's credit for coming a conclusion.

Third, letters of credit is good for Chinese government to control and manage in respects of foreign trade and foreign exchange. By means of letter of credit, under the export transactions, authorities can know real information of inflow of foreign exchange, avoiding foreign exchange outflow; under the import transactions, it is good for the authorities to control types and volumes of goods imported, and more importantly, avoiding effectively to gain foreign exchange by cheating.

Finally, letter of credit is the safest way for exchanging the proceeds and goods between the buyer and the seller over long distance or across the national boundaries. Bank acts as the bridge between the buyer and the seller so as to bring them together and come to the conclusion.

2. 2　Usage of Electronic Data Interchange

In the meantime, since the 1960's of last century, western countries already started to trial and promote to use technology of EDI in international trade i. e. non-paper trade, which greatly facilitate the development and efficiency of international trade payment.

EDI refers to Electronic Data Interchange, a combination of modern computer and data network technology, which is mainly used in automatically transmission of standardized commercial forms various computer system of organizations. Standard documents recognized in this system, such as order, contract, invoice, delivery order, customs clearance, license of import and export, etc. are to be transformed into digital structure, then can be identified and handled by computers. And such data can be interchanged through digital network between computer systems of different countries, regions and trades, so that business information is to be handled automatically, that is so-called E-commerce.

In an EDI system, when dealing with international firms, basic trade information is only one time to be imputed, and then handled automatically, e. g. placing order to the supplier, purchasing goods or parts, applying for license for import or export and origin, reserving ship space by carrier, effecting insurance and custom clearance, invoicing to the customer, obtaining proceeds from bank, and so on. Advantages of utilizing EDI are as follows:

(1) Speeding up information transmission

In EDI system, by transmitting information electronically and automatically, periods for placing order, creating documents for obtaining proceeds and transporting cargo will be shortened obviously and makes goods debuts on the market at the first time.

(2) Improving customer service

By connecting with customers through EDI, customer's inquiry can be answered as soon as possible, tying closely up the relationship of trade partners, having more business and increasing market share.

(3) Lowering costs of handling documents, improving quality of trade information and enhancing productivity

In traditional international trade, most of works, such as typing, copying, filling and checking, are to be made manually, which not only talks a plenty of energy and time, but also easily makes mistakes and increases costs. With EDI system, no need to input the same data repeatedly makes almost no delay and artificial errors by handling documents, so as to improve information quality and decline costs.

(4) Enabling to carry out new strategy of firms

Due to speeding up the goods turnover by using of EDI system, firms are able to carry out new commercial strategy, such as "real inventory" or "Zero inventory", thus cutting down inventory level and working cash.

In short, EDI is a very practical and profit-making commercial instrument, bring revolution in the field of international trade and management. Although EDI systems run in a small scale, it is predicted that in the near of future EDI will be widely used in international trade and settlement.

📖 Words & Expressions

1. settlement　　　　　结算
2. proceeds　　　　　　货款
3. counterpart　　　　　相对应的人
4. default　　　　　　　拒付
5. GDP　　　　　　　　国内生产总值
6. foreign exchange　　外汇
7. EDI　　　　　　　　　电子数据交换
8. inventory　　　　　　库存

📖 Notes

1. The essence of both the buyer and the seller's concerns is whether the counterpart fulfills the contract.
   买卖双方所关注的核心是对方能够履行合约。
2. Payment becomes the touchstone for checking performance sincerity of the two parties.
   支付成为检验双方行为真诚的试金石。
3. If one party of international trade insists that the counterpart's fulfilling of the contract be the prerequisite of his performance, the transactions would be aborted.
   如果国际贸易的一方坚持以另一方履行合约为先决条件，交易就可能告吹。
4. On a win-win basis, firstly, effective methods to supervise and even force counterpart to fulfill his obligation have to be defined.
   首先，建立在一个双赢基础上的有效管理甚至是迫使对方履行合约的方法必须予以规定。
5. The two parties must weigh and balance the effectiveness and costs of supervision, so as to smoothly obtain relative benefit from international trade.
   双方必须掂量和平衡管理的有效性和费用以便顺利从国际贸易中获得相关利益。
6. In international trade practice, due to the involvement of banks for a long time, people have created many effective methods which have been feasible to examine fulfillment of the parties.
   在国际贸易实践中，由于银行长期的参与，人们已创立了许多有效方法使之能够可行地核查双方对合同的履行。
7. Every participant in the transaction must carefully consider these issues, though they

will affect each differently and to a different degree.

尽管这些问题对任何一方的影响在程度上不同，但交易的任何一方必须认真细致地考虑这些问题。

8. Credit makes many such transactions possible.

信用使许多这样的交易成为可能。

9. Payment transaction costs mean total costs by using a certain payment method, including financial cost, fund transfer, expense, default risk of counterpart and exit risk of counterpart.

支付交易费用指的是使用某种支付方式的全部费用，包括财务费用、资金划拨、费用开支、交易对方拒付风险及对方逃逸风险。

10. Banking has vast penetrating power in modern economic society, and owns the reputation of blood vessel of national economy.

银行业在现代经济社会里具有巨大的渗透能力，因而享有国民经济中血管的盛誉。

11. In modern business world, without bank, we can not imagine how to make international trade payment with vast amount of money, not to conduct it efficiently.

在现代经济世界（商界）里，如果没有银行，我们难以想象，如此巨大金额的国际贸易结算如何能有效地进行。

12. Since the 1960's of last century, western countries have already started to trial and promote to use technology of EDI in international trade, i.e. non-paper trade, which greatly facilitate the development and efficiency of international trade payment.

自 20 世纪 60 年代以来，西方国家已经开始尝试和促进电子数据交换（EDI）技术在国际贸易中的运用，它极大地促进了国际贸易结算的发展和效率。

➤➤ Exercises

I. True or False

1. The domestic trade is almost the same as the international trade.

2. Without bank's participation, modern international trade payment system would not exist any more.

3. The essence of both buyers and sellers' concern is whether the counterpart fulfills the contract.

4. In today's international trade, commonly used payment systems are payment in advance, collections, letter of credit, open account, Factoring as well as Forfaiting.

5. In almost all business transactions the buyer prefers to obtain expensive credit terms.

6. The seller always has a priority to get his investment back.

7. In international trade, morality standard, maintaining and elevating self-reputation enable the businessmen do business with more people and earn more money.

8. The main motivation for the businessmen is profit rather than credit ratings.

9. Bank has vast penetrating power in modern economic society and owns the reputation of blood vessel of national economy.

10. EDI stands for Electronic Data Interchange.

II. Multiple Choice

1. At the _____ of every business transaction is the buyer and the seller.
   A. heart   B. space
   C. situation   D. circumstance

2. Both the buyer and the seller have one thing in common: _____.
   A. money and reputation   B. belief and reputation
   C. credit and profit   D. profit and the least risk

3. The essence of both the buyer and the seller's concerns is whether _____.
   A. the bank can bridge the gaps between them
   B. the third institution can help them
   C. the counterpart fulfills the contract
   D. there is no risk before them

4. International trade payment is not only a theory, but a _____.
   A. skill   B. practice
   C. tool   D. instrument

5. Credit gives the buyer the opportunity to _____ the goods before having to pay for them.
   A. distribute   B. obtain
   C. resell   D. store

6. Transaction costs of payment do not contain the expenses in respect _____.
   A. cost and freight
   B. production and transportation
   C. transportation and insurance
   D. production, transportation and insurance

7. Fund transfer expense means the expense used to transfer the _____ from the buyer to the seller.
   A. proceeds   B. profits
   C. credit   D. risks

8. In fact, fulfillment of contract rests on the _____.
   A. businessman's credits   B. businessman's reputation
   C. participant's awareness   D. participant's willingness

9. Bank has vast _____ power in modern economic society.
   A. persuading   B. penetrating
   C. forcing   D. keeping

10. Banking is _____ of today's economic society.
    A. engine   B. role-play
    C. tool   D. essence

Chapter 2

International Trade Terms

After learning this chapter, students will be able to understand the meaning and significance of the 11 trade terms in Incoterms 2010. Also, they will know some international conventions concerning international trade terms. Similarly, they also can identify different rights and obligations of importers and exporters under different trade terms. The more important thing is that students can tell the difference between Incoterms 2000 and Incoterms 2010. Finally, the students could easily apply some frequently-used trade terms and their derived ones in trade practice. On the other hand, they would fully understand factors that affects the selection of trade terms in international transactions.

Brainstorming

In international transactions, the seller and the buyer determine their respective responsibilities through negotiations. The seller's main responsibility is to deliver the qualified goods and related documents, while the buyer's equivalent obligation is to take the delivery of the goods together with the documents and pay for the goods. During the delivery, problems about risks, responsibilities, and costs are also the important issues that shall be solved while negotiating and concluding a contract.

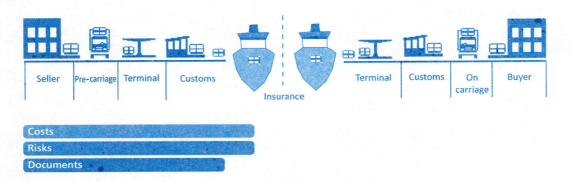

1. An Overview of Trade Terms

In the international trade, sellers and buyers are usually far away from each other and are separated by the boundary. And thus in the process of international cargo transportation and delivery, many procedures have to be handled, including paying for inspection, packing, loading and unloading, transportation, warehouse charges, insurance premium, import and export clearance, and some other miscellaneous charges, like taking charge of the risks of damage or losses during the transit, chartering a ship or booking shipping space, covering insurance, obtaining the import and export license, carrying out customs formalities, asking for inspection, etc. have to be considered. It will be expensive and time-consuming if the two parties decide everything through repeated consultations and will affect the conclusion and implementation of international contracts. In the international business practice, a set of special trade terms have been formulated to solve these problems and help to make international trade transactions go smoothly and effectively.

1.1 Meaning and Significance of Trade Terms

Trade terms, as an important component in the international cargo price, are also called price terms or delivery terms, each of which is a short form expression, e. g. Free On Board or a three-letter abbreviation FOB. Trade terms are used to explain the price structure, divide the related expenses, risks and responsibilities borne by the two parties, and help to define the relevant parties' obligations. The use of the trade terms greatly simplifies the contract negotiations and saves plenty of time and cost for the parties involved in the international business.

Trade terms usually are a part of international unit price, which is different from that of domestic trade. For example, U. S. $ 600 per M/T is a domestic one, while U. S. $ 600 per M/T is an international one. When two parties determine to adopt certain trade terms, all other clauses in the contract shall be in conformity with them. For example, if two parties decide to use CIF, then their contract is a CIF contract in which expenses, risks, and obligations are determined as per CIF regulations.

In international trade, the strike price does not only hinge on its own value, but also depends on some other issues such as carrying out the formalities, the division of risks, etc. The transaction price will be higher if the seller takes more responsibilities, costs, and risks. Whereas, the buyer can only accept a relatively lower price if he/she takes more. Thus trade terms have their dual nature. On one hand, trade terms define the delivery terms, explaining the division point of costs, risks and obligations; on the other hand, trade terms stand for one of the factors that construct international unit price.

In international trade practice, the significance of trade terms can be defined as follows:

Trade terms greatly simplify formalities of international transaction, shorten the time for business negotiation, and thus save the costs. Every trade term has its specific meaning, and has uniform explanation and regulation, stipulated by international conventions, which are widely accepted as rules of conduct in international trade practice.

Trade terms make price comparison easier and strengthen the price accounting. As trade terms can indicate the factors included in the unit price, when the two parties confirm their transaction price, they will definitely consider the incidental charges of the chosen trade term, such as freight, premium, charges for loading and unloading, customs expenses, VAT expenses, and other sundry expenses.

Trade terms can help us properly resolve trade disputes. When the two parties sign the contract, they may not define rights and obligations of the parties involved clearly which may cause disputes during the process of contract performance. On this occasion, the general explanation of trade terms can be quoted here.

1.2　International Conventions of Trade Terms

Trade terms came into being with the development of international trade practice. For quite a long time, there were no uniform explanations for trade terms in the trade practice. Then different countries and regions developed different interpretations for trade terms, and misunderstandings and disputes occurred frequently in the international business. As a consequence, time, energy and money were wasted, and the development of international trade was greatly prohibited. To solve these problems, international organizations, like ICC, ILA, etc., began to make efforts to formulate rules and regulations, known as trade conventions, to facilitate the international trade.

➤ Warsaw-Oxford Rules 1932

Warsaw-Oxford Rules 1932 is specially established to explain CIF contracts by ILA. In the mid-nineteenth century, CIF began to be widely adopted in the trade, but at that time, no uniform regulations or explanations were issued to define relevant parties' specific obligations under this term. Under this circumstance, ILA held a meeting in Warsaw in 1928, and worked out uniform rules for CIF contracts, called Warsaw-Rules 1928 including 22 clauses. Then it was revised at New York meeting in 1930, Paris meeting in 1931, Oxford conference in 1932 to 21 clauses, which is renamed Warsaw-Oxford Rules 1932. It is still in use nowadays in indicating the nature and characteristic of the CIF contracts.

➤ Revised American Foreign Trade Definitions 1941

It originated in U. S. Export Quotations and Abbreviations formulated by nine American commercial groups in 1919. Then it was revised in 1941 and renamed Revised American Foreign Trade Definitions 1941, which was approved by JNC selected from CCUS, AIA, and American National Foreign Trade Association. It defines the following six trade terms:

■　Ex (Point Of Origin)

■　FOB (Free On Board)

■　FAS (Free Along Side)

■ C & F (Cost and Freight)
■ CIF (Cost, Insurance and Freight)
■ Ex Dock—Ex Quay, Ex Pier (named port of importation)

These trade terms are often adopted by countries in America. The explanations for the second and the third trade term are quite different from those in INCOTERMS. Thus when transacting with American countries, companies shall pay more attention to the application of trade terms.

1. 3 Incoterms

Incoterms rules or International Commercial Terms are a series of pre-defined commercial terms published by International Chamber of Commerce (ICC). Widely used in the international transactions or procurement processes, Incoterms rules are intended primarily to clearly communicate the tasks, costs, and risks associated with the transportation and delivery of goods. Currently, Incoterms rules are accepted by governments, legal authorities and practitioners worldwide as the interpretation for international trade terms. Incoterms are intended to reduce or remove altogether uncertainties arising from different interpretation of the rules in different countries, and therefore they are regularly incorporated in the sales contracts worldwide.

In 1937, ICC worked out the first edition Incoterms 1936, and then revised Incoterms in 1953, 1982, 1990, and 2000 respectively. Incoterms rules help a lot in clarifying tasks, costs and risks involved in the delivery of goods from seller to buyer. Thus they are recognized by UNCITRAL as the global standard for the interpretation of the most common terms in the foreign trade. In view of some new situations, occurring in the international trade including the enlarging customs territory, the increasing use of telecommunication, the enhancing due care on security of goods in transit and the change of cargo transportation practice, ICC began to revise Incoterms 2000 in 2007 in order to bring the rules in line with current international trade practices.

Incoterms 2010 was proclaimed in September, 2010 and took effect on January, 1st, 2011. One point which we should always bear in the mind is that all contracts made under Incoterms 2000 or even any earlier versions of Incoterms remain valid after the application of Incoterms 2010 in trade practice, as Incoterms are rules and customary practice agreed by the parties involved in the contract, rather than laws enacted and bound by the governments. If you desire to use one of the enacted Incoterms, you have to clearly specify the version, like Incoterms 2010, Incoterms 2000 or any earlier versions in the contract. For example: "FOB Shanghai, Incoterms 2010" or "This contract is governed by Incoterms 2010" should be stipulated in the international sales contract.

2. Incoterms 2010

As all know, Incoterms 2010 is issued by International Chamber of Commerce and take effect in 2010. It is essential for traders to fully understand the main content and implication of Incoterms 2010.

2.1   Differences Between Incoterms 2000 and Incoterms 2010

Incoterms 2010 is the eighth set of pre-defined international contract terms published by the International Chamber of Commerce, with the first set having been published in 1936. Incoterms 2010 defines 11 terms, compared with the 13 terms defined in the Incoterms 2000. Four terms including DAF, DES, DEQ and DDU in Incoterms 2000, are replaced by two new terms: DAT (Delivered at Terminal) and DAP (Delivered at Place) in Incoterms 2010.

In Incoterms 2000, trade terms were divided into four categories, while the 11 pre-defined terms of Incoterms 2010 are subdivided into two categories based only on method of delivery. The larger group of the seven terms can be used regardless of the method of transport, with the smaller group of four terms applied only to sales, which solely involve transportation by water where the condition of the goods can be verified at the point of loading on board ship.

(1) Terms for Any or More Modes of Transport

EXW   Ex Works
FAC   Free Carrier
CPT   Carriage Paid To
CIP   Carriage and Insurance Paid To
DAT   Delivered At Terminal
DAP   Delivered At Place
DDP   Delivered Duty Paid

(2) Terms for Sea and Inland Waterway Transport

FAS   Free Alongside Ship
FOB   Free On Board
CFR   Cost and Freight
CIF   Cost and Freight

Terms in the first category suit any or more modes of transport in the international business. They can be used when no ocean transport is involved, and can also be applied when part of transport is marine transport. For example, on EXW term, the seller uses inland railway transport to carry the goods to the exporting country's nominated frontier, and delivers goods to the buyer in the adjoined country. On DDP term, the seller uses inland railway transport to carry the goods to the port of shipment, and transships them to the importer's port via marine transportation, then uses road transport to deliver the goods to the nominated place to make the delivery after unloading.

The four terms in the second category all take port to port of shipment or destination as the terminal of transportation at the buyer's premise and the place of delivery which makes sea and inland waterway transport applicable on their basis. As the majority of the international transactions adopt the ocean transportation, the three most commonly used terms in the new version are still FOB, CFR and CIF.

Incoterms 2010 Categories

Any or More Modes of Transport	**EXW**	Ex Works (... *named place of delivery*)
	FCA	Free Carrier (... *named place of delivery*)
	CPT	Carriage Paid To (... *named place of delivery*)
	CIP	Carriage and Insurance Paid To (... *named place of destination*)
	DAT	Delivered At Terminal (... *named terminal at port or place of destination*)
	DAP	Delivered At Place (... *named place of destination*)
	DDP	Delivered Duty Paid (... *named place of destination*)
Sea and Inland Waterway Transport Only	**FAS**	Free Alongside Ship (... *named port of shipment*)
	FOB	Free On Board (... *named port of shipment*)
	CFR	Cost and Freight (... *named port of destination*)
	CIF	Cost Insurance and Freight (... *named port of destination*)

In old versions, Incoterms regulate "passing ship's rail" as the place of delivery under the three commonly used terms: FOB, CFR and CIF, which indicate that the delivery is accomplished when the goods get across the ship's rail when the seller takes the goods on board at the port of shipment. The risk of damage and loses transfers from the seller to the buyer after the goods get across the ship's rail. But in international trade practice, under FOB, CFR and CIF terms, the buyer generally asks the seller to deliver the goods on board the vessel, and provides clean on board documents. In most cases, the seller will definitely approve the above requests, thus in the real practice, the place of delivery actually has extended from "the ship's rail" to "on board the vessel". Thus, in order to make the rules of Incoterms reflect modern commercial reality, Incoterms 2010 changes the seller's obligation of delivery as "deliver the goods on board the vessel at port of shipment".

Incoterms 2010 add some additional provisions concerning the seller's delivery obligations under FOB, CFR and CIF. Incoterms 2010 regulate that the seller's delivery obligation can be accomplished by "deliver the goods on board the vessel" or "procure the goods so delivered". This acknowledges "string sales", where goods in transit may be sold several times before arrival, by given the sellers at the intermediate position the option to "procure goods shipped" as the obligation to "ship the goods on board" can only be accomplished by the first seller. It is necessary to mention that in string sales, the goods can be resold by on FOB or CFR basis only if the vessel has not set sail yet; when the goods in transit are resold, CIF must be used as the seller must provide the reasonable insurance policy and the clean on board B/L. This rule is to encourage the use of Incoterms in commodities transactions.

Beside all of the above, some other rules have been changed. In Incoterms 2010, electronic communication gains the same status as paper communication under the consent of two parties, which makes the electronic documents legally binding as the paper ones. Beside the foreign trade, Incoterms 2010 can also be applied in the domestic trade if the relevant parties agree. All these differences have made Incoterms 2010 more practical and applicable in the modern domestic and international business.

It is necessary to notice that rules and explanations in Incoterms 2010 are usually international usages and customary practice, which means that they are not legally binding. The parties involved in the international transaction have rights to choose voluntarily a certain usage or even any regulations not included in the Incoterms and specify them in the contract, then all the issues or disputes can be resolved as per the contract. If the regulations on usages are ambiguous in the contract, then when the case is accused on court or resorts to arbitration, certain recognized or most influential international usages will be quoted by the court or arbitrator as the gist, e. g. Incoterms 2010.

2. 2   Specific Introduction to Incoterms 2010

In the international trade, not all trade terms are frequently used as the responsibilities shall be kept in stable equilibrium. Thus some of the terms are more frequently in use than others. It is very important for the foreign trade practitioners to get familiar with their meanings, obligations of the two parties involved, as well as some problems worth of their attention in foreign trade practice. The following interpretation of trade terms in Incoterms 2010 is done based on the significance and application frequency. The content in this part involves meanings, obligations of the two parties, division of risks and costs, and important issues about each of the terms. In order to give readers a complete understanding, the following figure is provided.

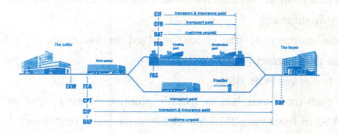

2.2.1　Six Major Trade Terms

FOB

Free On Board (… named port of shipment) is to be used only for sea or inland waterway transport. It means that the seller clears the goods for export and delivers them on board the vessel nominated by the buyer at the named port of shipment or procures the goods already so delivered. The risks of loss of or damage to the goods passes when the goods are on board the vessel and the buyer shall bear all costs from that moment onwards.

Here in Incoterms 2010, instead of accomplishing the delivery by delivering goods "across the ship's rail", the seller's responsibility of delivery is changed into "to deliver the goods on board the vessel, or to procure goods already so delivered". This rule is to cater to the needs of "string sales", where a single consignment may be resold multiple times during transit which is common in commodities transactions.

According to Incoterms 2010, the two parties' obligations are as follows:

(1) Seller's Main Responsibilities

■ Delivering the goods in compliance with the contract on board the nominated vessel by the buyer at the fixed port of shipment in the specific time or on a fixed date; or procuring the goods already so delivered, and sending sufficient advice to the buyer.

■ Obtaining export license or some other written authorization, and then carrying out all the formalities concerning customs clearance for export, when applicable.

■ Taking in charge of all the expenses and risks until all the goods are on board the vessel at the port of shipment.

■ Providing the commercial invoice and usual proof of on-board delivery.

(2) Buyer's Main Responsibilities

■ Paying for the goods as per the contract.

■ Chartering the vessel or booking shipping space and paying for the freight, then giving the seller sufficient notice on the vessel's name, place of shipment, and delivery time.

■ Obtaining import license or some other written authorization on one's own expenses and risks, and carrying out all formalities for import customs in one's own country or another country whose territory one shall pass through.

■ Taking in charge of all the expenses and risks after all the goods are on board the vessel at the port of shipment.

■ Taking the delivery of the goods involved in the contract, taking all documents conform to the contract.

(3) Important Issues on FOB Basis

In Incoterms, each trade term has its specific point of delivery, also called as the point for division of risks. FOB in Incoterms 2010 has changed the point of delivery from "ship's rail" to "on board the ship"; and added "or to procure the goods already so delivered" which caters to the "string sales" in bulk commodities' transaction. Actually, in trade practice, the division of cost is not necessary to be obeyed as "on board" which is decided by the structure of freight, custom of port, and agreement concluded by the two parties.

In FOB contract, the buyer is in charge of chartering the vessel or booking shipping space, and shall inform the seller the vessel's name and time of shipment; and the seller shall deliver the goods on board the named vessel within the stipulated period or on the nominated date. Here rises the problem of liking up the vessel and the goods. The buyer shall arrange the vessel to take the goods at the port of shipment within the given period. If the ship arrived on time, but the seller does not load the goods on board as cargo unprepared, the seller shall bear dead freight and demurrage thus resulted. Otherwise, if it is the buyer's fault, one shall bear the seller's additional warehouse expense, insurance premium, interest loss, and etc. In FOB practice, the seller could carry out all formalities concerning transport, but the seller shall compensate seller's expenditures afterwards. For example, the seller can book shipping space for the buyer while the risk of no shipping room shall still be borne by the buyer under such a circumstance.

Loading expense occurred at the port of shipment includes expense for loading the goods on board, related stowage charges and trimming charges. In FOB contract, if the buyer uses liners to transport the goods, the loading expense shall be borne by the buyer as liner charges includes loading expense at the port of shipment and the unloading expense at the port of destination. But in bulk commodities sales, the buyer usually has to charter ships, and then who shall bear the cost? In this case, some derived forms of FOB are introduced to solve the problem. Common FOB derived terms includes:

■ FOB Liner Terms

It means that loading expense shall be borne by the party in charge of the freight (the buyer) as liner transport.

■ FOB under Tackle

It only requires the seller to send and place the goods on the wharf within the reach of the ship's tackle. Loading expense thereafter shall be borne by the buyer.

■ FOB Stowed, FOBS

Under this term, the seller loads the goods into the ship's hold and pays the loading expense including stowing expenses.

■ FOB Trimmed, FOBBT

The seller pays all the loading expense including trimming expenses which actually also include stowing expenses.

As there are no uniform explanations to the variants of trade terms, in trade practice, when derived trade terms are necessary, their additional duties shall be specified in sales contact except the two parties have the same understanding on them. This tip is just to avoid future trade disputes in foreign trade.

CIF

Cost, Insurance and Freight (... named port of destination) is to be used only for sea or inland waterway transport. It means that the seller clears the goods for export and delivers them on board the vessel at the port of shipment, or procures the goods already so delivered. The risk of loss of or damage to the goods passes when the goods are on board the vessel or when the seller procures the goods already so delivered. The seller must contract for and pay the costs and freight necessary to bring the goods to the named port of destination. The seller also has to contract for and pay for the minimum cover insurance against the buyer's risk of loss of or damage to the goods during the carriage.

According to Incoterms 2010, the two parties' obligations are as follows:

(1) Seller's Main Responsibilities

■ Delivering the goods in compliance with the contract on board the nominated vessel by the buyer at the fixed port of shipment in the specific time or on a fixed date; or procuring the goods already so delivered, and sending sufficient advice to the buyer.

■ Obtaining export license or some other written authorization, and then carrying out all the formalities concerning customs clearance for export when applicable.

■ Chartering the vessel or booking shipping space and paying for the freight.

■ Covering insurance for cargo transportation, and paying for insurance premium.

■ Taking in charge of all the expenses and risks until all the goods are on board the vessel at the port of shipment.

■ Providing commercial invoice, insurance policy and all the usual proof of on-board delivery.

(2) Buyer's Main Responsibilities

■ Paying for the goods stipulated on the contract.

■ Obtaining import license or some other written authorization on one's own expenses and risks, and carrying out all formalities for import customs in one's own country or another country whose territory one shall pass through.

■ Taking in charge of all the expenses and risks after all the goods are on board the vessel at the port of shipment.

■ Taking the delivery of the goods involved in the contract, taking all documents conform to the contract.

(3) Important Issues on CIF Basis

Under CIF term, the seller must pay for the costs and freight necessary to bring the goods to the named destination, but the risk of loss of or damage to the goods as well as any additional costs due to events occurring after the time of delivery, are transferred from the seller to the buyer. Thus it is not the so-called "arrival contract", but a shipment one.

In CIF contract, the seller shall be in charge of contracting for and paying for transportation. But he only contract for transport according to usual practice, the buyer can not propose ant additional requests.

The seller is required to cover the insurance under CIF contract, but the seller only take the minimum insurance which is 10% higher than the invoice total value. Any additional requests shall be borne by the buyer himself.

In CIF contract, if the seller uses liners to transport the goods, the unloading expense shall be borne by the seller as liner charges includes unloading expense at the port of shipment and the unloading expense at the port of destination. But in bulk commodities sales, the seller usually has to charter ships, and then who shall bear the cost? In this case, some derived forms of CIF are introduced to solve the problem. Common CIF derived terms includes:

■ CIF Liner Terms

It means that the unloading expense shall be borne by the seller who is in charge of freight as that under the situation of liner transport;

■ CIF Ex Ship's Hold

It means that the buyer shall be in charge of the expense to unloading the goods from ship's hold to the wharf.

■ CIF Ex Tackle

It means the seller shall be in charge of the expense of unloading the goods from ship's hold off the tackle.

■ CIF Landed

It means that the seller shall be in charge of the expense of unloading the goods to the bank of the port of destination.

Under CIF contract, the seller can accomplish the delivery only by delivering the related transport documents including B/L, policy, and commercial invoice. When the seller delivers the documents, the goods are thought to be already delivered, which is called as "symbolic delivery". Although the buyer does not get the real goods, he/she shall pay against the documents received. It is important to point out that on CIF basis, the seller shall not be required to promise the arrival or the time of arrival, if it does, the contract can not be called as a CIF contract.

CFR

Cost and Freight (named port of destination) suits sea and inland waterway transport. It means that the seller clears the goods for export and delivers them on board the vessel at the port of shipment, or procures the goods already so delivered. The risk of loss of or damage to the goods passes when the goods are on board the vessel or when the seller procures the goods so delivered.

The seller must contract for and pay the costs and freight necessary to bring goods to the named port of destination but risk of loss of and damage to the goods, as well as any additional costs due to events occurring after the time of delivery, are transferred from the seller to the buyer. The seller must bear all risks and loss of or damage to the goods until such time until the goods are place don board the vessel at the port of shipment, while the buyer must accept delivery of the goods when they have been so delivered and receive them from carrier at the named port of destination. Under CFR, CIF, CPT and CIP, the seller fulfills its obligation to deliver when it hands the goods over to the carrier but not when the goods reach the destination.

The seller shall charter ships, book shipping space and pays for the cargo transport. When the goods are loaded on board, the seller shall send the shipping notice to the buyer.

Cargo insurance is to be effected by the buyer. The buyer receives the goods at the port of destination and pays for unloading expense at the port of destination unless such cost has been included in the freight.

Except the rule that under CFR the seller is not in charge of insurance premium and does not have to provide insurance policy, the responsibilities of the two parties under CFR contracts are exactly the same as those of CIF contracts. And as CIF, to solve the problem of unloading expenses, CFR also has four derived forms: CFR liner terms, CFR es ship's hold, CFR ex tackle and CFR landed, which has the same rules as those of CIF derived terms.

FCA

Free Carrier (... named place) can be used irrespective of the mode of transport selected and may also be used where more than one mode of transport is employed. It means that the seller delivers the goods, cleared for export, to the carrier specified by the buyer at the named place of delivery which in most cases is at the seller's premise or a named place. If delivery occurs at the seller's premise, the seller is responsible for loading. If delivery occurs at any other place, the seller is not responsible for unloading. Carrier means any person who, in a contract of carriage, undertakes to perform or to procure the performance of transport by air, road, rail, sea, inland waterway or by a combination of such modes.

When using FCA term, it is advisable to clearly specify in the contract of sale and carriage the precise point of delivery, as the risk passes to the buyer at that point. FCA is often used when making an initial quotation for the sales of goods.

CPT

Carriage Paid To (… named place of destination) may be used irrespective of the mode of transportation and can be applied where more than one mode of transport is employed. It means that the seller delivers the goods to the carrier or another person nominated by the seller at an agreed place of shipment (not the destination), and that the seller must contract for and pay the costs of carriage necessary to bring the goods to the named place of destination.

In CPT contracts, the seller shall be in charge of transport, while the buyer the transportation insurance. Thus in order to link the two actions up, the seller must dispatch a shipping notice in time to the buyer.

CPT is often used in sales where shipment is by air freight, containerized ocean freight, courier shipments of small parcels, and "ro-ro" shipments of motor vehicles. With CPT, if more than one carrier is used for carriage to the named place of destination, the risk passes when the goods have been delivered to the first carrier, but the seller still have to pay the freight from this point to the destination.

CIP

Carriage and Insurance Paid To (… named place of destination) is suitable for any or more modes of transport. It means that the seller delivers the goods to the carrier or another person nominated by the seller at an agreed place and that the seller must contract for and pay the costs of carriage necessary to bring the goods to the nominated place of destination. Obligations of the two parties are the same under CIP as those under CPT except that the seller also contracts for and pays for the minimum cover insurance which is 10% above the price on the commercial invoice.

2.2.2　Other Five Trade Terms

EXW

Ex Works (… named place) can be used irrespective of the mode of transport selected and may also be used where more than one mode of transport is employed. It means that the seller delivers when he places the goods at the disposal of the buyer at the seller's premise or another named place (i. e. Works, Factories) not cleared for export and not loaded on any collecting vehicle. Under this term, the buyer is in charge of all the expenses and risks after he has taken the delivery at the seller' premise. The term places greatest responsibilities on the buyer and minimum obligations on the seller.

FAS

Free Alongside the Ship (… named port of shipment) is to be used only for sea and inland waterway transport. It means the sellers delivers when the goods are placed alongside the vessel. Risks of loss or damage to the goods pass when the goods are alongside the ship, and the buyer bears all costs from that moment onwards.

Under FAS, the seller has the option to deliver the goods alongside the ship, or to procure goods already so delivered. It is commonly used in bulk commodity cargo like oil, grains, ore, and etc. If the shipment is containerized, common practice is to deliver the goods to the carrier at a terminal and not alongside a ship.

DAT

Delivered At Terminal (... named terminal at port of destination) can be used irrespective of the mode of transportation selected and may also be used where more than one mode of transportation is employed. It means that the seller delivers when the goods, once unloaded from the arriving means of transport, are placed at the disposal of the buyer at a named terminal at the named port or place of destination. Terminal here includes any place, whether covered or not, such as quay, warehouse, container yard, rail or air cargo terminal. The seller bears all risks before the goods are unloaded at the terminal at the named port or place of destination.

Under DAT, two parties shall specify a specific place as the terminal, or a specific point within the terminal as risks to that point are to the seller's account. Under DAT, the seller shall clear the customs for export but not for import, when applicable. DAT is the only term under which the seller is responsible for unloading.

DAP

Delivered At Place (... named place of destination) can be used irrespective of the mode of transportation selected and may also be used where more than one mode of transportation is employed. It means that the seller delivers when the goods are placed at the disposal of the buyer on the arriving means of transport ready for unloading at the named place of destination. The seller bears all risks involved in bringing the goods to the named place.

Under DAP, two parties shall specify a specific place as the terminal, or a specific point within the terminal as clearly as possible as risks to that point are to the seller's account. If the seller incurs any cost related to the unloading expense at the point of destination, the seller is not entitled to ask for compensation.

DAP requires the seller to clear the goods for export, where applicable, whereas the seller does not have to clear the goods for import. If the buyer wishes the seller to clear the goods for import and pay for import duties, or carry out the import formalities, then the term DDP should be applied.

DDP

Delivered Duty Paid (... named place of destination) can be used irrespective of the mode of transportation selected and may also be used where more than one mode of transportation is employed. It means that the seller delivers the goods when the goods are placed at the disposal of the buyer, cleared for import on the arriving means of transport ready for unloading at the named place if destination. The seller bears all the costs and risks involved in bringing the goods to the place of destination and has the obligation to clear the goods not only for export but also for import, to pay any duty for both export and import and to carry out all customs formalities.

DDP represents the maximum obligation for the seller. The two parties shall specify a specific place as the terminal, or a specific point within the terminal as clearly as possible as risks to that point are to the seller's account. If the seller incurs any cost related to the unloading expense at the point of destination, the seller is not entitled to ask for compensation.

The parties are well advised not to use DDP if the seller is unable directly or indirectly to obtain import clearance. Any VAT or other taxes payable upon import are for the seller's account unless otherwise agreed in the sales contract.

3. Main Factors Concerning Selection of Trade Terms

In the international business transactions, following factor are usually concerned in choosing the trading term when signing the contract.

3. 1　Transport Conditions

When the two parties decide which term to apply, the first factor to be considered is the transportation mode. If the party has competent transport ability and the transportation is economic, the party can adopt group F to import and group C to export; otherwise, it shall use group F to import while group C to import.

3. 2　Supply Market

In the international trade, goods involved are various and different goods have different characters, and usually there are different requests as for the transportation, which makes the freight totally different. And the size of the orders can also count, so when the party chooses the trade terms, this factor shall be considered.

3. 3　Freight

Freight is one of the factors added to the unit price. When two parties decide the trade terms, they shall consider the freight along the root as well as the increase of freight. Generally when the freight is on the rise, in order to avoid risks, the party shall choose C group to import while F group to export.

3. 4　Risks During Transit

During international carriage, the transacted goods have to experience long-term transportation; the goods will encounter various natural disasters, accidents, or even wars which make the risks during transit great. Thus when the two parties decide trade terms, risks in different periods, roots, and transport modes shall be considered.

3.5 Difficulty in Carrying out Customs Formalities

In the international trade, some countries may forbid the foreign party to clear customs for the local party. For example, if the buyer can not carry out the export formalities in its partner's country, then EXW shall not be applied; if the seller can not carry out the import formalities directly or indirectly, then DDP is not advisable.

Key Terms

Arbitration 仲裁

Commercial invoice 商业发票

Commodities transactions 大宗商品交易

Customs clearance 清关税

Customs formalities 结关手续

Dead freight 空仓费

Demurrage 滞期费

Electronic communication 电子通讯

Equilibrium 平衡

Loading and unloading 装卸

Miscellaneous charges 杂费

International usages 国际惯例

Insurance premium 保险费

Port of destination 目的港

Port of shipment 装运港

Shipping space 仓位

Ship's rail 船舷

String sales 转售

Stowage charges 理舱费

Symbolic delivery 象征性交货

Trade terms 贸易术语

Unit price 单价

Abbreviations

ICC (International Chamber of Commerce) 国际商会

ILA (International Law Association) 国际法协会

B/L (Bill of Lading) 提单

INCOTERMS (International Rules for Interpretation of Trade Terms) 国际贸易术语解释通则

JNC (Joint National Committee) 联合委员会

CCUS (Chamber of Commerce of the U. S.) 美国商会

UNCITRAL (United Nations Commission on International Trade Law) 联合国国际贸易法委员会

VAT (Value Added Tax) 增值税

 ### Case Study

CIF or Not?

One year, a Chinese exporter sold 1000 M/T of walnut to several British clients on CIF basis, which they agreed to pay by irrevocable sight L/C. As walnut is a kind of seasonal commodity, the prompt delivery is especially important cause that will affect the selling price in the market. Thus the following clause on time of delivery was stipulated in the contract: "The goods shall be shipped in October at the Chinese port of shipment, the seller shall guarantee the arrival of the cargo vessel at the port of destination in Britain on December 2nd. If the cargo vessel arrives later than the deadline, the seller must agree to cancel the contract under the buyer's request. Then the buyer shall be entitled to get the refund if the goods are paid in advance."

After the contract is concluded, our Chinese exporter shipped the goods in the middle of October, and received the full payment from the bank against the shipping documents stipulated on L/C. Accidentally, during the transit, the vessel's main engine was damaged thus could not sail ahead any more.

In order to ensure the prompt delivery, we used lots of money to rent a high-powered tugboat to tow the ship ahead. But the tugboat encountered great sound storm on the sea which resulted in the cargo vessel's lateness for 3 days. At that time, the market price of walnuts was decreasing, most of the clients in Britain asked for cancellation of contracts except two companies. The Chinese exporter suffered a disastrous financial loss.

📖 Discussion

1. Is the contract involved a CIF contract? Why or why not?
2. What are the main barriers that challenge you while reading? Linguistic barriers or lack of professional knowledge in the international business?
3. What can you learn from this case?

≫ Exercises

I. True or False

1. Incoterms 2010 differs from Incoterms 2000 only in the number of involved trade terms.
2. Trade terms define the responsibilities and expenses of both the seller and the buyer.
3. The risks transfer from the seller to the buyer on FOB basis when the goods are delivered across the ship's rail according to Incoterms 2010.
4. "London" in the price "U. S. $ 800 per M/T CIF London" is the named port of shipment.
5. Electronic communications now has the same status as that of the paper communications in

today's international trade as per Incoterms 2010.

6. In string sales, the goods shall be resold under FOB after the cargo vessel has set off.

7. Carrier in FCA refers to any person who undertakes transportation by rail, air, sea, etc., in a contract of carriage.

8. CFR derived terms are defined to indicate the responsibility of loading expense.

9. CIF is a shipment term.

10. In DDP, the seller's responsibilities are maximized.

II. Mutiple Choice

1. The term FOB should be followed by _____.

    A. point of origin   B. port of importation

    C. port of discharge   D. port of exportation

2. If delivery occurs at the seller's premise under FCA, the _____ is responsible for the loading.

    A. seller   B. buyer

    C. carrier   D. shipper

3. The term EXW should be followed by _____.

    A. point of origin   B. point of shipment

    C. port of importation   D. port of exportation

4. Under DDP, _____ shall clear the customs for import and carry out import formalities.

    A. the buyer   B. the agent

    C. the seller   D. the importing country

5. _____ refers to the action to resell the goods during transit.

    A. Foreign trade   B. Distribution

    C. Wholesaling   D. String sales

III. Answer Questions

1. What means by trade terms? Why shall we use them in international trade?

2. Compared with Incoterms 2000, what are the changes in Incoterms 2010?

Chapter 3 Remittance

This chapter mainly introduces the different methods of fund transfer in international trade. It is important for traders to familiarize with the parties, procedures and function of remittance. As well as international transferring and clearing system and laws, rules and uniform customs relating to international trade payment.

Remittance is one of banking customer services, in which funds will be transferred from one person to another. When two persons live in the same country, this type remittance is called domestic remittance, while the remittance will be a foreign banking business if two persons live in different countries, which will be our attention in this chapter.

Taking an exporter remitting fund to importer abroad as an example, the brief process of international remittance is: firstly, importer applies for transferring money at a local bank; then, pays money to the bank. After accepting the application, the local bank will transfer the money to the exporters account through its correspondent bank.

1. Overview of Remittance

Remittance is a kind of commercial settlement used in international trade and settlement. Normally, after conclusion of a sales contract, the buyer may effect the payment by remittance. It means that the buyer applies to his bank for paying a specific amount to the seller either by Mail Transfer, or Telegraphic Transfer. Sometimes, the payment is adopted by means of Demand Draft.

Remittance advice is a letter sent by a customer to a supplier, to inform the supplier that their invoice has been paid. If the customer is paying by cheque, the remittance advice often accompanies the check. The advice may consist of a literal letter (e. g. , "Gentlemen: Your shipment of the 10th was received in good order; accompanying is our remittance of $ 52. 47 per invoice No 83046") or of a voucher attached to the side or top of the check.

Remittance advice is not mandatory, however they are seen as a courtesy because they help the accounts—receivable department to match invoices with payments. The remittance advice should therefore specify the invoice numbers for which payment is tendered.

In countries where checks are still used, most companies' invoices are designed so that customers return a portion of the invoice, called a remittance advice, with their payment. In countries where wire transfer is the predominant payment method, invoices are commonly accompanied by standardized bank transfer order forms (like accept giros (Dutch) (Netherlands) and Überweisungen (German) (German)) which include a field into which the invoice or client number can be encoded, usually in a computer-readable way. The payer fills in his account details and hands the form to a clerk at, or mails it to, his bank, which will then transfer the money.

The employee who opens the incoming mail should initially compare the amount of cash received with the amount shown on the remittance advice. If the customer does not return a remittance advice, an employee prepares one. Like the cash register tape, the remittance advice serves as a record of cash initially received. Modern systems will often scan a paper remittance advice into a computer system where data entry will be performed. Modern remittance advice can include dozens, or hundreds of invoice numbers, and other information.

1. 1 Parties to a Remittance

Originally, there are four parties involved in this business, i. e. (1) Remitter: who applies to transfer money to another person. (2) Payee or Beneficiary: to whom the money will be transmitted. (3) Remitting Bank: who is entrusted to remit the funds outward. (4) Paying Bank: who is entrusted by the remitting bank to make payment to the payee.

1. 2 Type of Remittance

Based on the manner by which the payment instruction is transmitted from remitting bank to paying bank, there are 3 types of remittance, i. e. Telegraphic Transfer (T/T), Mail Transfer (M/T) and Demand Draft (D/D). In practice, type of remittance is determined by the client himself when he fills in the remittance application form a bank. For Telegraphic Transfer, Mail Transfer and Demand Draft, application forms are the same and in duplicate. After filling in the forms, the remitter should hand over them to bank clerk. And the bank clerk will give one copy of the forms back after checking and stamping, which means that bank is to commit to this business.

1. 2. 1 Telegraphic Transfer (T/T)

By Telegraphic Transfer, payment instruction given by the remitting bank to the paying bank will be transmitted by telecommunication, such as cable, telex or computer system. The key point is that the paying bank must authenticate whether the instruction is given really by the remitting bank indicated in the telecommunication, for the funds should eventually be reimbursed by this remitting bank to the paying bank. In the history of international banking, there were numerous cases of cheating money by fake instruction in the name of a remitting bank. The method of authenticating the remitting bank is to check its test key. After receiving the instruction from the remitting bank, the paying bank will, firstly, check the test key according to the predetermined rule. The paying bank would refuse to inform the payee if the test key is incorrect.

(1) The main messages in a remittance by T/T are as follows:

a. Test-key of the remitting bank

b. Name and address of the remitter

c. Name and address of the payee

d. Currency and amount of funds

e. Reimbursement of remittance cover

f. Telegraphic transfer procedure

(2) The main procedure

a. Applying: The remitter fills in the application form and gives the funds to be transferred.

b. Instructing: The remitting bank will check out the amount, if the remitter has opened an account with this bank, then, debits remitter's account, in the amount to be remitted plus commission, and send payment instruction by means of telecommunication to its correspondent bank.

c. Paying: Upon receipt of the instruction, the paying bank will verify the test-key of remitting bank in question, notify the beneficiary, pay to him, and claim reimbursement from the remitting bank.

d. Advising: Paying bank should advise the debiting against the remitting bank.

(3) The whole procedure of T/T

The whole procedure could be illustrated by following Figure 3.1.

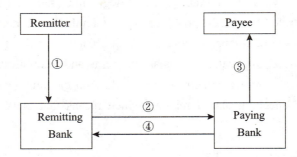

Figure 3.1　Procedure of Telegraphic Transfer

1.2.2　Mail Transfer (M/T)

A Mail Transfer mean that payment instruction given by the remitting bank is transmitted by mail given by the remitting bank is transmitted by mail or by courier. Payment instruction is in a form of Payment Order illustrated in Specimen 1. Procedure of M/T is almost the same as the T/T. (See Figure 3.1), except that the truthfulness of the instruction received should be authenticated by means of authorized signature pre-agreed instead of test-key. Owing to the mail time being much longer than that of telecommunication, the M/T is not broadly used in international trade.

Bank of China
Payment Order

Hubei

To:

No. of payment order	To be paid or credited to	Amount

Amount in words

Remarks

By order of

☐ You are authorized to debit our account with you

☐ We have credited your a/c with us

Bank of China, Hubei, Branch

Specimen 1　Payment Order

1.2.3　Demand Draft

Demand Draft is called also remittance by Banker's demand draft. The payment instruction is written down directly on the surface of the bank draft. A bank draft is a negotiable instrument drawn by the remitting bank in its overseas correspondent bank, ordering the latter to pay on demand the stated amount to the holder of the draft. It is often used when the client wants to control the founds—transfer. After being issued, the bank draft should be handed over to the remitter, who may dispatch or even bring it to the beneficiary abroad. Upon receipt of the draft, the payee can either present it for payment at the counter of the drawee bank or collect it through his account bank. Specimen of a bank demand draft is shown by Specimen 2.

Bank of China

This draft is valid   No. 1123044

for one year from

the date of issue

Amount: USD 30,855,00

Pay To: Management Rationalization Research Centre Aug. 25, 2002

.... (Date)

(Place)

The Sum of U. S. Dollars Thirty Thousand Eight

....

Hundred and fifty-five only

To: Bank of China, Singapore

....

Pay against this draft to the   Bank of China

Debit of our   account   Shandong Branch

Specimen 2 Bank Demand Draft

Little different from T/T, the procedure of D/D is shown in Figure 3. 2 and explained as follows:

a. Applying: The remitter fills with a remittance form and deliver funds to be transferred.

b. Issuing: The remitting bank issues the draft and hands over it to the remitter.

c. Sending: The remitter forwards the draft to the payee by post or in person.

d. Presenting: The payee presents the draft to the drawee bank for payment.

e. Paying: The paying bank verified the signatures on the draft face and make payment.

f. Advising: The paying bank advises that they have debited remitting bank's Nostro account.

The procedure of D/D is illustrated by Figure 3. 2.

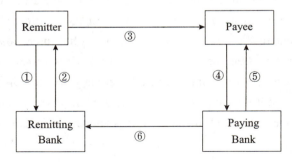

Figure 3. 2 Procedure of Demand Draft

2. Reimbursement of the Remittance Cover

Under remittance, the paying bank credits the funds against the payee's account, which should be reimbursed by the remitting bank prior to or after the payment. Reimbursement or booking remittance cover under a remittance refers to keep books on the current accounts or other appointed accounts. Booking manner, namely, debiting or crediting, should be instructed in the payment order given by the remitting bank. Net amount payable or receivable to the banks involved will be calculated in a certain time interval (say, one day), and be cleared through inter-bank clearing system. Cover can be constructed as funds in this context.

2. 1 Bank Instruction

Under each remittance, the remitting bank has to instruct the paying bank clearly how to handle the "remittance cover". Methods of reimbursement are specified in the telegraphic text under a T/T, or in the payment order under a M/T, or on the face of bank draft under a D/D. based on the relationship of banks, there are different manners to handle the cover as follows:

If both the remitting bank and paying bank are the correspondent banks each other, i. e. having an account relationship, the cover instruction given by the remitting bank could be either "In cover, we have credited your a/c with us" or "In cover, please debit our a/c with you." In practice, the remitting bank prefers to choose the latter scheme, because the paying bank will debit the remitting bank's account with it only after the paying bank has made the payment to the payee, eliminating the uncertainty in the remittance. The former scheme means that the remitting bank has credited paying bank's account before its payment to the payee, which decreases liquidity of the remitting bank.

2. 2 Relationship Between Correspondent Banks

If remitting bank and paying bank do not have direct account relationship with each other, but both have opened accounts with the same correspondent bank, say, Bank X, for facilitating funds transfer. The remitting bank may advise this correspondent Bank X to keep books on both accounts with them. The wording in the instruction to the paying bank could be "In cover, we have authorized Bank X to debit our a/c and credit your a/c with them." Even though both banks have opened accounts with each other, they would entrust a correspondent which is located in the world financial center (New York or London) to handle funds between the. So as to speed up the clearance.

If the remitting bank and paying bank have neither a direct account relationship nor a common correspondent bank like in case mentioned above, things become much complicated. The procedure might be, the remitting bank firstly advising its correspondent bank, say, Bank X to transfer the funds to the Bank Y, correspondent bank from paying bank side in favor of the paying bank, and at the meantime, to instruct the paying bank with the wording like "In cover, we have instruct Bank X to remit proceeds to you."

According to the above situations, more convenient and less cost is to transfer funds when remitting bank and paying bank are correspondent each other. From firm's point of view, delegating to a transactional bank which has worldwide network of branches, subsidiaries and correspondent banks, to conduct its international trade settlement would get more benefit in cost, time, financial products as well as quality of service.

3. International Transferring and Clearing System

3. 1　Clearing Principles

A bank usually has a lot of overseas relational banks, with which it opens account and entrusts business. In Vostro accounts of a bank, some banks have receivables, and the others have payables. In an agreed interval, such bank should pay all banks with new receivables and demand payment from all banks with net payables. And other banks should also do in this way, which, no doubt, are time-and-energy-consuming works. In today's banking, banks having close ties each other normally open accounts with the same clearing instruction (national central bank or special clearing house), and keep certain sum of funds. A bank, which still has net debit after netting all receivables and payables to other banks, it named net paying bank, while a bank still having net credit is named net receiving bank. Only the net paying bank will make payment ultimately. The further question would be raised, to whom should the net paying bank make the payment? Figure 3. 3 below explains the clearing principles.

Paying bank / Receiving bank	A	B	C	D	E	Sum of receivables	Net debit
A	0	10	20	30	40	100	—
B	10	0	20	30	40	100	—
C	10	20	0	30	40	100	0
D	10	20	30	0	40	100	30
E	10	20	30	40	0	100	60
Sum of payable	40	70	100	130	160	500	
Net credit	60	30	0		—		90

Figure 3. 3　Inter-bank Clearing Principles

Consider, there are five member banks, A, B, C, D, E belonging to a clearing house. Among of them, Bank A should collect proceeds in amounts 10, 20, 30, and 40 from Banks B, C, D, and E respectively, totally 100 units of receivables, while it should also pay in amounts of 10 units to each bank, totally 40 units payables. Therefore it has net credit at 60 units (100 receivables minus 40 payables). The same as Bank A, Bank B has 30 units of net credits. Thus Bank A and Bank B are net receiving banks. Bank C's receivables it just equal to the payables, and Bank C does nothing. Bank E has 1010 units of receivables and 160 units of payables totally, so it should pay net 60 units. Hence, Banks D and E are net paying banks. The sum of receivables of all banks should be equal to the sum of payables, i. e. 500 units. And the net credits of the net receiving banks should be equal to net debits of all net paying banks, i. e.... 90 units. After matching and netting, Bank D pays 30 and Bank E pays 60 to the clearing house which in turn transfers funds 60 to Bank A and 30 to Banks merely. In other words, only 90 units of money should be moved physically instead of 500 units, by which it saves not only manpower, material resources, but also working capital.

3. 2 World Leading Payment and Clearing Systems

In the past, the most of debits and credits to be cleared probably in the form of paper instruments, which were cleared manually, tanking several days, or even weeks, accordingly slowing down turnover of banks and exposing foreign exchange. Along with the ever-changing business environment and rapidly developed information technology, transferring funds between banks mainly are implemented through electronic funds transfer systems. Funds of being debited will be transferred and settled from the sending participants (say, remitting bank's) account to the recipient's, e. g. the paying bank's account, in real-time, almost without time interruption, and without manual operation. And the recipient bank can use the funds transferred to its account immediately. Final clearing can be done in one day interval. Nowadays, there are four vital electronic funds transfer systems, they are CHIPS, CHAPS, SWIFT and TARGET.

3. 2. 1 CHIPS

CHIPS, abbreviation of Clearing House Inter-Bank Payment System, developed 1971 by the New York Clearing House Association for transfer of international dollar payments, operated real-time, final payment system for business-to-business transactions, linking about 140 depository institutions, called also settling banks, that have offices or affiliates in New York City. Clients of settling banks (participants) have their own accounts and UIN in the system, but are not to clear their accounts by the end of business day directly, which will be done in the name of their settling bank.

CHIPS transfers an average total value of USD1. 2 trillion daily, clearing and settling 242,000 transactions on an average day, handling over 95% of all U. S. dollars payments moving among countries worldwide in 2000.

The core of CHIPS is Universal Identifier Database (UID), in which all corporate customers of the member's bank has its own Universal Identification Number, a unique identifier that tells the CHIPS system what private account and bank information to use for processing payments. It allows straight-through processing without manual lookups or costly delays.

In each business day, at 7 o'clock CHIPS starts to receive the participant's instructions, verifying UIN, matching and sending them to the receivers concerned. Immediately following the closing of the CHIPS network at 16:30 (Eastern Standard Time), the CHIPS computer produces a settlement report showing the net debit or credit position of each participant. Then, the settling participants (non-settling participant is netted against the position of its correspondent settling participant) with net debit positions have until 17:45 to transfer their debit amounts through FEDWIRE, operated by the Federal Reserve and used for domestic money transfers, to the CHIPS settlement account on the books of the New York Fed. The CHIP then transfers those funds via FEDWIRE, out of the settlement account to those settling participants with net credit positions. The process usually is completed by 18:00.

3.2.2 CHAPS

CHAPS (Clearing House Automated Payment System) is an electronic transfer system for sending same-day value payments from bank to bank. It operates in partnership with the Bank of England in providing the payment and settlement service.

CHAPS was developed in 1984, and is one of the largest real-time gross settlement systems in the world, second only to FEBWIRE in the USA. Since 4 January 1999, the CHAPS clearing company has operated two separate clearings, CHAPS Sterling and CHAPS Euro. In 2000, CHAPS Sterling processed an average daily volume 81,738 with a daily average value of USD189 billion.

There are 21 member banks currently participating in the Euro and/or sterling clearing, such as Bank of England, Deutshe Bank, Dresdner Bank, HSBC Bank, Citybank, Standard Chartered Bank, Bank of Tokyo-Mitsubishi, and so on.

3.2.3 SWIFT

SWIFT, standing for the Society for World Inter-bank Financial Telecommunication, has over 7,000 financial institutions in 192 countries, based in the Netherlands, Hong Kong, the United Kingdom, and the United States. It provides worldwide, 24 hours a day, 7 days a week, assistance in more than 10 languages. SWIFT provides messaging services to banks, broker-dealers and investment managers, as well as to market infrastructures (means here clearing and settling house) in cover transfer, international trade payments, treasury, securities, foreign exchange transactions, and so on.

SWIFT has carried 1.2 billion message in 2000, i.e. 330,000 average daily transaction, and the average daily value of payment messages is estimated to be above USD 5 trillion. Since 1982 Bank of China is the member of the SWIFT, while several hundreds of Chinese banks and their branches became its members.

SWIFT was born in 1973 at the centre of Brussels, supported only by 239 banks in 15 countries at its beginning, started the mission of creating a shared worldwide data processing and communications link and a common language for international financial transactions. However, no any messages were transmitted by this system until Albert, Prince of Belgium, sent the first message via this system in 1977.

To safely and efficiently transfer customer's message and settle the funds cover, SWIFT introduces a series of standard formats for a variety of financial message. For example, MT100 is a customer transfer message which is used for a funds transfer instruction in which at least one of the end-parties' is a non-financial institution, MT700 to issue a documentary credit, indicating the terms and conditions of a Documentary Credit.

In order to ensure error-free identification of parties in automated systems, SWIFT developed the Bank Identifier Code (BIC), which identifies precisely the financial institution involved in financial transactions. The BIC is made of eight or eleven consecutive alphanumeric characters, without any spaces or other characters, the first four-character code is called the Bank Code. It is unique to each financial institution and can only be made up of letters. The 5th and 6th code are country code identifying the country in which the financial institution is located, which are followed by the last two location code, maybe alphabetical or numeral, providing geographical distinction within a country , e. g. cities, states, provinces and time zones. Only a SWIFT BIC can appear in the header of a SWIFT message as Sender or Receiver.

3.2.4   TARGET

TARGET, which stands for the Trans-European Automated Real-time Gross Settlement Express Transfer system, is the real-time gross settlement system for the Euro, which commenced operation on 4 January 1999.

TARGET consists of 15 national real-time gross settlement (RTGS) systems and the ECB payment mechanism (EPM), which are interlinked so as to provide an uniform platform for the processing of cross-border payments. The cross-border part (i. e. that involving two interlinked RTGS systems) represents approximately 40% in terms of value and 20% in terms of volume of all TARGET payments (both cross-border and domestic payments).

There are more than 5,000 RTGS participants in TARGET and almost all Ell Credit Institutions are accessible via TARGET, including those countries which have not adopted the Euro as their currency (Non-euro area countries).

In March 2000 the number of payments processed in TARGET as a whole, i. e. cross-border and domestic payments taken together, amounted to more than 187,000 as daily average (of which 39,000 were cross-border). At the same time, the average daily value processed in

TARGET as a whole reached EUR 1,040 billion (of which the value of cross-border payments was EUR 436 billion), which is equivalent to a 69% share of all large-value payment systems operating in Euro. These figures show that TARGET is already one of the largest payment systems in the world. Usually, payment instruction takes at most several minutes, even though within several seconds, to be debited with the sending bank's account.

SWIFT was chosen as the network service provider for TARGET. Special agreements have been concluded with SWIFT with a view to providing the best support in term of speed, capacity, availability and security.

Each clearing system introduced previously has it own characteristics as well as limitation. CHIPS and CHAPS are connected with their own central bank respectively, easily clearing the net position for its settling members, yet limit the numbers of participating member on the base of qualification or location and the operating only in the local business time. Transferring Euro only in the Ell member states, including Euro-area countries and non-Euro-area countries, limits the worldwide use of TARGET. With working in different currencies, in more than 10 languages, 24 hours in 7 days per week, SWIFT is the most popular international payment in the world, even though it can not yet make the ultimate net debit or credit settlement at moment.

4. Laws, Rules and Uniform Customs

4.1　Relating to International Trade Payment

As well-known, commercial parties in international trade live in different countries or regions, many service companies, such as transport companies, banks etc., are needed for doing foreign business. Hence, international trade is a complicated process where different parties are involved, and political, legal environment and trade customs have impacts on it. The interpretation to the same practice differs from person to person, or even becomes a matter of debate, hindering from doing business, increasing transaction costs and making trouble to the businessperson. Therefore, uniform commercial usages widely recognized by nations are needed. International customs refer to particular usages within some trade established worldwide through a long social practice.

Generally, customs should have such characteristics as follows:

(1) they are used by people in certain trade constantly and repeatedly;

(2) they contain clear and acceptable contents;

(3) they are recognized by this circle and are able to bind people concerned.

Though international customs can bind people's behaviors, they are not laws. Customs are disciplines commonly followed by the non-government organizations and people in certain trade, while laws are behavior standard worked out and approved by the state authorities, embodying the will of state, being carried out compulsorily. International customs restrain people's behavior in a certain extend, but they are not compulsory implemented by the state authority. The reasonability of the international customs are, by avoiding differences of culture, especially political and legal system of countries, to recognize the common usages from long commercial practice. Those customs, as a non-official arrangement of institution, normally are to be observed on professional's own will and have longer life.

As a arrangement of institution, international customs can fill in gaps and shortage of laws. First, they standardize commercial practice of traders, so as to decline transaction costs; second, by stating to comply with international customs, commercial parties can show their internationalization and raise their trade credit; third, international customs are often used by the court for judgment or arbitrator for arbitration on trade disputes. Many countries clearly recognize international customs and apply them in legal practice.

4.2 The International Customs

The first international customs was about international cargo. ICC (International Chamber of Commerce) worked out for the first time INCOTERMS in 1936, now this term is the most influent and widely used custom in the world.

Because of long period between the conclusion and completion of a contract, traders are easy to have suspicions on mutual credit. The success of trade, at a large extend, rest on the credit, either trade credit or bank credit. Trade credit is the key factor of successful transaction, while the bank credit is necessary supplement. No matter using trade credit or bank credit, the purpose is all ensuring that buyers pay to the seller for goods or services and sellers provide goods or services in accordance with contract. Accordingly, traders and bankers established payment of collections based on the trade credit and payment of L/C based on bank credit. Gradually, international rules and customs for international trade payment have been developed and recognized worldwide, i. e. "Uniform Rules for Collections" and "Uniform Customs and Practice for Documentary Credits".

In addition, with the innovation of international trade contracts for large construction projects and international purchase are, normally, conducted by means of international bidding. Success of those high value transactions relies on trade credit as well as bank credit. Bank's guarantee is needed for ensuring that the trader will fulfill the contract. In order to standardize practice and usage of bank guarantee, ICC worked out "Uniform Rules for Contract Guarantee", and "Uniform Rules Demand Guarantee", specifying rights and obligations of related parties in bank guarantee, promoting the success of transactions.

In international payment, China has been doing in line with international practice, recognizing and observing uniform rules and customs for international payment.

Closely related to international trade payment are also laws on instruments. Owing to obvious law differences between British Commonwealth Countries and European Continental Countries, there are no worldwide uniform customs for instruments. Therefore, pay attention to the applications of laws for instruments relating to the party's location.

📖 Words & Expressions

1. remittance 汇款业务
2. party 当事人
3. remitter 汇款人
4. payee 收款人
5. remitting bank 汇出行
6. paying bank 付款行
7. T/T 电汇
8. reimbursement 偿付/拨付
9. cover 头寸
10. debit 借汇
11. credit 贷汇
12. D/D 票汇
13. M/T 信汇
14. clearing system 清算系统
15. CHIPS 美国纽约票据交换所银行同业支付系统
16. CHAPS 英国伦敦票据交换所银行同业支付系统
17. SWIFT 环球银行间金融电讯协会
18. TARGET 欧元自动拨付与清算系统
19. Uniform Customs 统一惯例
20. "Uniform Rules for Collections"《托收统一规则》
21. "Uniform Customs and Practice for Documentary Credits"《跟单信用证统一惯例》
22. "Uniform Rules for Contract Guarantee"《合约保函统一规则》
23. "Uniform Rules for Demand Guarantee"《见索即付保函统一规则》
24. British Commonwealth countries 英美法系
25. European Continental countries 大陆法系
26. Vostro 来账
27. Nostro 往账

📖 Notes

1. Remittance is one of banking customer services, in which funds will be transferred from one person to another.

   汇付是银行客户服务方式之一，是将资金从一方转移至交易的另一方。

2. The remitting bank will check out the amount, if the remitter has opened an account with this bank, then, debits remitter's account, in the amount to be remitted plus commission, and send payment instruction by means of telecommunication to its correspondent bank.

汇出行将核实总额，如果汇款人在该行已开户，然后借记汇款人账户（以汇付金额加佣金），最后通过电讯方式将付款指令传送到它的代理行。

3. Procedure of M/T is almost the same as the T/T, except that the truthfulness of the instruction should be authenticated by means of authorized signature pre-agreed instead of test-key.

除了所接受指令的真伪性借助于双方预先同意的签名而不是密押予以证实外，信汇的程序和电汇的程序几乎相同。

4. A bank draft is a negotiable instrument drawn by the remitting bank on its overseas correspondent bank, ordering the latter to pay on demand the stated amount to the holder of the draft.

一张银行汇票是一份可转让的票据，它是由汇款行开立给它的海外代理行，且命令后者即期支付所述金额给汇票的持票人。

5. Under each remittance, the remitting bank has to instruct the paying bank clearly how to handle the "remittance cover".

在任何一种汇付情况下，汇款行必须清楚地批示付款行如何处置"汇付头寸"。

6. In Vostro accounts of a bank, some banks have receivables, and the others have payables.

在一家银行的来往账户里，一些银行有应收款，而其他银行有应付款。

7. In today's banking, banks having close ties each other normally open accounts with the same clearing instruction (national central bank or special clearing house), and keep certain sum of funds.

在当今的金融业，相互有密切联系的银行通常在相同的清算机构（国家中央银行或专门清算行）开立账户并保持一定金额的资金。

8. In the past, the most of debits and credits to be cleared probably in the form of paper instruments, which were cleared manually, taking several days, or even weeks, accordingly slowing down turn over of banks and exposing foreign exchange.

在过去，大多数借记和贷记或许都是以低票据形式清算，这种清算由手工完成，花费若干乃至若干星期相应地降低了银行营业额并产生外汇风险。

9. To safely and efficiently transfer customer's message and settle the funds cover, SWIFT introduces a series of standard formats for a variety of financial message.

为了安全和有效地发送客户住处和结算资金头寸，SWIFT 系统引入了一系列标准格式用于众多的财务信息。

10. In order to ensure error-free identification of parties in automated systems, SWIFT developed the Bank Identifier Code (BIC), which identifies precisely the financial

institution involved in financial transactions.

为了确保在自动化系统里有关当事人的无错识别，SWIFT 系统开发出了银行识别码，它能精确识别涉及金融交易的金融机构。

11. In addition, with the innovation of international trade contracts for large construction projects and international purchase are, normally, conducted by means of international bidding.

此外，随着国际贸易的进步，大型建设项目和跨国采购合同一般都借助于国际招标而予以实施。

12. In order to standardize practice and usage of bank guarantee, ICC worked out "Uniform Rules for Contract Guarantee" and "Uniform Rules for Demand Guarantee", specifying rights and obligations of related parties in bank guarantee, promoting the success of transactions.

为了使银行保函的实行和用途标准化，国际商会制订了《合约保函统一规则》和《见索即付保函统一规则》，特别强调了银行保函业务中相关当事人的权利和义务，促进了交易的成功进行。

≫≫ Exercises

I. True or False

1. D/D stands for Demand Draft.

2. M/T is a quicker method of payment than a banker's draft.

3. Among T/T, M/T and D/D, T/T is the cheapest method of payment.

4. A further advantage of T/T over M/T is that there is no danger of instructions being delayed or lost in the post.

5. In the case of M/T, the remitting bank issues a draft to its customer, and directs its foreign branch or correspondent by mail to make the payment to the beneficiary.

6. Banks keep two types of international account, Vostro and Nostro accounts.

7. SWIFT stands for Society for Worldwide Inter-bank Financial Telecommunications.

8. CHIPS is almost the same as CHAPS.

9. SWIFT is the most convenient for transferring funds.

10. The operation of a telegraphic transfer is just the same as the mail transfer.

II. Multiple Choice

1. If the London's bank makes a payment to a correspondent abroad, ＿＿＿＿＿＿.

   A. it will remit the sum abroad

   B. the foreign bank's Vostro account will be credited

   C. the London bank's nostro account will be credited

D. either A or B

2. If Bank of England instructs Citybank to pay a sum of USD 100,000 to Midland, its Nostro account should be _____.

   A. credited   B. debited   C. increased   D. deceased

3. When a customer asks its bank to make a T/T to a beneficiary abroad, the charges may _____.

   A. be paid by either the remitter

   B. be debited against the nostro account

   C. be credited to the Vostro account

   D. be paid by the remitting bank

4. If an importer in Britain asks his bank to make a T/T to an exporter abroad, he should _____.

   A. pay the home currency equivalent of the sum in foreign currency

   B. pay the banks commission

   C. get a permission from authorities

   D. pay the bank in foreign currency

5. SWIFT is _____.

   A. in the United States

   B. a governmental organization

   C. an institution of the United Nations

   D. a kind of communications belonging to T/T system for interbank's fund transfer

6. M/T is sent to the correspondent bank _____, unless otherwise instructed by client.

   A. by courier service   B. by ordinary mail

   C. by airmail   D. by seamail

7. The various methods of settlement all involve the same book keeping, The only difference is _____.

   A. the method by which the overseas bank is advised about the transfer

   B. the method by which the beneficiary is advised about the transfer

   C. the speed

   D. the beneficiary

8. Suppose that a UK firm which is to pay a debt to a German Supplier in Euro dollar the firm will give a written instruction to its bank in the UK to issue a mail transfer. Then the UK bank _____.

   A. debits the UK firm's account as authorized

   B. credits the UK firm's account as authorized

   C. debits the account of German bank

   D. credits the German supplier's account

9. Large payments should be made by _____.

  A. T/T   B. SWIFT   C. M/T   D. A or B

10. A _____ payment does not take as long as an M/T payment.

  A. SWIFT   B. T/T   C. D/D   D. A or B

Chapter 4

Instrument

This chapter demonstrates the definition, implications and function of financial document, called also instruments which are widely used in international trade payment. It is essential for us to recognize and use them correctly and properly in order that we can facilitate the transfer of credits and do more business with foreigners.

As we know, just owing to various documents being created and used, banks are capable of taking part in international trade payment. Among the documents, financial document, called also instruments, is a kind of certificate in writing which aims at obtaining a certain amount of proceeds. It clearly records currency to certain extend, circulating among participants, facilitating the transfer of credits, acting as payment and credit tools in merchandise exchange.

In international trade, the main instruments of payment in settlement of the purchase price are the currency and bills (i. e. bill of exchange, promissory note, and check).

1. Overview of Instruments

Many documents guaranteeing the completion of obligations are properties, e. g. bill of exchange, bill of lading and so on. Briefly, there are two categories of property, i. e. real property and personal properly. The former refers to the property like land and house, which can not be moved from one place to another, while the latter could be taken away by the owner of property. The personal property in turn can be classified into chose in action and chose in possession.

A chose in action is property which does not physically exist and consequently can not be effectively protected by physical means, only by court action. Therefore, it is often referred to as intangible property. Examples include rights in bill of exchange, bill of lading, patents, copyrights, shares and life policies. A chose in procession is property with a physical existence, such property can therefore be physically possessed and protected, books in your book shelf or clothes in your wardrobe for examples.

The proof of title to a chose in action is certificate of title, or document of title, sometimes also called broad instrument, which can be transferred from one holder to another by some legal actions. On certificate of title, debtor who should pay money or deliver goods in a certain amount has to be stated in writing. Generally, the title can be transferred from transferor to transferee in three ways, namely, negotiation, semi-negotiation and assignment.

1. 1   Negotiation

Negotiation means that the title can be transferred merely by delivering the certificate of title or by endorsement on the certificate completed by delivery. This kind of document of title is named negotiable instrument, or financial document, or in short term, instruments, being used for obtaining a certain sum of money.

Negotiable instruments are payment tools as well as credit tools for domestic and international transactions, which can substitute cash in certain extent, but more convenient than it. Strictly speaking, a negotiable instrument is an unconditional order or promise to pay an amount of money, easily transferable from one person to another. Bill of exchange, promissory note and check are good examples.

A negotiable instrument has three vital significant features:

(1) The transfee in good faith and for value can acquire a better title than that held by all his prior parties.

(2) The holder need not give notice of the transfer to prior parties, especial to original debtor, to establish their title.

(3) The holders can sue in their own names.

A person taking a transfer of a negotiable instrument in good faith and for value, called also holder in due course or bona fide transferee, is unaffected by any defects of the title of the transferor or any other prior parties. For instance, a person, say, A who acquired the instrument by fraud has only an empty title to it, but a bona fide transfee, say, person B, for value from that person A acquire a perfect title. Importance in practice is that a holder in due course like person B acquires an absolute right to payment of the full amount of the negotiable instrument and can enforce this right against all parties to the instrument if the instrument is not paid by the drawee. The advantage of a person as a holder in due course is particularly vital to a bank involved in international business. Imagine, a bank paid a certain sum of money for obtaining a bill of exchange, becoming a bona fide transferee, if the importer refused to pay the money under the contract with a number of reasons, the bank should be reimbursed at least by the drawer, i. e. exporter, so that benefit of the bank would be protected.

Debtor being indicated on a negotiable instrument should assume instrument obligations, while the creditor enjoys the instrument rights. Instrument obligations mean that the instrument debtor has the obligation to pay the instrument amount to the holder, while the instrument rights refers that the creditor has title to demand debtor for paying the sum of instrument, including demand right, recourse right and transfer right. The instruments are produced, transferred and terminated along with the issuance, transfer and termination of the instrument.

1. 2　Semi-negotiation

A title certificate which can be transferred in the way of semi-negotiation is quite similar to the negotiable instrument. In general, title is transferable just by delivering the certificate or by endorsement on the certificate completed by delivery, needless to give notice of the action to prior party to recognize the transferee's title. However, the transferee can not acquire a better title than his prior party i. e. any defect in the transferor's title is also transferred. The good examples for semi-negotiable certificate of title are bill of lading, warehouse receipt, not negotiable crossed cheque and demand draft.

1. 3　Assignment

Assignment, one type of transferring legal title, is effected by sending the appropriate transfer form signed by the transferor and the relevant certificate to the organization which issued the securities for details of the new ownership to be entered on the register. A new certificate is then issued in favor of the transferee. The certificate of title like share, life policies, debenture should be transferred in the form of assignment.

Chose in action used for international trade payment are negotiable instruments, for example, bill of exchange, promissory note and check and semi-negotiable instruments, for instance, bill of lading and insurance policy.

Wide usage of instruments owes to their special economic functions of instruments summarized as follows: (1) they act as payment tool. Most of international trades are settled by means of non-cash, which need some payment tools; instruments are good tools to meet this requirement. (2) they act as a credit tool. One side of a transaction may ask the counterpart for providing credit as the promise of fulfilling the contract beforehand. For instance, in order to make the seller believe that payment will be made one month after shipment, the buyer can issue a promissory note payable one month later to the seller. With this promissory note, the seller most likely is willing to prepare products for shipment. Therefore, an international trade would be made successfully. (3) they act as circulating tool. Instruments can be transferred by endorsement, and the rights associated can be transferred also, functioning as a circulating tool and being generally accepted.

Instruments themselves, however, are not currency, even though they can substitute currency to certain extent. The main differences between instruments are currency are as follows:

(1) Instruments rely on private credit of issuer, acceptor or endorser without mandatory circulation of legal currency.

(2) The creditor has to accept when the debtor repays with the legal currency, but he has title to refuse accepting the instruments as repayment if he does not agree.

（3）Instruments can be restricted by time, limitation, and I validity, instruments can play the roles of payment and credit, they will no longer have those currency functions following their termination.

2. Currency and Bill of Exchange

Normally, during the payment of international trade, there are three cases in using currency for direct settlement between the creditors and debtors; adopting the currency of seller's country, or that of the buyer's country, or even that of a third country.

When both the buyer and the seller decide which currency should be used, they should take the following two points into consideration; one is the convertibility and stability of the currency; the other is the tendency of fluctuation of the currency adopted.

The bill of exchange or draft has played a vital part in the world's commercial and financial life for some countries. Also, it is widely used for settlement in international trade.

A bill of exchange or draft is an unconditional order in writing prepared by one party (the drawer) and addressed to another (the drawee) directing the drawee to pay a specified sum of money to the order of a third person (the payee), or to the bearer, on demand or at a fixed and determinable future time.

In conjunction with the definition, Figure 4.1 Specimen Bill of Exchange may be dissected as follows:

（1）An unconditional order in writing.

（2）Addressed by one person/party (the drawer), Thomas Jones.

（3）To another (the drawee), James Arthur, Manchester.

（4）Signed by the person (the drawer) giving it.

（5）Requiring the person to whom it is addressed (the drawee or payer) to pay.

（6）On demand, or at a fixed or determinable future time.

（7）A sum certain in money, $ 100.

（8）To, or to the order of, a specified person, or to bearer (the payee), John Wood.

No. 9340
USD100

London, 15 July 2016

On demand pay to John Wood or bearer the sum of U. S. dollars one hundred only.

(Signed) Thomas Jones

To: Mr. James Arthur
Manchester

Figure 4.1   Specimen: Bill of Exchange

2. 1   Parties to a Bill of Exchange

It will be seen that there are three parties to a bill of exchange:

(1) The drawer, i. e., the person who draws the bill and he is usually the exporter or his banker in international trade.

(2) The drawee (payer), i. e., the person who is to pay the money and he is usually the importer or the appointed banker under a letter of credit in international trade.

(3) The payee, i. e., the person who is to receive the money, he may be, and often is, the same person as the drawer and he is usually the exporter himself or his appointed banker in international trade or he may be the bearer of the bill.

2. 2   Key Elements of a Bill of Exchange

To be a valid negotiable instrument, a bill of exchange or draft has to be drawn properly. According to the Bill of Exchange Act 1882, a bill of exchange or draft must conform to the following requirements:

(1) It must contain the wording like Draft or even Bill of Exchange.

(2) It must write unambiguously the name and address of the drawee.

(3) It must contain an unconditional order to pay a definite sum of money.

(4) It must be in writing and signed by the drawer.

(5) It must be payable on demand or at a fixed or determinable future time.

(6) It must be payable to or to the order of a specific person or to bearer.

(7) It must indicate the amount to be paid in words and in figures. Besides above key elements, there are also some other elements to be written in the draft, e. g. :

(8) Number of bill of exchange: Those bills have the same contents, if one of them is paid, the others will be null and void, such wording can be seen in the first copy of exchange in duplicate: "Second of the same tenor and date unpaid", and in the second copy could be " First of the same tenor and date unpaid."

(9) Reason of issuing: Drafts under L/C normally indicate the reason of issuance, i. e., according to which L/C of which bank the bills of exchange are issued. ("Drawn under L/C No. 569547 of Bank Brussels Lambert, 18 Rafles Place HEX 42-00 OUB Center Singapore 048616, Dated December 18, 1998")

2. 3   Classification of Bill of Exchange

2. 3. 1   Clean or Documentary Drafts

A documentary draft is one that is accompanied by the relevant documents that are needed to complete the export transaction.

A clean draft is one that has no documents attached and is usually handed to a bank for collection in a foreign country. Such a draft may be drawn for many purposes, among which are the collection of an open account, the sale of stocks and bonds, payment for services, and other transactions that arise in international trade but for which no shipping documents exist. Bank drafts are usually clean drafts.

2. 3. 2　Sight or Time Drafts

Drafts may be drawn either at sight or at a specified number of days after sight. The time at which payment is to be made is called the tenor or usance of the draft. As its name implies, the sight draft is supposed to be paid when it is first seen by the drawee. In some countries, however, a grace period of a specified number of days is allowed. Time drafts are those that specify payment a certain number of days after sight.

In some countries it is customary for the drawee to delay payment of a sight draft until the merchandise arrives. For this reason the exporter should always have an understanding with the customer as to whether he will accept or pay a sight draft immediately or whether acceptance or payment may be delayed until the arrival of the merchandise.

2. 3. 3　Trade or Bank Drafts

A trade draft is one issued by a trader on another trader or on a bank, while a bank draft is in effect a check drawn by one bank on another. Normally, trade drafts are frequently used in international trade, which are issued on the basis of terms and conditions of the L/C.

2. 3. 4　With or Without Recourse

When financing is without recourse this means that the purchase by a bank or another financial institution of drafts is made with the understanding that the bank has no recourse to the drawer of the drafts if such drafts are dishonored. In other words, the bank that purchases drafts or bills of exchange assumes full responsibility for payment, discharges the exporter of his or her obligation as guarantor, and looks to the consignee to accept the draft and to pay it at the due date.

The term with the recourse means the exact opposite — the bank does not, in the usual sense of the term, buy or purchase the draft.

The transaction is simply that the bank lends a certain amount of money to the exporter against a clean or documentary draft. If the consignee fails for any reason to meet the draft at the due date, the bank immediately has recourse to the original drawer of the draft when the draft is discounted or sold with recourse, the drawer assumes full responsibility for the payment of the draft.

3. Legal Acts on Instruments

Legal Acts on Instruments refers to the formal actions to be taken for undertaking the obligations specified in an instrument, examples are issue, endorsement, presentation acceptance, payment and so on. Issue is the key action among them.

3. 1 Issue

To issue a draft comprises two acts to be performed by the drawer. One is to write and sign a draft, the other is to deliver it to the payee or to the payer for acceptance or payment. Delivery means to pass the draft to the payee personally or to send it by mail. Only writing a draft without delivering is invalid. Delivery is an essential act. It states in *Bill of Exchange Act*, whatever acts such as issue, endorsement or acceptance without delivering would be invalid acts. After being drawn and delivered to the payee, the draft becomes irrevocable and in the meantime the drawer engages to the payee and related holder that the draft should be paid or accepted. If it is dishonored by the drawee, the holder has the right of recourse against the drawer who is primarily liable thereon.

3. 2 Endorsement

Endorsement is the signature of the endorser on the draft, who should be the payee or a subsequent holder. The signature indicates the holder's intention to transfer his or her rights in the bill of exchange or draft. To be valid, an endorsement must satisfy the following criteria:

(1) It must be written on the back of the bill.

(2) It must be of the entire bill and not part.

If there are two or more payees, all must endorse, unless one is authorized to endorse for the others. There are three types of endorsement:

(1) Blank endorsement: An endorsement in blank is where the transferor merely signs the bill on its back. The bill becomes payable to bearer.

(2) Order endorsement: An order endorsement is where the transferor adds a direction to pay a particular person. The bill becomes payable to, or to the order of the person specified, e. g. say, "X signed Y."

(3) Restrictive endorsement: That is where the endorsement prohibits further transfer of the bill, i. e. the transferee can not transfer his right to payment. An example of a restrictive endorsement would be "Pay X only, signed Y."

An important point to remember is that any endorsement on a bearer bill is irrelevant and of no effect in this context. It can be ignored. Thus, a bill drawn as a bearer bill remains as such it can not be converted in an order bill by a special endorsement. Conversely, a bill drawn as an order bill and converted a bearer bill by an endorsement in blank can be converted back to an order bill by any holder writing an order to pay specific person above the signature of the endorser.

3. 3   Presentation

Act of submitting bill to the payer for acceptance or payment is called presentation. As bill is a kind of chose in action, the bill holder has to show the bill to the payer, so as to proof his right to payment. There are two types of presentation, presentation for acceptance and presentation for payment. A time bill needs to be presented for acceptance, while a sight bill or an accepted time bill needs to be presented for payment. In other words, a sight bill needs presentation once, a time bill needs presentation twice: first one for acceptance, second one for payment. Presentation has to be done within the agreed period. For the payment presentation of a sight bill and acceptance presentation of a time bill. British Acts specifies that it should be done within a reasonable time, in practice, not more than half a year. Geneva Uniform Laws specifies one year, but for the payment presentation of an accepted time bill, it should be done at or two days later of the maturity. Bill holder will lose right of recourse to the prior parties when he fails to present within limitation period.

There are three channels to make presentation: the first one is to do over the counter of the paying bank; the second one is to exchange the bill through a clearing house; and the third one is to dispatch the bill to the paying bank for acceptance or payment.

3. 4   Acceptance

Acceptance is an act by which the drawee promises to make payment at the bill maturity. Acceptance includes two acts too, that are writing and delivering. By signing his name on the bill, the payer engages that he will make payment when the bill falls due. More significantly is that the drawee is known as the acceptor and becomes primarily liable for the payment after having signed his acceptance. Keep in mind, the bill drawer is the party primarily liable before the bill is paid in case of sight bill or accepted in case of time bill.

Acceptance can be classified into general acceptance and qualified acceptance. A general acceptance is an acceptance by which the drawee confirms the order given by the drawer without ant qualification. For example, "Accepted, June 18, 2001, for bank of Tokyo LTD". A qualified acceptance is an acceptance by which the drawee accepts the bill with conditions that is, he revises the terms of the original bill. There are four qualified acceptance.

(1) Conditional acceptance: payment to be made by the acceptor depends on the fulfillment

of some conditions, for example, "Accepted, June 18, 2001, payable after receiving the bill of lading."

(2) Partial acceptance: by which the acceptor will pay only part of the bill amount stated thereon. For example, "Accepted, June 18, 2001, payable for the amount of USD 7,500 only" where the whole amount stated thereon, say, is USD 8,600.

(3) Local acceptance: the payment will be made only at a particular place specified by the acceptor.

(4) Time acceptance: time of payment will be changed in comparison with the tenor stated in the original bill, it could be deferred or ahead of time.

Bill holder is entitled to refuse such qualified acceptance. The bill can be considered as dishonored if the holder refuses to agree such restriction. The holder will lose his right of recourse when he is not authorized to take qualified acceptance by the issuer and all endorsers beforehand and afterwards, in other words, the obligations of all prior parties are canceled.

3.5 Payment

Act taken by the payer to pay the bill to the holder at agreed time and place is the act of payment. The so-called payment in due course signifies the payment made by the drawee in good faith on or after the maturity date to the holder thereof without perceiving his title defect. If the drawee or the acceptor does pay some person other than the holder, it does not mean the payment in due course. And so he will be compelled to pay again to the true owner. But if he does pay the holder, whether the latter is the true owner or not, he will no longer be liable to any other party, for he has obtained the paid draft as a receipt.

3.6 Dishonor

Act of dishonor is a failure or refusal of acceptance on or payment of a bill of exchange when presented. When a bill duly presented for acceptance is not accepted within a customary time, the presenting person must treat it as dishonored by non-acceptance, while presented for payment, the holder must treat it as dishonored by non-payment. When a bill is dishonored by non-acceptance, an immediate right of recourse against the drawee and the endorsers accrues to the holder, and presentation for payment at maturity is not needed. If the drawee assents conditionally to the payment, the holder can take it or consider it as non-acceptance.

3.7 Notice of Dishonor

Notice of dishonor is an advising act taken by the holder to all endorsers about the dishonor. According to British Bills of Exchange Act, when a bill has been dishonored by non-cacceptance or by non-payment, a notice of dishonor must be given to the drawer and each endorser, otherwise the holder shall be discharged of the right of recourse against the drawer and all the endorsers.

If the holder gives the notice of dishonor to his prior endorser only, the latter shall do so in quick succession, doing so till it is given to the drawer.

The notice may be given in writing or in words. The return of a dishonored draft to the party liable thereon may be an appropriate notice of dishonor.

3.8　Protest

According to British Bills of Exchange Act, if a foreign bill is dishonored by the payer, the holder has to make protest within one working day. If a non-acceptance bill is protested, no presentation for payment is needed and needless to protest non-payment.

Protest should be made by a notary public in the dishonor place, the holder carries out his right of recourse by means of such protest.

Charges for protest paid to the notary public should be for the account of issuer may add wording "Protest waived", so that the holder can carry out his recourse right without protest. Charges should be for the account of holder when he has made protest on the bill with indication of protest waived.

3.9　Recourse

The term of recourse is used to signify the right of a draft holder to compel his prior endorsers or the drawer to perform their legal obligations of payment if dishonored by the drawee. The holder can claim the payment and related fees in succession of endorsers; alternatively he can claim payment from any endorser, or even directly to the drawer. It needs to stress that the recourse claim should be enforced within the legal limit of time, which differs from country to country. According to British Bills of Exchange Act it is 6 years; according to Geneva Uniform Laws it is 1 year.

All of the legal acts explained above apply to all negotiable instruments, i. e. bill of exchange, Promissory note and check with some exceptions which will be stated in related section hereunder.

4. Promissory Notes

A promissory note is an unconditional promise in writing made by one person (the maker) to another (the payee or the holder) signed by the maker engaging to pay on demand or at a fixed or determinable future time a sum certain in money to or to the order of a specified person or bearer.

From definition of promissory note, it is easy to find that there is no acceptor, only the maker and the other parties are the payee, endorser, bearer and holder. The maker has prime liability while the other parties have second liability. Should the promissory note be made by two persons, then they are jointly and severally liable on the note according to its tenor.

Bill of treasuries, bank notes and so on are daily used examples of promissory note.

4. 1　Essentials to a Promissory Note

Main contents are stated as follows:

(1) The words "Promissory Note" clearly indicated

(2) An unconditional promise to pay

(3) Name of the payee or his order

(4) Maker's signature

(5) Place and date of issuing

(6) Tenor of payment

(7) A certain amount of money

The details are shown in Figure 4. 2.

Promissory Note

　　　　　　　　　　　　　　　　　　　　　　　　Leicester

USD700　　　　　　　　　　　　　　　　　　　August 31, 2016

　　Ninety days after sight we promise to pay William Smith or order the sum of U. S. Dollars seven hundred only.

　　　　　　　　　　　　　　　　　　　　　James Harrison

　　　　　　　　　　　　　　　　　　　　　John Martin

　　　　　　　　　　　　　　　　　　　　　Florence Brown

Figure 4. 2　Promissory Note

4. 2　Classification of Promissory Notes

According to the maker, promissory notes can be classified as bank promissory note and trade promissory note. The former is issued by a bank; the latter is issued by a business.

According to the tenor, promissory notes can be classified as sight promissory note and time promissory note. The former is payable at sight or on demand, the latter is payable at a fixed future date or a determinable future date.

Trade promissory notes are sometimes used in international trade, especially in capital goods trade, by which the amount due is very large and the payment effects in installments. For example, under forfaiting business, the importer can issue a series of promissory notes with different tenors which should be guaranteed by his bank. Upon receipt of guaranteed promissory notes the seller will sell them to the forfaiting bank for cash.

All of the legal acts except for acceptance described in section of Bills of Exchange apply to promissory note. Promissory note itself can be considered as a guarantee made by the payer to effect payment. Therefore, legal acts will not be repeated here again.

5. Checks

A check is defined as an unconditional order in writing drawn on a bank signed by the drawer, requiring a bank to pay on demand a sum certain in money to the order of a named person or to the bearer.

The meaning of the different parts of the definition are:

(1) Unconditional; payment can not hinge on certain conditions being met, for example "Pay Mr. Jones USD50 provided my salary check has been paid into my account".

(2) Writing: it must be in writing, pen, biro, print, even pencil can be used although the latter is not recommended because details can easily be altered.

(3) Signed: a check must be signed by the drawer who is the person paying the money.

(4) On demand: it is expected that the check will be paid as soon as it is presented to the other bank.

(5) A sum certain: the amount of the check must be definitive, both in words and figures.

(6) Named person or bearer: the check must be payable to someone by name or payable to "the bearer".

5. 1　The Main Parties Involved in a Check

Initially, there are three parties are involved in a check:

(1) Drawer: the person who makes out the check

(2) Drawee: the person to whom the check is addressed, it must be a bank

(3) Payee: the person to whom the check is made payable

A couple of important points have to be noted in the following:

(1) The drawee of a check is always a bank

(2) Unlike a bill of exchange, there is no legal acts of acceptance because a check is merely an instrument payable on demand or at sight. In other words, a check is never accepted by the bank on which it is drawn, more importantly, it means that a bank is never liable to the

check holder if it does not yet pay it. The drawer remains the party primarily liable, and any endorsers are sureties for the drawer's payment.

5. 2　Essential Elements of a Check

Basically, there are five essential elements in a check. They are mentioned as follows: Wording "cheque" or "check".

(1) Detailed name of the drawee, i. e. the paying bank

(2) Name and signature of the drawee

(3) Date and place of issuance

(4) Currency and a certain amount

(5) Date of issuing a check is critical, used as the basis of calculating its validity.

A check should be presented within its validity, otherwise it is null and void. It, however, does not mean that the payment obligation to the maker is canceled. Period of validity set by Geneva Uniform Laws is 8 days from the issuing date inner a nation, 20 days inner a continent, and 70 days beyond a continent; the period set by the British Act is not clearly defined, but within a reasonable time, Laws of People's Republic of China on Negotiable Instruments specifies: "Check holder should present for payment within 10 days from the issuing date".

5. 3　Classification of Checks

5. 3. 1　Crossing Check and Non-crossing Check

Some checks bear two bold parallel lines across their face. This is the crossing, which implicates that the payee can collect the check proceeds only through a bank institution called collecting bank rather than ask for payment in cash directly on counter of the drawee bank. In contrast, an uncrossed check namely, open check, does not have to be paid through a bank account, payment can be made over the counter, i. e. in cash. Thus a person finding or even stealing an uncrossed check would be able to obtain payment over the counter at the drawee bank provided that person had reasonable identification as the payee and provided that the payee was not personally known to the bank. Contrast the position with a crossed check, suppose that a person, getting crossed check fraudulently and attempting to obtain the proceeds under this check, has to have one reason or can persuade someone else with a bank account to pay in the check and to make suitable endorsement. The transferee should let a bank collect that check. No doubt, it makes considerably more difficult and risky, because the applying of a crossing increases the time available for discovering the fraudulent activity and gives the drawer more time to stop payment of any stolen check. Furthermore, even if payment has been made before loss or fraud is discovered, it can almost always be recovered from the person, that is the rogue himself or his successor, for whom it collected since that person would have to have an account at the collecting bank. Crossed check can be in turn categorized in two types as below:

General crossing. A general crossing consists of two parallel transverse, or more common, bevel lines across the face of check without indicating the name of collecting bank. There are 5 general crossings as shown in Figure 4.3. A. blank in between of two lines, which are the most common crossing checks; B. adding the words of "and Co.", being banking conventionality, no significance; C. adding the words of "not negotiable" in between, which does not mean it is not transferable, but not transferred in negotiation, i. e. the right of transferee is not more preferential than his prior party, belonging to the semi-negotiable; D. adding the words of "A/C payee" in between, instruct the collecting bank to credit payee's account after proceeds having collected. In principle, such check can not be transferred because the collecting bank can only credit payee's account, not somebody else; E. adding the words of "not negotiable A/C payee" in between.

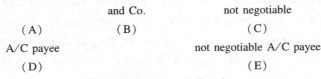

Figure 4.3   General Crossing

5.3.2 Special Crossing

A special crossing consists of the name of a particular bank and often a particular branch, which is entitled to present the check for payment. There are 4 special crossings as shown in Figure 4.4. A. only the collecting bank is indicated in between; B. besides collecting bank's name, adding the words of "not negotiable"; C. adding the words of "not negotiable". D. adding the words of "not negotiable" and "A/C payee". Note, only one collecting bank is to be indicated, by more than one, the paying bank is entitled to refuse to pay.

ABC Bank	ABC Bank	ABC Bank
	A/C Payee	Not Negotiable
(A)	(B)	(C)

ABC Bank
Not Negotiable A/C Payee
(D)

Figure 4.4   Special Crossing

5.3.3 Order Check and Bearer Check

The same as the classification of bills of exchange. Order check is one which indicates the name of the payee and can be transferred by endorsing, while the bearer check is one not indicating a particular person as the payee, being transferred merely by delivery and payable to any holder by the paying bank.

5. 3. 4　Confirmed Check

A confirmed check is one with adding of seal of "confirmed", which will be definitely paid when presented. In fact, the check amount is already transferred from maker's account to a bank's special account. Such confirmed check, normally, will be not dishonored. After adding its confirmation to the check, the paying bank becomes the primary liable; obligations of holder and endorser are terminated.

5. 4　Legal Acts on a Check

The key legal act on a check is still issuing. Under a check, there are also acts, such as endorsement, payment, dishonor, notice of dishonor and recourse, etc., but without act of acceptance because of being payable at sight. Dishonoring check happens also somewhat often despite of bank being the payer. This, however, will not hurt the credit reputation of banks because they are never the debtor of check (except for confirmed check). Dishonor normally arises out of the wrongful acts of issuing, endorsing and so on. The probable reason of dishonor could be:

Signature not in consistent with the agreed one

(1) Insufficient funds

(2) Amount in words and in figures not consistent

(3) Post dated

(4) Out of date or stale

(5) Lack of amounts in words

(6) Lack of payee's endorsement

(7) Incorrect issuing.

📖 Words & Expressions

1. instrument 票据
2. bill of exchange 汇票
3. bill of lading 提单
4. chose in action 权利动产
5. chose in possession 占有动产
6. copyrights 著作权
7. share 股票
8. life policies 人寿保险单

9. certificate of title 权利凭证

10. negotiation 流通转让

11. semi-negotiation 准流通转让

12. assignment 过户转让

13. holder 持票人

14. prior party 前手

15. debtor 债务人

16. creditor 债权人

17. bill of exchange 汇票

18. issue 出票

19. endorsement 背书

20. presentation 提示

21. acceptance 承兑

22. dishonor 退票

23. notice of dishonor 退票通知

24. protest 拒绝证书

25. recourse 追索

26. drawer 出票人

27. drawee 受票人

28. payer 付款人

29. payee 收款人

30. promissory note 本票

31. maker 出票人

32. check 支票

33. crossing check 划线支票(又称为平行线支票或模线支票)

34. non-crossing check 非划线支票

35. general crossing 普通划线

36. special crossing 特殊划线

37. order check 记名支票

38. bearer check 来人支票

39. confirmed check 保付支票

40. legal acts 行为

41. chose in action 权利动产

42. chose in possession 占有动产

📖 Notes

1. Among the documents, financial document, called also instruments, is a kind of
   certificate in writing which aims at obtaining a certain amount of proceeds.

在所有单据中，金融单据又称为票据，是一种书面凭证。它的目的就是获取一定金额货款。

2. The personal property in turn can be classified into chose in chose in action and chose in possession.

动产依次可以分为权利动产和占有动产。

3. A chose in action is property which does not physically exist and consequently can not be effectively protected by physical means, only by court action.

权利动产是指尚未实际占有的，不以物质形态存在的，通过法律行为可以获得的财产。

4. The proof of title to a chose in action is certificate of title, or document of title, sometimes also called broad instrument, which can be transferred from one holder to another by some legal actions.

对权利财产享有所有权的证明就是权利凭证，有时也称为广义票据。权利凭证可以通过一定的法律行为从一个人转移到另一个人。

5. The title can be transferred from transferor to transferee on three ways, namely, negotiation, semi-negotiation and assignment.

权利凭证可以从转让人转移到受让人通过三种方式，即流通转让，准流通转让和过户转让。

6. Negotiable instruments are payment tools as well as credit tools for domestic and international transactions, which can substitute cash in certain extent, but more convenient than it.

流通票据既是支付工具又是信用工具用于国内和国际贸易。它能在一定的程度上替代现金，但比现金更方便。

7. The transferee in good faith and for value can acquire a better title than that held by all his prior parties.

一个善意的、付了对价的受让人能获得优于他所有前手的权利。

8. The holder need not give notice of the transfer to prior parties, especial to original debtor to establish their title.

持票人无需通知他的前手进行转让，特别是无需通知原始的债务人，以建立他们的权利。

9. A person taking a transfer of a negotiable instrument in good faith and for value, called also holder in due course or bona fide transferee, is unaffected by any defects of the title of the transferor or any other prior parties.

一个善意的、付了对价的接受了可流通票据的受让人，又称作正式持票人或合法持票人，其权利不受转让人以及任何前手权利缺陷的影响。

10. However, the transferee can not acquire a better title than his prior party, i. e. any defect in the transferor's title is also transferred.

然而，受让人所获得的权利并不优于前手，也就是说，转让人的权利缺陷也同时转让给了受让人。

11. Assignment, one type of transferring legal title, is effected by sending the appropriate transfer form signed by the transferor and relevant certificate to the organization which issued the securities for details of the new ownership to be entered on the register. A new certificate is then issued in favor of the transferee.

过户转让，转让权利方式之一。必须将有转让人签字的转让书及原始凭证寄送到签发该凭证的机构，并由该机构登记新的凭证持有人，转让才告完成。新凭证必须以受让人为受益人。

12. The creditor has to accept when the debtor repays with the legal currency, but he has title to refuse accepting the instruments as repayment if he does not agree.

当债务人以法定货币清偿债务时，债权人不能拒绝，但如债务人以票据清偿债务时，则必须征得债权人的同意，否则债权人可以拒绝接受。

13. Protest should be made by a notary public in the dishonor place. The holder carries out his right of recourse by means of such protest.

拒绝证书必须在拒绝地点由公证机构作出。持票凭此拒绝证书追索自己应享有的权利。

14. In order to save this expenditure, issuer may add wording "protest waived", so that the holder can carry out his recourse right without protest.

为了节省费用，出票人可能增加书写文字"放弃拒绝证书"，以便持票人没有拒绝证书即可行使他的追索权。

>>> **Exercises**

I. True or False

1. A bill of exchange is a conditional order in writing.

2. Trade bills are usually documentary bills.

3. The person who draws the bill is called the drawer.

4. There is no acceptor in a promissory note.

5. There is only one drawee in a promissory note.

6. A promissory note is an unconditional order in writing.

7. The payment of a check can not hinge on certain conditions being met.

8. In check transaction, the drawer and the payer are the same person.

9. A check is a demand bank draft.

10. A crossed check can be cashed over the counter.

II. Multiple Choice

1. When financing is without recourse, this means that the bank has no recourse to the _____ if such drafts are dishonored.

   A. drawee   B. payee

C. payer   D. drawer

2. Only be endorsement the interest in the bill of exchange can be transferred by _____.

   A. the drawee   B. the drawer

   C. the holder   D. any person

3. Usually, the drawer and _____ are the same person.

   A. the payee   B. the payer

   C. the drawee   D. the holder

4. The _____ of a promissory note has prime liability while the other parties have secondary liability.

   A. drawer   B. drawee

   C. maker   D. acceptor

5. A _____ is drawn by the exporter and sent to the buyer.

   A. draft   B. promissory

   C. I. O. U.   D. check

6. _____ are shipping documents.

   A. Bills of Exchange   B. Promissory Notes

   C. Checks   D. Bills of Lading

7. A check must be signed by _____.

   A. the drawer   B. the drawee

   C. the payer   D. the payee

8. The person paying the money is a _____ of a check.

   A. payee   B. drawer

   C. endorser   D. endorsee

9. _____ check can be cashed over the counter.

   A. An open   B. Crossed

   C. A general crossing   D. A special crossing

10. The role of the _____ bank is to debit the check to the customer's account.

    A. paying   B. collecting

    C. advising   D. confirming

III. Answer Questions

1. How to understand three vital significant features of a negotiable instrument?

2. Explain the main differences between a bill of exchange and a check.

3. Try to point out the significance of negotiable instrument substituting for the cash in international trade.

Collections

This chapter shows the definition of both clean and documentary collection. In the meantime, it emphasizes upon the details and procedure of various kinds of documentary collection used in international trade. Finally, it tries to make readers or learners be familiar with the main ideas and key issues relevant to Uniform Rules for Collection issued by ICC.

Collection means instructing others to collection money. Generally speaking, collections serve as a compromise between open account and payment in advance in settlement of international trade. Under a collection, banking in a position of commission assists creditor to obtain proceeds from the debtor in another country.

1. Overview of Collections

Collection is a kind of payment system, in which creditors submit financial documents or commercial documents or both for obtaining proceeds to the remitting bank and ask it to entrust his relational bank (collecting bank) to make the documents available to the payer.

From standing point of banking, collection, as defined in "Uniform Rules for Collections" i. e. URC522 set by ICC, means the handling by banks of documents in accordance with instructions received, in order to obtain payment and/or acceptance, or deliver documents against payment and/or against acceptance, or deliver documents on other terms and conditions.

Documents, as defined by ICC, refer to financial documents and commercial documents, the former means bills of exchange, promissory notes, check or other similar instruments used for obtaining the payment of money; the latter means invoices, transport documents, documents of title or any other documents whatsoever, not being financial documents.

Due to the participation of banking in collections, direct exchange of goods and proceeds between buyers and sellers is changed to the exchange of goods and documents. This exchange, however, takes place in the importer's country. In principle, importer should not yet see the arrival of goods before he effects payment or acceptance.

1. 1　The Main Parties Involved in Collection

Normally, there are four main parties which are involved in collection (it mainly refers to documentary collection in international trade. Note below that each party has several names. This is because business persons and banks each have their own way of thinking about and naming each party to the transaction. For example, as far as business people are concerned, there are just buyers and sellers and the buyer's bank and the seller's bank. Banks, however, are not concerned with buying and selling. They are concerned with remitting (sending) documents from the principal (seller) and presenting drafts (order to pay) to the drawee (buyer) for payment. The four main parties are:

(1) The Principle (Seller/Exporter/Drawer)

The principal is generally the seller/exporter as well as the party that prepares documents (collection documents) and submits (remits) them to his bank (remitting bank) with a collection order for payment from the buyer/drawee.

(2) The Remitting Bank (Principal's/Seller's Bank)

The remitting bank receives documentation (collection documents) from the seller (principal). For forwarding (remitting) to the buyer's bank (collecting/presenting bank) along with instructions for payment.

(3) The Collecting/Presenting Bank

This is the bank that presents the documents to the buyer and collects cash payment (payment of a bank draft) or a promise to pay in the future (acceptance of draft) from the buyer (drawee of the draft) in exchange for the documents.

(4) The Drawee (Buyer/Importer)

The drawee (buyer/importer) is the party that makes cash payment or signs a draft according to the terms of the collection order in exchange for the documents from the presenting or collecting bank and takes possession of the goods. The drawee is the one on whom a draft is drawn and who owes the indicated amount.

1.2 Basic Documentary Collection Procedure

The documentary collection procedure involves the step-by-step exchange of documents giving title to goods for either cash or a contracted promise to pay at a later time.

(1) Buyer and Seller

Both the buyer and seller agree on the terms of sale of goods: a. specifying a documentary collection as the means of payment; b. naming a collecting/presenting and c. listing required documents.

(2) Principal or Seller

The seller (principal) ships the goods to the buyer (drawee) and obtains a negotiable transport document (i. e. bill of lading) from the shipping firm/agent.

Normally, the seller (principal) prepares and presents a document package to his bank (the remitting bank) which consists of collection order specifying the terms and conditions under which the bank is to hand over documents to the buyer and receive payment. Also, the negotiable transport document (B/L), and other documents (e. g. insurance document, certificate of origin, inspection certificate, etc.) are required by the buyer.

(3) Remitting Bank

It is clear that the remitting bank sends the documentation package by mail or by courier to the designated collecting/presenting bank in the buyer's country with instructions to present them to the drawee (buyer) and collect payment.

(4) Collecting Bank

The collecting (presenting) bank should review the documents making certain that they are in conformity with the collection order. Also, it must notify the buyer (drawee) about the terms and conditions of the collection order, and release the documents once the payment conditions have been met.

(5) Buyer/Drawee

Usually, the buyer (drawee) should make a cash payment (signing the draft), or if the collection order allows, sign an acceptance (promise to pay at a future date) and receive the documents and takes possession of the shipment.

(6) Collecting Bank

It is sure that the collecting bank need to pay the remitting bank either with an immediate payment or, at the maturity date of the accepted bill of exchange (draft).

(7) Remitting Bank

Finally, when the remitting bank gets the proceeds from the collecting bank, the remitting bank then should pay the seller (principal) in time.

The whole procedure of documentary collection is shown by Figure 5. 1.

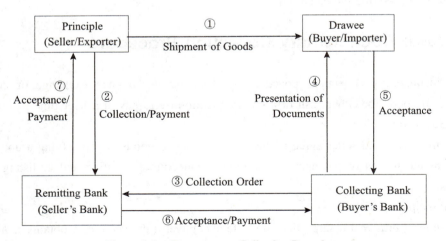

Figure 5. 1   Documentary Collection Procedure

It is worth knowing that the remitting bank may find it necessary or desirable to use an intermediary bank (called a correspondent bank) rather than sending the collection order and documents directly to the collecting bank. For example, the collecting bank may be very small or may not have an established relationship with the remitting bank.

2. Classification of Collections

Generally speaking, collections used in international trade can be sorted into two categories, i. e. clean collection and documentary collection.

2.1 Clean Collection

Clean collection refers to collection of financial documents not accompanied by commercial documents. It is often used to collect remaining funds, advance in cash, sample expenses, etc. in international trade payment. The seller draws merely kills of exchange on buyer, not accompanied by any shipping documents, and entrust bank to collect funds from the buyer. Under normal circumstance, the clean collection is mainly used for transaction of invisible goods because the transaction is not involved with documents such as inspection certificate, ocean bill of lading, insurance documents etc.

2.2 Documentary Collections

Documentary collections means a collection of financial documents accompanied by commercial documents or commercial documents not accompanied by the financial documents. Documentary collection is broadly used in international trade payment, which will be introduced as follows:

2.2.1 Documents Against Payment (D/P)

Under the term of Documents Against Payment, the collecting bank releases the documents to the buyer only upon his full and immediate cash payment. This type of collection offers the greatest safety to the seller among documentary collections. D/P can be further divided into following two categories.

2.2.1.1 D/P at Sight

After shipment of the goods, the exporter (seller) shall draw a sight bill of exchange and send it as well as shipping documents to his bank (remitting bank), through which and whose correspondent bank the documentary draft is presented to the importer. The importer (buyer) shall pay against the documentary draft drawn by the seller at sight. Actually, D/P at sight requires immediate payment by the importer to get hold of the documents.

The whole procedure of D/P at Sight is shown by Figure 5. 2.

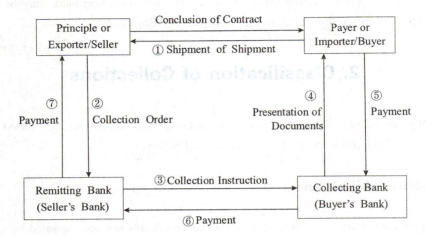

Figure 5. 2   Procedure of D/P at Sight

Explanations:

①After conclusion of contract, the exporter makes the goods available and effects the shipment of goods as per the terms and conditions of contract.

②After shipment, the exporter applies to the remitting bank for collecting the invoice value by sending an application, a sight draft and shipping documents to the remitting bank.

③The remitting bank draw up a collection order and transfers it as well as the sight draft and shipping documents to the collecting bank.

④The collecting bank present the draft and shipping documents to the importer according to the instructions in the collection order.

⑤The importer pays the purchase price at sight to the collecting bank.

⑥The collecting bank delivers the documents to the importer.

⑦The collecting bank transfers the funds (proceeds) to the remitting bank.

⑧The remitting bank transfers the funds to the principal (seller/exporter).

2.2.1.2   D/P after Sight

After shipment of the goods, the exporter shall draw a usance draft and send it as well as ship to his bank (remitting bank), through which and whose correspondent bank (collecting bank) the documentary draft is presented to the importer. The importer shall accept the usance draft, and make payment on the due date of the usance draft.

Under D/P after Sight, the importer is given a certain period to make payment, such as 30, 45, 60 or 90 days after the first presentation of the documents, but he is not allowed to get hold of the documents until he pays.

In this case, in order to push sales of the goods in time, the importer may consult with the collecting bank to borrow the bills of lading before the maturity of the drafts against the trust receipt（T/R）, and make payment on the due dates of drafts. This method is called accommodation.

The so-called "Trust Receipt" is a written guaranty provided by the importer to the collecting bank for the purchase of borrowing B/L from the latter, in which the importer declares that he will take delivery of the goods, declare to the customs, store the goods, take out insurance on and push sales of the goods as the consignee of the collecting bank, and acknowledge the title to the goods and proceeds of the sale belonging to the collecting bank and with guarantee to make the payment on the date due.

The whole procedure of D/P at Sight is shown by Figure 5. 3.

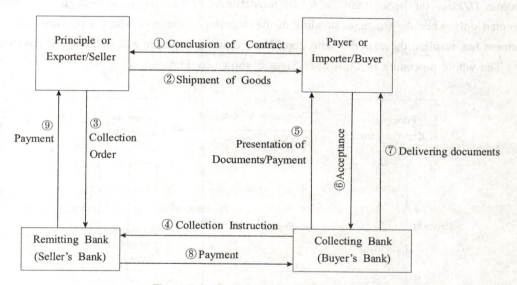

Figure 5. 3　Procedure of D/P after Sight

Explanations：

①The buyer and the seller conclude the contract and agree on payment in D/P after Sight.

②After conclusion of contract, the exporter makes the goods available and effects the shipment of goods as per the terms and conditions of contract.

③After shipment, the exporter applied to the remitting bank for collecting the invoice value by sending an application, a time draft and shipping documents to the remitting bank.

④The remitting bank draws up a collection order and transfers it as well as the time draft and shipping documents to the collecting bank.

⑤The collecting bank presents the drafts and shipping documents to the improper and the importer accepts the draft.

⑥The importer accepts the draft on seeing the draft during first presentation and pays in due course to the collecting bank.

⑦The collecting bank delivers the documents to the importer.

⑧Then, the collecting bank transfers funds to the remitting bank.

Finally, the remitting bank transfers funds to the principal.

2. 2. 2　Documents Against Acceptance (D/A)

D/A calls for delivery of documents against acceptance of the draft drawn by the draft drawn by the exporter. D/A is always after sight.

D/A makes the importer get hold of shipping documents and take delivery of the goods before payment. So the exporter would have to take great risks.

As far as the seller's benefit is concerned, D/P at sight is better than D/P after sight, whereas D/P is far better than D/A. In international trade, payment through collection is accepted only when the financial standing of the importer is sound or where a previous course of business has inspired the exporter with confidence that the importer will be good for payment.

The whole procedure of D/A after Sight is shown by Figure 5. 4.

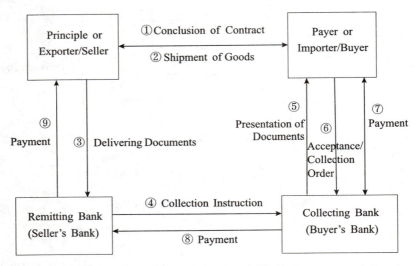

Figure 5. 4　Procedure of D/A

Explanations:

①The buyer and the seller conclude the contract and agree on payment in D/A.

②After conclusion of contract, the exporter makes the goods available and effects the shipment of goods as per the terms and conditions of contract.

③After shipment, the exporter applies to the remitting bank for collecting the invoice value by sending an application, a time draft and shipping documents to the remitting bank.

④The remitting bank draws up a collection order and transfers it as well as the time draft and shipping documents to the remitting bank.

⑤The collecting bank presents the draft and documents to the importer.

⑥The importer accepts the draft. So the bank will deliver the shipping documents to the importer while taking back the accepted draft.

⑦The importer pays the purchase price at the maturity of accepted draft.

⑧The collecting bank transfers funds to the remitting bank.

Finally, the remitting bank transfers funds to the principal.

To sum up, the classification of types of collection is shown in following diagram:

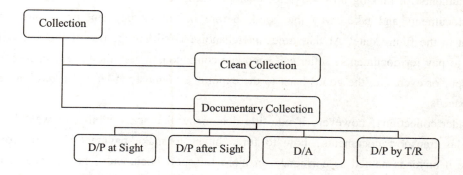

3. Documents Under Collection

Initially, there are two types of documents which are necessary for documentary collection in international trade. They are explained as follows:

3.1 Transaction Documents

The documents required under a documentary collection are fundamentally the same as those in a documentary letter of credit transaction. In the original agreement between the buyer and the seller specifies documents that (1) make it possible to secure the shipment from the shipping company (B/L), (2) secure release from the customs authority (certificates of origin, commercial invoice, etc.), and (3) offer some guarantee of quality and count (inspection certificates).

3.1.1 Bills of Exchange

Clean collection, D/P by T/R and D/A contain either sight bill of exchange or time bills of exchange issued by sellers. Under D/P it may or may not contain bills of exchange. Reason for the absence of bill of exchange is that some countries impose stamp duties. Therefore, importers of such countries often ask exporters not to draw drafts so as to evade tax. There are two reasons why exporters are willing to issue bills of exchange. First, bill of exchange is a good evidence that payer shall perform his obligation of payment, typically under D/P. Second, laws regarding negotiable instruments are complete and perfect. Strongly protecting parties involved under collections, especially protecting all rights including recourse of the endorsers, transferees and others.

3. 1. 2 Transport Documents

In order to control the ownership of goods under collections, exporter normally attaches the title documents for picking up goods, for example, full set of ocean B/L. buyer is not able to obtain documents and take away the goods before he makes payment or promises to make payment in the future date. At that time, merchandise is still properties of the seller. If buyer refuses to pay for documents, seller can negotiate continuously with the buyer, or look for other purchaser, or even ship the goods back to the exporter's country, at least not loss both of goods and proceeds.

Under collections, however, if non-title documents like sea waybill, air waybill and road waybill as transport documents, how to force buyer to make payment must be considered. Because if buyer is named as consignee on those transport documents, he can take delivery of the goods against goods arrival notice given by the carrier at the destination and his identity certificate rather than original transport documents. In other words, it is not inescapable that buyer has to get documents from the collecting bank, that means to pay or promise to pay, for picking up the goods. In this case exporter or collecting bank could not control the goods even though they have original documents on hand. When transport documents are not title to the goods, seller can make out of collecting bank as consignee, which can transfer the right of picking up goods by issuing a Delivery Order after buyer made payment or acceptance. But seller and remitting bank can do so only based on the agreement of the collecting bank, otherwise the collecting bank bears no obligations for the goods shipped to it.

It would be better to use the methods such as payment in advance or letter of credit rather than collection when exporter has no enough trust to the buyer and meanwhile, collecting bank does not agree to accept goods for the time being.

3. 1. 3 Other Documents

Besides the documents mentioned above, other documents such as commercial invoice, packing list, certificate of origin insurance policy, inspection certificate and export license may be required. Transaction contract may specify the documents' requirements in relative clauses.

3. 2 The Collection Order

The collection order is the key document prepared by the seller specifying the terms and conditions of the documentary collection. It must be prepared with great care and precision as the banks are only permitted to act upon the instructions given in the order and not on instructions from past transactions or verbal understandings. On the following sample collection order and below are notes for key provisions of the document.

(1) The payment period as agreed with the buyer.

(2) The name and address of the buyer.

(3) The buyer's bank.

(4) Instructions, if any, about what to do with the accepted bill of exchange.

(5) Notation concerning payment of charges for the documentary collection.

(6) Notation/instructions for the lodging of a protest in the event of nonacceptance or nonpayment.

(7) Instructions for notification of agent or representative in the buyer's country.

Sender									Documentary Collection	
									....	
									Place/Date	
Our Reference:									Registered: Swiss Bank Corporation Documentary Collections	
We send you here with the following documents for collection.										
Amount			Maturity ①						Drawee ②	
									Drawee's bank ③	
Draft	Invoice	I. cert	Cert. origin	Waybill	B/L	Packing list	Postage receipt		Other documents	
Goods: by: from: to: on:										
Please follow the instructions marked "X".										
Documents/goods to be delivered against payment acceptance.		Draft ④ To be sent back against acceptance							State the exact due date To be collected on due date	
You charges for drawee's account if refused.		Waive charges							Do not deliver documents.	
Your correspondent's charges are for drawee's account. If refused.		Waive charges							Do not deliver documents.	
Protest in case of	Nonpayment	Nonacceptance		Do not protest in case of		Nonpayment			Nonacceptance	
Advise	Nonpayment	Nonacceptance		By airmail		By cable			Giving reasons	
Please credit proceeds as follows: To our _____ account No. Remit to: Remarks:										
Endorsures: Signature:										

Figure 5.5 Collection Order

4. Uniform Rules for Collection

It is clear that there are some rules which can effectively regulate all activities involved in international trade. For traders, they should be aware of those specific rules and guide their trade transaction during adopting documentary collection or clean collection.

4.1　Summary of the Provisions of URC

URC (The Uniform Rules for Collections) form an internationally accepted code of practice covering documentary collections. URC are not incorporated in national or international law, but become binding on all parties because all bank authorities (especially the collection order) will state that the collection is subject to URC. URC will apply unless the collection order states otherwise or the laws in one of the countries concerned specifically contradict them. We must have a good knowledge of URC.

(1)The four main parties to a documentary collection are:

a. The principal, i. e. the exporter.

b. The remitting bank. This is the bank to which the principal entrusts the collection order. This is normally the exporter's own bank.

c. The collecting bank. This is any bank other than the remitting bank which is involved with the collection. Normally, this will be a bank in the importer's country.

d. The presenting bank. This is the bank which notifies the drawee of the arrival of the collection and which requests payment or acceptance from him/her. The collecting and presenting bank will normally be the same bank, but they could be different banks. This example will clarify:

An exporter hands in a documentary collection to his bank (Barclays), drawn on an importer in New York. If the principal does not specify which collecting bank to use, Barclays will choose their New York office. However, if the importer banks at Chemical Bank, Barclays, New York may well ask Chemical Bank to attend to the actual presentation. In this case the four parties are:

Principal	The exporter
Remitting Bank	Barclays
Collecting Bank	Barclays, New York
Presenting Bank	Chemical Bank

(2)Documents are of two types:

a. Financial documents — the instruments used for the purpose of obtaining money (e. g. bills of exchange).

b. Commercial documents — the documents relating to goods for which the financial documents are to secure payment (e. g. Bill of Lading, Insurance Document.)

Clean collections. Financial documents which are not accompanied by commercial documents. In the meantime, commercial documents which may or may not be accompanied by financial documents.

(1) Articles 1 and 2 state that banks will act in good faith and exercise with reasonable care. Bank must check that they appear to have received the documents which are specified in the collection order, but they have no obligation to examine the documents any further. (In practice banks do check the documents for common errors.)

(2) Article 3   Where the principal specifies a collecting bank, the remitting bank will choose a collecting bank. In practice, it is better for the choice to be left to the remitting bank. Not all overseas banks can be relied upon, and it is much safer for the remitting bank to select one of the collecting overseas banks which it knows will carry out instructions properly.

(3) Article 4   Banks have no liability for any delay or loss caused by postal or telex failure.

(4) Article 6   Goods should not be dispatched direct to the address of a bank or consigned to a bank without prior agreement on the part of that bank. In the event of goods being dispatched direct to the address of a bank or consigned to a bank for delivery to a drawee against payment or acceptance or upon other terms without prior agreement on the part of that bank, the bank has no obligation to take delivery of the goods, which remain at the risk and responsibility of the party dispatching the goods.

(5) Article 8   The principal should insert the complete address of the drawee on the collection order. Of the complete address is not shown, the collecting bank may try and ascertain the information, but it is under no obligation to do so.

Any loss or delay caused by an incomplete drawee's address will rest with the principal. In practice the remitting bank should check that the full address appears on the collection order.

(6) Article 10   The collection order should indicate D/A or D/P. in the absence of such a statement, documents can only be released on payment.

(7) Article 17   The collection order should give specific instructions about whether or not to protest in the event of non-payment or non-acceptance. In the absence of such instructions, no protest need be made. Any legal fees incurred by the presenting bank in a protest will be charged to the remitting bank who will debit the principal's account.

(8) Article 18   Where the collection order indicates a case of need (i. e. an agent of the exporter who is resident in the importer's country, his powers must be clearly stated. The collection order specifies either to follow the instructions of the case of need for guidance, or to accept the instructions of that case of need. In the absence of such indication banks will not accept any instructions from the case of need.

(9) Articles 21, 22, 23   A collection order must state whether charges and interest can be

waived if refused. If the collection order does not say whether charges and interest can be waived if refused, the position is as follows:

Details on collection order and bill of exchange	Position if charges refused by drawee, but face value payment offered
(1) Collection order claims charges, no reference to charges on bill of exchanges on bill of exchange. (2) No reference to charges on collection order, but the bill of exchange claims charges in addition to the face value.	(1) The collection is treated as being honored, assuming the collection order does not forbid waiving of charges. (2) The collection is treated as dishonored unless all charges are paid.

4.2   Legal and Practical Position Regarding the Duties of Remitting Bank

The bank's legal liability is set out in the URC. Banks must check that they appear to have received the documents specified in the collection order, but they have no liability to examine the documents in more detail.

However, in practice, the remitting bank will make the following additional checks before it sends the documents abroad:

a. Make sure the bill of exchange is correctly drawn, signed and endorsed.

b. Ensure that the amount of the bill of exchange agrees with the invoice (and collection order if applicable).

c. If the bills of lading is made out to order it must be endorsed in blank by the shipper (who is usually the exporter).

d. If the bills of lading are used, a full set would normally be required. If any are missing, an explanation should be obtained and the collecting bank must be advised accordingly.

e. Ensure that the shipping marks tie up on all documents.

f. If the invoice shows which incoterms apply, check that the documents conform to it e. g. with CIF, the bill of lading must be marked "freight paid" and an insurance documents should be present.

g. Make sure that the instructions on the collection order are logical, e. g. release documents on payment with sight draft.

h. Check the bank's reference book to see if there are any special documentary requirements in the importer's country.

i. Ensure that the customer signs the collection order.

4. 3   The Theory Involved in Collection

The exporter should be able to make an accurate assessment of when payment can be expected with sight drafts, the payment should be made as soon as the documents reach the presenting bank. The only additional delay will be if a payment may be deferred pending arrival of goods clause applies. There may be some delay whilst the importer is contacted by the presenting bank, but usually the importer will be eager to obtain the documents, and hence the goods, as quickly as possible.

The same timing considerations apply with term bills except that the period allowed after sight must be added.

4. 4   Timing of Payment: the Practice

Some banks publish a list of countries with the average length of time which can be expected to elapse from:

a. remittance of the collection from the United Kingdom when it is a sight draft;

b. number of days after due date when it is term draft.

Obviously, the time taken will depend on the method of remittance of proceeds (Mail Transfer SWIFT, or Telegraphic Transfer).

The chief Examiner states, "Most experienced exporting companies appreciate that when they sell goods in a foreign country, a sight bill means, in effect, giving 20 to 30 days' credit, and similarly 20 to 30 days can be added on to the due date of any usance bill. This is simply due to the delay in receiving funds".

4. 5   Acceptance Pour Aval

This is an alternative to straightward D/A. if the collection states release documents against acceptance pour aval, it means that the bill of exchange must be accepted by the drawee and then guaranteed for payment at a maturity by the drawee's bankers. Only then may the documents be released.

The benefit to the exporter is that:

a. the drawee's bank is liable on the bill, thus eliminating risk of non-payment if the bank is sound;

b. funds will be remitted on the due date, thus reducing the 20-30 days delay normally met.

The prior permission of the importers and their banks should be obtained before submitting such a collection.

4. 6   Risks to Exporter Selling Documents

The risks are the same s for open account, i. e. country risk and transit risk. As with all of the terms of payment, the exchange risks applies if the exporter invoices in foreign currency.

a. How to further reduce the buyer risk with D/P collections.

Provided that documents of title are used, the buyer can not obtain the goods without paying the bill of exchange (or where a bill of exchange is not included, paying the amount specified on invoice/ collection order).

However, where a buyer refuses to pay the physical goods are at the overseas port, in danger of being damaged or stolen and possibly incurring demurrage (demurrage means charges levied by port authorities for goods which are not collected).

To overcome this problem a store and insure clause should be incorporated on the collection schedule. The exporter knows that the goods will then be protected until an alternative buyer can be found.

If the exporter has a reliable agent, he can insert details of a case of need on the collection order. If the agent is reliable, the collection order will give him full authority to sell the goods on behalf of the exporter.

With air freight the airway bill could show that the goods are consigned to the presenting bank. The bank's prior permission is required, however, and this will not often be forthcoming.

b. How to reduce the risk with D/A collections

The additional risk with a D/A collection is that the documents, and therefore the goods, are released on acceptance, with no guarantee that the payment will be forthcoming at maturity.

Once the bill of exchange has been accepted, the exporter is in no better position than under open account terms, except that there is an accepted bill of change on which he can sue the buyer if it is dishonored at maturity.

However, if the exporter, importer and importer's bank agree beforehand, the collection order could stipulate release documents against acceptance pour aval. This means the importer's bank will accept the bill of exchange and hence guarantee payment.

📖 Words & Expressions

1. clean collection 光票托收
2. documentary collection 跟单托收
3. URC 托收统一规则
4. principal 委托人
5. remitting bank 托收行
6. collecting bank 代收行
7. collection order 托收申请书

8. D/P at Sight 即期付款交单
9. D/P after Sight 远期付款交单
10. D/A 承兑交单
11. D/P by T/R 远期付款凭信托收据交单
12. tenor 期限
13. usance 支付外国汇票的习惯期限
14. acceptance pour aval 第三者担保承兑
15. case of need 需要时的代理人

Notes

1. Collections serve as a compromise between open account and payment in advance in settlement of international trade.

   托收主要作为介于国际贸易结算中寄售业务和预付货款之间的一种折中或妥协。

2. Under a collection, banking in a position of commission assists creditor to obtain proceeds from the debtor in another country.

   在托收业务里，处于经纪人地位的银行帮助债权人从另一国家的债务人那儿获取货款。

3. Collection is a kind of payment system, in which creditors submit financial documents or commercial documents or both for obtaining proceeds to the remitting bank and ask it to entrust his relational bank (collecting bank) to make the documents available to the payer.

   托收是一种支付制度。其中债权人向托收行交付金融单据或商业票据，或二者一起收取货款，并要求托收行委托它的代理行（代收行）让付款人支付单据。

4. Documents, as defined by ICC, refer to financial documents and commercial documents, the former means bills of exchange, promissory notes, cheques, or other similar instruments used for obtaining the payment of money; the latter means invoices, transport documents, documents of titles or any other documents whatsoever, not being financial documents.

   单据，正如国际商会所定义的那样，指的是金融票据和商业票据。前者指的是汇票、本票支票或其他类似用于获取金钱支付的票据。后者指的是商业发票、运输单据、权利凭证或任何其他非金融票据以外所使用的其他单据。

5. The principal is generally the seller/exporter as well as the party that prepares documents (collection documents) and submits (remits) them to his bank (remitting bank) with a collection order for payment from the buyer/drawee.

   委托人一般是卖方/出口商，也是准备单据（托收单据）和交付单据连同托收指示一起给托收行的当事人，要求从买方/受票人那儿获得付款。

6. This is the bank that presents the documents to the buyer and collects cash payment (payment of a bank draft) or a promise to pay in the future (acceptance of draft) from the buyer (drawee of the draft) in exchange for the documents.

这是一家银行，它提示单据给买方并从买方(汇票受票人)(一张银行汇票的支付)和得到一个远期付款的承兑(汇票的承兑)以交换所有单据。

7. The drawee (buyer/importer) is the party that make cash payment or signs a draft according to the terms of the collection order in exchange for the documents from the presenting or collecting bank and takes possession of the goods.

受票人(买方/进口商)是一位当事人，他支付现金或签署一张汇票(根据托收指示的术语)用以从托收行那儿交换单据，从而获取货物。

8. Collection can be sorted into two categories, i. e. clean collection and documentary collection.

托收可以分为两类，即光票托收和跟单托收。

9. The seller draws merely bills of exchange on buyer, not accompanied by any shipping documents, and entrust bank to collect funds from the buyer.

卖方仅仅是向买方开具汇票而不用伴随任何其他装运单据，并委托银行从买方托收资金。

10. Documentary collection means a collection of financial documents accompanied by commercial documents or commercial documents not accompanied by the financial documents.

跟单托收是一种金融单据伴随着商业单据或者商业单据无金融单据伴随的托收。

11. Under the term of Documents Against Payment, the collecting bank releases the documents to the buyer only upon his full and immediate cash payment.

在付款交单术语里，代收行仅凭买方金额即时付款才交付所有单据。

12. The so-called "Trust Receipt" is a written guaranty provided by the importer to the collecting bank for the purpose of borrowing B/L from the latter, in which the importer declares that he will take delivery of the goods.

所谓"信托收据"是一份书面保函，进口商交给代收行目的是要从代收行借出提单。保函中声明进口商将提取货物。

⟫⟫⟫ Exercises

I. True or False

1. Under documentary collection, the remitting bank has no obligation to examine documents.

2. A documentary collection is an arrangement whereby the seller draws only a draft on buyer for the value of the goods and presents the draft to his bank.

3. Drafts which are payable at a future date are called demand drafts.

4. If the instructions are D/P the importer's bank will be release the documents to the importer against payment.

5. Normally D/P will apply with sight drafts and D/A will apply with usance drafts.

6. The four main parties to a documentary arte the principal, the remitting bank, the collecting bank and the drawee.

7. The principal is usually the importer.

8. Banks have no obligation to take any actions in respect of the goods to which a documentary collection relates.

9. Banks have no liability for any delay or loss caused by postal or telex failure.

10. Goods should not be dispatched direct to the address of a bank or consigned to a bank without prior agreement on the part of that bank.

II. Multiple Choice

1. After the goods have been shipped, the exporters present the documents to _____.

    A. the remitting bank   B. the collecting bank

    C. the reimbursing bank   D. the opening bank

2. Detailed instructions must be sent to the collecting bank _____.

    A. in the application form   B. in the collection order

    C. in the documents   D. both A and B

3. Banks are obligated to verify the documents received to see that _____.

    A. they are authentic

    B. they are regular

    C. in the documents

    D. they are those listed in the collection order

4. The collecting bank will make a protest only when _____.

    A. the documents are rejected

    B. a case of need is nominated

    C. specific instructions concerning protest are given

    D. protective measures in respect of the goods are taken

5. If it is not stated as D/A or D/P, the documents can be released _____.

    A. against payment   B. against acceptance

    C. in either way   D. against acceptance pour aval

6. The operation of collection begins with _____.

    A. the customer and the remitting bank

    B. the remitting bank and the collecting bank

    C. the presenting bank and the drawee

    D. the collecting bank and the presenting bank

7. The documents will not be delivered to the buyer until _____.

    A. the goods have arrived   B. the bill is paid or accepted

    C. the buyer has cleared the goods   D. both A and B

8. It will be more convenient if the collecting bank appointed by the seller _____.

A. is a large bank

B. is the remitting bank's correspondent in the place of the importer.

C. is in the exporter's country

D. acts on the importer's instructions

9. A bill of exchange which is accompanied by commercial documents of title to goods is known as _____.

A. a clean bill   B. a documentary bill

C. a clean collection   D. a documentary collection

10. _____ has the right of first choice in selecting a collecting bank.

A. The presenting bank   B. The drawee

C. The remitting bank   D. The principal

Chapter 6

Documentary Credits

This chapter really illustrates the essence of documentary credit operation in international trade. To familiarize with the procedure and classifications of documentary credits would be helpful for us to do business with foreigners. It is not difficult to find that to use L/C settlement properly will be the key to the success of business between the buyer and the seller.

The most commonly used method of payment in the financial business of international trade is the letter of credit which is a reliable and safe method of payment, facilitating trade between unknown parties and giving protection to both the buyer and the seller.

1. Overview of Documentary Credits

A documentary credit is the written promise of a bank, undertaken on behalf of a buyer to pay the seller the amount specified in the credit provided the seller complies with the terms and conditions set forth in the credit. The terms and conditions of a documentary credit revolve around two issues: the presentation of documents, that evidence title to goods shipped by the seller and payment.

In simple term, banks act as intermediaries to collect payment from the buyer in exchange for the transfer of documents that enable the holder to take possession of the goods.

Documentary credits provide a high level of protection and security to both buyers and sellers engaged in international trade. The seller is assured that payment will be made by a party independent of the buyer so long as the terms and conditions of the credit are met. The buyer is assured that payment will be released to the seller only after the bank has received the title documents called for in the credit.

Documentary credits are so named because of the importance of documents in the transaction letter of credit (L/C) is the historic and popular term used for a documentary credit because such credits were and are transmitted in the form of a letter from the buyer's bank. Both "documentary credit" and "letter of credit" will be used for subsequent discussions.

1. 1   The Feature Common to All Kinds of L/C

The feature common to all kinds of L/C is that the buyer arranges with a bank to provide finance for the exporter in the country of the latter on delivery of the shipping documents. On presentation of the shipping documents, the bank will pay purchase price, normally by paying a sight draft or by accepting a time draft drawn on the buyer. There is no doubt that under L/C operation, issuing bank plays a very important role in protecting both buyer (applicant) and the seller's (beneficiary) interest. Therefore, it assures the smooth conduct of international trade.

For applicant, if he can initiate the application of L/C and pay the proceeds to issuing bank, he would be sure that the issuing bank would deliver all documents to him, which could be used for taking deliver at the port of destination.

For beneficiary, if could effect the shipment of goods and present perfectly right documents required by L/C, the issuing bank will guarantee to pay him the relevant proceeds.

1. 2   Role of Banks Under Documentary Credits

It is important to note, and not for the last time, that a fundamental principle of documentary credits is that banks deal with documents and not goods. Banks are responsible for issues relating to documents and the specific wording of the documentary credit as opposed to issues relating to the goods themselves.

Therefore, banks are not concerned if a shipment is in conformity to the working with the credit. This principle should be paid attention to.

It is important to note that documentary credit procedures are not infalliable. Things can and do go wrong. Since banks act as intermediaries between the buyer and seller, both took to the banks as protectors of their interests. However, while banks have clear cut responsibilities, they are also shielded from certain problems deemed to be out of their control or responsibility. For example, since banks deal with documents and not goods, they assume no responsibility regarding the quantity or quality of goods shipped. They are only concerned that documents presented appear on their face to be consistent with the terms and conditions of the documentary credit. Any dispute as to quality or quantity of goods delivered must be settled between the buyer and the seller. So long as the documents presented to the banks appear on their face to comply with the terms and conditions of the credit, banks may accept them and initiate the payment process as stipulated in the documentary credit.

It is obvious that if there are any conclusions to be made between the buyer and the seller, first, the buyer and the seller should know each other and have at least some basis of trust to be doing business in the first place, and second, all parties to the transaction should take responsibility to follow through on their part carefully.

1.3　Limitations of Documentary Credits

Although documentary credits provide good protection and are the preferred means of payment in many international transactions, they do have limitations. They do not, for example, ensure that the goods actually shipped are as ordered, nor do they insulate buyers and sellers from other disagreements or complaints arising from their relationship. It is up to the parties to settle questions of this nature between themselves.

As we know, documentary credits are not foolproof. There are layers of protections for both the buyer and the seller, but opportunities for fraud do exist. Many of the opportunities for fraud center around the facts that banks deal with documents rather than goods, and therefore the seller has the opportunity for presenting fraudulent documents. Obviously, the seller will have difficulty doing this more than once or twice as no bank will repeatedly accept documents from a supplier accused of such practices. Also, almost every country has criminal statutes against fraud and the seller will eventually get caught, but perhaps only after you have been defrauded.

As a reminder, it is always best to know your counterpart and the banks involved and to exercise caution and common sense in making decisions.

The situations listed below are extremely uncommon, but do exist.

(1) Sellers have reported receiving an advice or a confirmation of a documentary credit from non-existing banks. The perpetrator of the fraud attempts to get the seller to ship goods and present documents for payment to a bank that does not exist. By the time the seller is aware of the fraud, the "buyer" has received the goods.

(2) Buyers have reported receiving empty crates or crates filled with sand instead of the merchandise they ordered. By the time they received the shipment the banks had already paid the "supplier".

(3) Buyers have reported receiving defective merchandise from sellers. While there may be some latitude for interpretation of what constitutes "defective", it is clear that some suppliers have purposefully shipped incorrect or substandard goods.

(4) Buyers have reported being short-shipped. In some cases buyers have ordered a valuable commodity sold by weight and were shortchanged by being charged for the gross weight rather than the net weight. They were charged the commodity price per kilogram for the packing materials.

(5) Buyers of commodities, especially gray market goods, have reported being defrauded by the seller's providing fraudulent shipping documents, evidencing shipment on a nonexistent ship.

1.4　The Uniform Customs and Practice for Documentary Credits

Although documentary credits, in one form or another, have been in use for a long time, questions arose about how to effect transactions in a practical fair and uniform manner. The Uniform Customs and Practice for Documentary Credits (UCP) is the internationally recognized codification of rules unifying banking practice regarding documentary credits. The UCP was developed by wording committee attached to the International Chamber of Commerce (ICC) in Paris. It is revised and updated from time to time: the current valid version is ICC publication No. 600.

2. The Operation of Documentary Credit

2.1   Main Parties to Documentary Credit

There are four main parties to a basic documentary letter of credit transaction. Note that each party has multiple names. The name used for each party depends on who is speaking. Normally, business-people like to use the names buyer, seller, buyer's bank and seller's bank. The banks prefer to use the names applicant, issuing bank, advising bank, and beneficiary, The four parties are:

2.1.1   The Applicant (Buyer/Importer)

The buyer initiates the documentary credit process by applying to his bank to issue a documentary credit naming the seller as the beneficiary. The buyer, therefore, maybe called the buyer in commercial terms, the importer in economic terms, and the applicant in banking terms. They are all one and the same.

2.1.2   The Issuing Bank (Buyer's bank)

Upon instructions from the buyer, the issuing bank (typically the buyer's regular business bank) issues a documentary credit naming the seller as the beneficiary and sends it to the advising bank (typically the Seller's bank)

2.1.3   The Advising Bank (Seller's bank)

Upon instructions from the issuing bank and the buyer, the advising bank (typically the seller's bank) advises the seller of the credit. The advising bank is typically the seller's regular business bank and is in the seller's country.

2.1.4   The Beneficiary (Seller/Exporter)

The beneficiary receives notification (advice) of the credit from the advising bank, complies with the terms and conditions of the credit and gets paid. The seller is the beneficiary of the documentary credit. The seller, therefore, may be called in commercial terms, the exporter in economic terms, and the beneficiary in banking terms. They are all one and the same.

2. 2　Procedure of Documentary Credit

Procedure of documentary credit is shown in Figure 6. 1. Keep in mind, there are important variations on this basic procedure, which is related to confirmation of the payment or the availability of the payment. In addition, such procedure would be changed when discrepancies are checked out by banks and correspondences take place several rounds between parties involved.

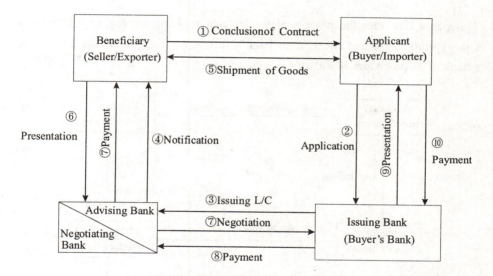

Figure 6. 1　Procedure of L/C Operation

Explanations:

①The buyer and the seller agree to conclude the contract on the payment terms by L/C.

②The importer/buyer/applicant applies to his bank (issuing bank) for issuing a L/C in favor of the exporter (seller/beneficiary), and provides a certain amount of deposit and formality fees.

③The issuing bank sends a L/C opened to the advising bank.

④The advising bank authenticates L/C and transfers it to the exporter.

⑤After examining the L/C, the exporter effects the shipment according to the stipulations of L/C. After shipment, the exporter makes out a draft and draws up the documents in accordance with the L/C.

⑥The exporter delivers documents as well as shipping documents to the negotiating bank within its validity.

⑦If the documents are in conformity with the L/C, the negotiation or the negotiating bank will advance the purchase price to the exporter. At the same time, the negotiating bank negotiates the documents to issuing bank and asks for payment.

⑧The issuing bank will pay to the negotiating bank after examining the documents.

⑨The issuing bank informs the applicant and asks him to make payment so as to get hold of the shipping documents.

⑩The applicant makes payment to get hold of shipping document and takes delivery of the goods against documents at the port of destination.

2. 3   L/C Issuance

L/C issuance describes the process of the buyer's applying for and issuing a documentary credit at the issuing bank and the issuing bank's formal notification of the seller through the advising bank. The procedure is shown by Figure 6. 2.

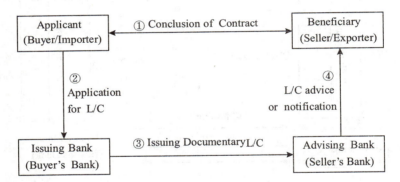

Figure 6. 2   Procedure of L/C Issuance

Explanations:

①The buyer and the seller agree on the terms of sale: specifying a documentary credit as the means of payment, naming an advising bank, and listing required documents.

②The buyer applies to issuing bank for opening a documentary credit naming the seller as beneficiary based on specific terms and conditions that are listed in the credit.

③The issuing bank issues the documentary credit to the advising bank named in the credit.

④The advising bank informs the seller of the documentary credit.

2. 4   L/C Amendment

When the seller receives the documentary credit it must be examined closely to determine if the terms and conditions reflect the agreement of the buyer and the seller, and can be met within the time stipulated.

Upon examination, the seller may find some problems. In this case, amendment is necessary for the seller to fulfill his obligation under documentary credit.

Amendment describes the process whereby the terms and conditions of a documentary credit may be modified after the credit has been issued. The whole procedure is shown by Figure 6. 3.

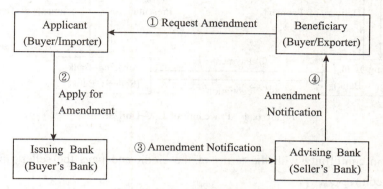

Figure 6. 3   Procedure of L/C Amendment

Explanations:

①The seller requests that the buyer makes an amendment to the credit. This can be effected by a telephone call, a fax or by face-to-face negotiation.

②If the buyer agrees, he orders the issuing bank to issue the amendment accordingly.

③The issuing bank amends the credit as per the buyer's instructions and notifies the advising bank of the amendment.

④The advising bank notifies the seller of the amendment.

2.5   L/C Utilization

Utilization describes the procedure for the seller's shipping of the goods, the transfer of documents from the seller to the buyer through the banks, and the transfer of the payment from the buyer to the seller through the banks.

The whole procedure is shown by Figure 6. 4.

Explanations:

①The seller (beneficiary) effects the shipment to the buyer and obtains a negotiable transport document (negotiable bill of lading) from the shipping firm/agent.

②The seller prepares and presents a document package to his bank (the advising bank or the negotiating bank) consisting of the negotiable transport document, and other documents (e. g. commercial invoice, packing list; insurance policy, certificate of origin and inspection certificate, etc.) are required by the buyer in the documentary credit.

③The advising bank or negotiating bank reviews the document package making certain the

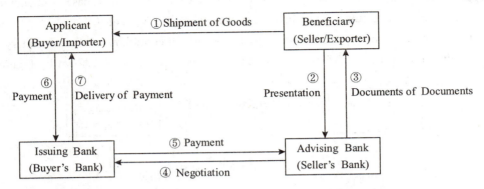

Figure 6. 4　Procedure of L/C Utilization

documents are in conformity with the terms of the credit and pays the seller (based upon the terms of the credit).

④The advising bank or negotiating bank sends the documentation package by mail or by courier to the issuing bank.

⑤The issuing bank reviews the document package making certain the documents are in conformity with the terms of the credit. pays the advising bank or negotiating bank (based upon the terms of the credit), and advises the buyer that the documents have arrived.

⑥The buyer reviews the document package making certain the documents are in conformity with the terms of the credit, and makes a cash payment (signs a sight draft) to the issuing bank, or if the collection order allows, signs an acceptance (promise to pay at a future date).

⑦The issuing bank sends the document package by mail or courier to the buyer who then takes possession of the shipment.

2. 6　Settlement (Making Payment)

Settlement refers to the process of payment of the beneficiary to the credit after presentation of documents under the credit. Utilization, availability of payment and settlement are all closely related and often the terms are used interchangeably.

Utilization is the process of the seller shipping the goods, presenting documentation and getting paid. Availability of payment and settlement are part of the process, but refer more specifically to the seller getting paid.

Generally speaking, there are three primary means of payment: settlement by payment, settlement by acceptance, and settlement by negotiation.

2. 6. 1　Settlement by Payment

If the credit is an irrevocable, confirmed credit, the value of the credit is available to the beneficiary as soon as the terms and condition of the credit have been met (as soon as the prescribed document package has been presented to and checked by the confirmed bank). In an unconfirmed credit the value of the credit is made available to the beneficiary once the advising bank has received the funds from the issuing bank.

The whole procedure of settlement by payment is shown by Figure 6. 5.

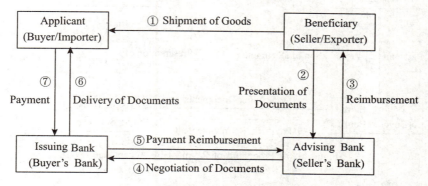

Figure 6. 5　Procedure of Settlement by Payment

Explanations：

①The seller (beneficiary) effects the shipment to the buyer and obtains a negotiable transport documents (negotiable bill of lading) from the shipping firm/agent.

②The seller prepares and presents a document package to the advising/confirming bank consisting of the negotiable transport document and other documents (e. g. commercial invoice, packing list, insurance policy, certificate of origin and inspection certificate, etc.) as required by the buyer in the documentary credit.

③ The advising/confirming bank reviews the document package making certain the documents are in conformity with the terms of the credit, and pays the seller.

④The advising/confirming bank then sends the documentation package by mail or by courier to the issuing bank.

⑤The issuing bank reviews the document package making certain the documents are in conformity with the terms of the credit and pays or reimburses the advising/confirming bank as previously agreed in the documentary credit.

⑥The issuing bank sends the document package by mail or by courier to the buyer.

⑦The buyer pays or reimburses the issuing bank as previous agreed.

2. 6. 2　Settlement by Acceptance

In settlement by acceptance the beneficiary presents the required documentation package to the bank along with a time draft drawn on the issuing, advising, or a third bank for the value of the credit. Once the documents have made their way to the buyer and found to be in order, the draft is accepted by the bank upon which it is drawn (the draft is now called a bank acceptance) and it is returned to the seller who holds it until maturity.

The whole procedure of settlement by acceptance is shown by Figure 6. 6.

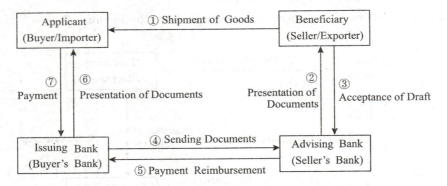

Figure 6. 6 Procedure of Payment by Acceptance

Explanations:

①The seller (beneficiary) effects the shipment to the buyer and obtains a negotiable transport document (negotiable bill of lading) from the shipping firm/agent.

②The seller prepares and presents a document package to the advising/confirming bank consisting of the negotiable transport document, other documents (e. g. commercial invoice, packing list, insurance policy, etc.) as required by the buyer in the credit, and a draft drawn on the buyer at the specific tenor (maturity date).

③ The advising/confirming bank reviews the document package making certain the documents are in conformity with the terms of the documentary credit, and accepts the draft and returns it to the seller.

④ The advising/confirming bank then sends the documentation package along with a statement that it has accepted the draft by mail or by courier to the issuing bank.

⑤The issuing bank reviews the document package making certain the documents are in conformity with the terms of the documentary credit and at maturity of the draft pays or reimburses the advising/confirming bank as previously agreed in the documentary credit.

⑥The issuing bank sends the document package by mail or by courier to the buyer.

⑦The buyer pays or reimburses the issuing bank as previously agreed in the documentary credit.

2. 6. 3 Settlement by Negotiation

In settlement by negotiation the buyer accepts the documents and agrees to pay the bank after a set period of time. Essentially, this gives the buyer time (a grace period) between delivery of the goods and payment. The issuing bank makes the payment at the specified time, when the terms and conditions of the credit have been met.

The whole procedure of payment by negotiation is shown by Figure 6. 7.

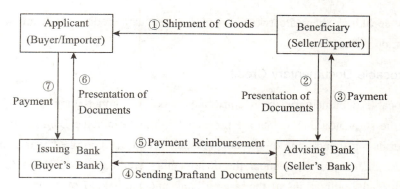

Figure 6. 7   Procedure of Payment by Negotiation

Explanations:

①The seller (beneficiary) effects the shipment to the buyer and obtains a negotiable transport document (negotiable bill of lading) from the shipping firm/agent.

②The seller prepares and presents a document package to the advising/confirming bank consisting of the negotiable transport document, other documents (e. g. commercial invoice, packing list, insurance policy, certificate of origin and inspection certificate, etc.) as required by the buyer in the credit, and a draft drawn on the bank. The advising/confirming bank reviews the document package making certain the documents are in conformity with the terms of the documentary credit, and pays the seller.

③The advising/confirming bank then sends the documentation package by mail or by courier to the issuing bank.

④The issuing bank reviews the document package making certain the documents are in conformity with the terms of the documentary credit and pays or reimburses the advising/confirming bank as previously agreed in the documentary credit.

⑤The issuing bank sends the document package by mail or by courier to the buyer.

⑥The buyer pays or reimburses the issuing bank as previously agreed in the documentary credit.

3. Types and Uses of Documentary Credits

There is no doubt that different types documentary credits are widely used in international trade. On the other hand, different documentary credits may adopt various usage according to the specific requirements from both the buyer and the seller.

3. 1   Types of Documentary Credits

Generally speaking, there are two types of documentary credits which are widely used in international trade. They are:

3. 1. 1   Irrevocable Documentary Credit

An irrevocable documentary credit constitutes a definite undertaking of the issuing bank, provided that the stipulated documents are presented to the Nominated Bank or to Issuing Bank and that the terms and conditions of the documentary credit are complied with, to say, accept draft and/or documents presented under the documentary credit (see UCP 500 Article 9, for a full description of the obligations of the issuing bank under this kind of documentary credit.)

An irrevocable documentary credit gives the beneficiary greater assurance of payment, however, he remains dependent on an undertaking of a foreign issuing bank. The issuing bank irrevocably commits itself to honor the exporter's draft and/or documents provided that the stipulated documents are presented and all the stipulations of documentary credit are complied with. The irrevocable documentary credit can not be canceled/modified without the express consent of the issuing bank, the confirming bank (if any) and the beneficiary.

3. 1. 2   Revocable Documentary Credit

A revocable documentary credit is issued in favor of the beneficiary in accordance with the instructions of the applicant and gives the buyer maximum flexibility, since it can be amended, revoked or canceled without the beneficiary's consent and even without prior notice to the beneficiary up to the moment of payment by the bank at which the issuing bank has made the documentary credit available.

The revocable documentary credit involves risks to the beneficiary since the documentary credit may be amended or canceled while the goods are in transit and before the documents are presented, or, although documents may have been presented, before payment has been made, or, in the case of a deferred payment documentary credit, before documents have been taken up. The seller then faces the problem of obtaining payment directly from the buyer.

The revocable documentary credit is normally accepted as usage between affiliated parties or subsidiary companies, or as a usage of a particular trade, or as a substitute for a promise to pay or a payment order.

3. 2   Uses of Documentary Credit

Usually, there are ten different uses of documentary credits which could effectively solve some concrete problems.

3. 2. 1　Irrevocable Straight Documentary Credit

An irrevocable straight documentary credit conveys a commitment by the issuing bank to only honor draft or documents presented by the beneficiary of the credit.

This means that the beneficiary of the documentary credit is supposed to deal directly with the issuing bank in presenting drafts and documents under the terms of the credit.

It is quite normal for banks and other financial institutions to purchase the drafts and documents of a beneficiary at a discount. For example, a seller may possess a draft obligating the issuing bank to pay a stated sum in 90 days. If the seller needs the money he may wish to sell it to his bank at discount for immediate cash. In an irrevocable straight documentary credit the issuing bank has no formal obligation to such a purchaser/holder of the draft.

The irrevocable straight documentary credit is typically used in domestic trade and for standby credit, both situations where confirmation or negotiation is considered unnecessary because of the reputation of the issuing bank.

The irrevocable straight documentary credit is of greatest advantage to the buyer who does not incur a liability to pay the seller until his own bank reviews the documents.

The obligation of the issuing bank in an irrevocable straight documentary credit is typically stated in the credit itself with wording such as:

"We hereby engaged with you that each draft drawn and presented to us under and in compliance with the terms of this documentary credit will be duly honored by us".

Sample　**Irrevocable Straight Documentary Credit**

The French Issuing Bank

38 rue Francois Ler

75008 Paris, France

Date of Issuing: Paris, 1 January 2016.

Place of Expiry: At out counter

Applicant:	Beneficiary:
The French Importer Co.	The American Exporter Co. Inc.
89 rue du commerce	17 Main Street
Paris, France	Tampa, Florida

Amount: USD 100,000. One Hundred Thousand US Dollars

Credit available with the French Issuing Bank,

Paries, France by payment of Beneficiary's draft at sight drawn on The French Issuing Bank for 100 percent of invoice value accompanied by the documents detailed herein.

Partial shipments: Allowed

Transshipment: Not allowed

From: Tampa, Florida To: Paris, France

Not later than December 15, 2016

Documents to be presented:

Original and three signed copied of commercial invoice.

Clean Ocean Bill of Lading consigned to applicant marked freight collection, notify applicant.

Covering: Merchandise as per Proforma Invoice

No. 1234, FOB New York

Insurance effected by the applicant

Documents must be presented at place of expiration not later than 10 days after date of shipment and within documentary validity.

Documents must be forwarded to us in one parcel and be mailed to The French Issuing Bank, 38 rue Francois ler, 75008 Paris, France.

Drafts must indicate the number and date of this credit.

Each draft presented here under must be accompanied by this original credit for our endorsement thereon of the amount of such draft.

This credit is subject to the uniform customs and practice for documentary credits (1993 revision), International Chamber of Commerce, Publication Number 500.

We hereby engage with you that each draft drawn and presented to us under and in compliance with the terms of this documentary credit will be duly honored by us.

The French Issuing Bank

3. 2. 2   Irrevocable Negotiation Documentary Dredit

Under the irrevocable negotiation documentary credit, the issuing banks engagement is extended to third parties who negotiate or purchase the beneficiary's draft/documents presented under the documentary credit. This assures anyone who is authorized to negotiate drafts/documents under the documentary credit that these drafts/documents will be duly honored by the issuing bank provided the terms and conditions of the documentary credit are complied with. A bank which effectively negotiates drafts/documents buy them from the beneficiary, thereby becoming a holder in due course.

The engagement of the issuing bank is normally indicated in the documentary credit as available for negotiation by a nominated bank and expiring for presentation of documents at the offices of such a nominated bank. Alternatively, the engagement of the issuing bank may be stated more explicitly as follows:

"We hereby agree with the drawers, endorsers and bona fide holders of drafts/documents drawn under and in compliance with the terms and conditions of the credit that such drafts/documents will be duly honored on due presentation if negotiated or presented at this office on or before the expiry date."

Sample Irrevocable Negotiation Documentary Credit

The Trade Bank

525 Market Street, 25th Floor

San Francisco, California, USA

To: Indonesia Export Bank

Jakarta, Indonesia

We hereby issue our irrevocable documentary credit No. 12345678

Date of issue: May 15, 2016

Date of expiry: July 7, 2016

Place of expiry: Indonesia

Applicant:	Beneficiary:
US Coffee Importer	ABC Coffee Exporter
San Francisco, California, USA	Jakarta, Indonesia

Amount: USD 65,000. Sixty-five thousand US dollars.

Credit available with any bank, by negotiation for payment of beneficiary's draft at sight drawn on The Trade Bank for 100 percent of invoice value.

Partial shipments: Not allowed

Transshipment: Allowed

Shipment from Indonesia no later than June 16, 1998 to San Francisco, California, USA

Goods: Fifteen metric tons of 60-kilo bags of new crop Sumatra Mandheling Arabica Grade 1 green coffee as per buyer's purchase order CIF San Francisco, California, USA

Documents required

(1) Original and four copies of signed commercial invoice

(2) Negotiable insurance policy or certificate and 2 copied for at least 110 percent of invoice value, covering marine risks and all risks, indicating loss, if any, payable in the United States in US dollars.

(3) Full set of clean "on board" ocean bill of lading to the order of shipper blank endorsed marked "freight prepaid" showing "notify John Smith & Company 123 Main Street San Francisco, CA 94123."

Drafts must indicate the number and date of this credit. The amount of each draft negotiated under this credit must be endorsed on the reverse of this credit and the presentation of any such draft to us shall be a warranty by the presenting bank, that such endorsement has been made.

Documents must be forwarded to us by courier in one parcel and may be mailed to The Trade Bank 525 Marked Street, San Francisco, CA USA.

This credit is subject to the uniform customs and practice for documentary credits (1993 Revision), International Chamber of Commerce, Publication Number 500, and engages us in accordance with the terms thereof.

Charges: All charges of banks other than ours are for beneficiary's account. However, our out of pocket expenses incurred in effecting any payment hereunder are also for beneficiary's account.

Period for presentation: Documents must be presented at place of expiration no later than 21 days after date of shipment and within documentary credit validity.

Confirmation instructions: Without

The Trade Bank

3. 2. 3   Irrevocable Documentary Credit (Unconfirmed)

The issuing bank's irrevocable documentary credit is advised through an advising bank. Usually, the advising bank acts as agent of the issuing bank and does not assume any responsibility to the beneficiary under the documentary credit except for taking reasonable care to check the apparent authenticity of the documentary credit which it advises. The advising bank will inform the beneficiary that it is passing on the issuing bank's documentary credit and will add to this advice the following:

"This notification and the enclosed advice are sent to you without any engagement on our part".

3. 2. 4   Irrevocable Confirmed Documentary Credit

A confirmation of an irrevocable documentary credit by a bank (the confirming bank) upon the authorization or request of the issuing bank constitutes a definite undertaking of the confirming bank, in addition to that of the issuing bank, provided that the stipulated documents are presented to the confirming bank or to any other nominated bank on or before the expiry date and terms and conditions of the documentary credit are complied with, to pay, to accept drafts or to negotiate.

a. A double assurance of payment

An irrevocable confirmed documentary credit gives the beneficiary a double assurance of payment, since it represents both the undertaking of the issuing bank and the undertaking of the confirming bank. The second obligor (the confirming bank) engages that the drawings under the documentary credit will be duly honored in accordance with the terms and conditions of the documentary credit.

Normally, one considers the classification of the credit and the financial standing of the issuing bank. If an issuing bank is considered to be a first class bank, there may not be any need to have its documentary credit confirmed by another bank. Nevertheless, the beneficiary may desire that the documentary credit and payment thereunder be guaranteed by a bank located in his own country. In such a situation, such confirming bank becomes legally liable to the beneficiary to the same extent that the issuing bank does. Despite the fact that UCP 500 Article 2 states "…… For the purpose of these Articles, branches of a bank in different countries are considered another bank", the beneficiary should review the confirmation of a documentary credit given by a branch or a subsidiary of the issuing bank to see whether it is indeed another separate and distinct bank obligation under the documentary credit.

b.　　　　　*Sample*　**Irrevocable confirmed documentary credit**

Turkish Export/Import Bank

Ankara, Turkey

To: The Trade Bank, 525 Market Street, 25th Floor, San Francisco, CA USA

We hereby issue our irrevocable documentary credit No. 3456789

Date of Issue: July 15, 2016

Date of expiry: October 12, 2016

Place of expiry: USA

Applicant:　　　　　　　　　　　　Beneficiary:

Turkey Medical Equipment Importer　　American Medical Equipment Exporter

Ankara, Turkey　　　　　　　　　　Houston, Texas USA

Amount: USD 12,000, twelve thousand US Dollars credit available at sight with the Trade Bank, 525 Market street, San Francisco, California, USA by payment.

Partial shipments: Allowed

Transshipment: Allowed

Shipment from any USA airport, for transportation to Esenboga airport, Ankara, Turkey by plane.

Latest day of shipment: September 20, 2016

Description of goods: Blood plasa machine as per Proforma Invoice No. 123

Quantity: One

Unit price: USD 12,000, Total price USD 12,000

Terms of price: FOB Texas

Documents required

1. Signed commercial invoice in original and 2 copies that merchandise is in strict conformity with Proforma Invoice and indicating quantity, quality and unit price.

2. Certificate of origin, legalized by local chamber of commerce in 2 copies indicating that the goods are of USA origin.

3. Copy of fax send to us on shipment date about expedition details as description, value, loaded quantity of merchandise and characteristics of transport vehicle (fight No.) our fax No. 0-312-1234567.

4. Clean air waybill, in 3 copies consigned to Turkish Export/Import Bank and marked notify applicant and freight collection.

5. Beneficiary's written statement showing that 1 original invoice, 1 certificate of origin legalized by local chamber of commerce, 1 original clean air waybill have been sent together

with the goods. Additional conditions: Insurance will be covered by applicant.

Original documents will be sent to us by courier "DHL".

All documents should bear our and the negotiating/presenting bank's reference numbers.

Charges: All charges outsides Turkey are for beneficiary's account.

Period of presentation: Documents to be presented within 21 days after shipment date.

Confirmation instructions: Confirm

Reimbursement bank: New York Bank, New York, NY USA

If presented documents contain discrepancies USD 100, or equivalent in the documentary credit currency will be deducted from proceeds as additional processing fees.

Advise through bank: The Trade Bank, San Francisco, California USA

This credit is subject to the Uniform Customs and Practice for Documentary Credit (1993 Revision), International Chamber of Commerce, Publication Number 600, and engages us in accordance with the terms thereof.

Turkish Export/Import Bank

3. 2. 5 Revolving Documentary Credit

A revolving documentary credit is one by which, under the terms and conditions thereof, the amount is renewed or reinstated without specific amendments to the documentary credit being required. The revolving documentary credit may be revocable or irrevocable, and may revolve in relation to time or value.

In the case of a documentary credit that revolves in relation to time, e. g. which is initially available for up to USD 15,000 per month during a fixed period of time, say, six months, the documentary credit is automatically available for USD 15,000 each month irrespective of whether any sum was drawn during the previous month. A documentary credit of this nature can be cumulative or non-cumulative. If it is stated to be "cumulative", any sum not utilized during the first period carries over and may be utilized during a subsequent period. If it is "non-cumulative", any sum not utilized in a period ceases to be available, that is, it is not carried over to a subsequence period. It must be remembered that under this kind of documentary credit and following this example, the obligations of the issuing bank would be for USD 90,000, i. e. six revolving periods each for USD 15,000, so while the face value of the documentary credit is given as USD 15,000 the total undertaking of the issuing bank is for the full value that might be drawn.

In the case of a documentary credit that revolves in relation to value, the amount is reinstated upon utilization within a given overall period of validity. The documentary credit may provide for automatic reinstatement immediately upon presentation of the specified documents, or it may provide for reinstatement only after receipt by the issuing bank of those documents or another stated condition. This kind of documentary credit involves the buyer and the banks in an incalculable liability. For that reason, it is not in common use. To maintain a degree of control, it would be necessary to specify the overall amount that may be drawn under the documentary credit. Such amount would have to be decided by the buyer and the seller to meet their requirements, and would have to agree to by the issuing bank.

3.2.6　Red Clause Documentary Credit

A red clause documentary credit is a documentary credit with a special condition incorporated into it that authorizes the confirming bank or other nominated bank to make advances to the beneficiary before presentation of the documents.

The clause is incorporated at the specific request of the applicant, and the wording is dependent upon his requirements. The red documentary credit is so called because the clause was originally written in red ink to draw attention to the unique nature of this documentary credit. The clause specifies the amount of the advance authorized, which, in some instances, may be for the full amount of the documentary credit.

The red clause documentary credit is often used as a method of providing the seller with funds prior to shipment. Therefore, it is of value to middlemen and dealers in areas of commerce that require a form of pre-financing and when a buyer would be willing to make special concessions of this nature.

For example, a furniture manufacturer in Taiwan area (the buyer/importer) through an issuing bank in Taiwan opens a red clause documentary credit naming a hardwood lumber dealer in Indonesia as beneficiary, with the dealer's Indonesian bank as the confirming bank. The hardwood dealers draws against the red clause credit, obtaining funds from the bank to pay his supplier as he finds lumber that meets the needs of the furniture manufacturer in Taiwan.

If the hardwood dealer is unable to ship the lumber according to the terms and condition of the original credit, the confirming bank in Indonesia has recourse to the issuing bank in Taiwan, which also has recourse to the beneficiary (seller/hardwood dealer) in Indonesia.

This kind of arrangement places the onus of final repayment on the applicant, who would be liable for repayment of the advances if the beneficiary failed to present the documents called for under the documentary credit, and who would also be liable for all costs — such as interest or foreign exchange hedging — incurred by the issuing bank, the confirming bank, the confirming bank, if any, or any other nominated bank.

3.2.7　Standby Credit

The standby credit is a documentary credit or similar arrangement, however, named or described, which represents an obligation to the beneficiary on the part of the issuing bank to:

a. repay money borrowed by the applicant, or advanced to or for the account of the applicant;

b. make payment on account of any indebtedness undertaken by the applicant; or

c. make payment on account of any default by the applicant in the performance of an obligation.

The standby credit thus serves as a back-up or secondary means of payment, though it is recognized as a primary obligation of the issuing bank. In both types of usage, commercial or standby documentary credits alike, the underlying purpose of the issuing bank is to pay for goods supplied or services furnished, as required by the contract between the parties. The difference in application can be expressed by saying that the commercial documentary credits is activated by the "performance" of the beneficiary. The standby credit, by contract, supports the beneficiary in the event of a "default".

Exporters may be asked to provide a standby documentary credit as a requirement of working on complicated infrastructure projects abroad or as an assurance under a contractual obligation that they will perform as agreed. If the goods are provided, or the service performed as agreed the standby documentary credit will expire unused. The exporter must also be certain that the documents submitted are exactly as required in the documentary credit.

3.2.8   Transferable Documentary Credit

A transferable documentary credit is one where the beneficiary may request that part of the proceeds (payment) of the credit be transferred to one or more other parties who become second beneficiaries.

A transferable credit is used by "middleman" who acts as an intermediary between a buyer and a seller to earn a profit for structuring the transaction.

The buyer opens a documentary credit naming the intermediary as the beneficiary. The intermediary then transfers both the obligation to supply the goods and part of the proceeds of the credit to the actual supplier.

In the process, the intermediary commits little or no funds to the transaction where the intermediary does not wish the buyer and actual supplier to know each other's identity.

a. Permitted changes to the credit

A transferable credit can be transferred only under the terms stated in the original credit.

However, the intermediary may transfer the credit with the following changes:

(1) The name and address of the intermediary may be substituted for that of the original buyer (applicant of the credit).

(2) Unit prices and total amount of the credit may be reduced to enable the intermediary an allowance for profit.

(3) The expiration date, the final shipment date, and the final date for presentation of documents may all be shortened to allow the intermediary time to meet obligations under the original credit.

(4) Insurance coverage may be increased in order to provide the percentage amount of cover stipulated in the original credit.

b. Amendments to a transferable credit

Since the ultimate buyer and the actual seller/supplier are separated by the intermediary there is the question of how to deal with amendments. Do amendments by the buyer get sent (advised) to the second beneficiary?

The intermediary, therefore, must establish irrevocably, at the time of the request for transfer of the credit, and prior to the actual transfer of the credit, whether the transferring bank may advise amendments to the seller (second beneficiary).

Options for transfer rights on amendments include full or partial transfer of the credit with

(1) retainment of rights on amendments

(2) partial waiver of rights on amendments

(3) waiver of rights on amendments

If the transferring bank agrees to the transfer, it must advise the seller (second beneficiary) of the intermediary's amendment instructions.

Basically, transferable documentary credits are used as a financing tool in transactions where the buyer trusts the intermediary.

The whole procedure of transferable credit issuance is shown by Figure 6. 8

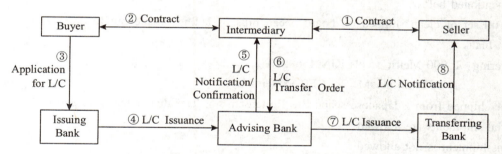

Figure 6. 8   Procedure of Transferable Credit Issuance

Explanations:

①Intermediary (first beneficiary) concludes the contract with seller (second beneficiary) to purchase goods.

②Intermediary concludes the contract to seller goods to buyer (end-user)

③Buyer applies to issuing bank for opening a documentary L/C

④ Issuing bank issues the documentary L/C as per the intermediary's instructions and forwards it to advising bank.

⑤Advising bank authenticates the L/C and informs intermediary of documentary L/C.

⑥Intermediary orders transfer of documentary L/C to seller (second beneficiary).

⑦Advising bank transfers credit (L/C) in care of transferring (seller's) bank.

⑧Transferring bank notifies seller (second beneficiary) of documentary credit.

Sample   **Transferable Documentary Credit**

To: The Transferring Bank

  Swiss Bank Corporation

Reference: Issuing Bank's Documentary Credit Number

   Doc. Credit No. 173896

   Advising Bank's Reference No.

   L/C /5 39284

Amount: USD 386,000   Three hundred eighty-six thousand US dollars only

Validity: January 15, 2016

Applicant:	Beneficiary:
Schmitt & Co. Ltd.	Transito Ltd.
Hinterlindenstrasse 47	Rheinalee 183
Frankfurt 34	4002 Basel

Documents Required

1. Invoice — 3 copies

2. Inspection certificate, evidencing that the goods are in accordance with the specifications mentioned below.

3. Full set of clean shipped on board ocean bills of lading, made out to order and endorsed in blank

Covering: 1,000 Metric steels KIN 456/243

   at USD386 per M. T, CFR Rotterdam

to be shipped from a Japanese seaport to Rotterdam not later than January 1, 2016

Partial shipments are allowed

Transshipment is not allowed

Documents to be presented not later than 15 days after date of shipment

This documentary credit is transferable

We confirm this documentary credit to you as irrevocably valid until January 15, 2001.

The Trade Bank

3.2.9   Assignment of Proceeds

In accordance with UCP500 Article 49, the fact that a documentary credit is not stated to be transferable shall not affect the beneficiary's right to assign any proceeds to which he may be, or may become, entitled under such documentary credit in accordance with the applicable law. This provision relates only to the assignment of proceeds and not to the assignment of the right to perform under the documentary credit itself.

  a. How to control an effective assignment of proceeds

Written notification by the beneficiary to the nominated bank, giving his instructions for the assignment of the proceeds must be irrevocable and in writing, in which instructions obligates the beneficiary himself vis-à-vis the nominated bank to present the required drafts and/or documents under the documentary credit and that payment, if and when effected, is to be made in accordance with those instructions.

The beneficiary's instructions should be manually signed and bear a bank's guarantee which confirms the authenticity and authority of the signer of that document.

The nominated bank, if it agrees to such instructions, must acknowledge and notify the assignee of the instructions lodged and the nominated bank's agreement to perform in accordance therewith.

The nominated bank which is authorized to negotiate or pay should bear in mind that, if it decides to pay or negotiate the drafts and/or documents drawn under the documentary credit, it must disburse the funds as instructed.

If an advising bank or another nominated bank (not the issuing bank or the confirming bank) is instructed by the beneficiary to accept such instructions. However, if such advising bank or nominated bank does accept such instructions for assignment of proceeds, such bank should not mislead the assignee into believing that he has that bank's irrevocable obligation to pay as a result of those instructions.

The statement to the assignee from such a bank should be phrased in such a manner that the assignee is aware of that bank's limited undertaking.

b. The whole procedure of transferable assignment proceeds is shown by Figure 6. 9.

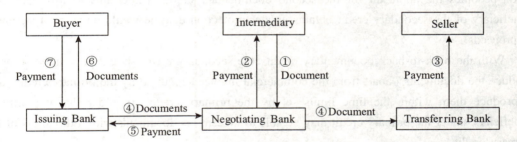

Figure 6. 9   Procedure of Transferable Assignment of Proceeds

Explanations:

①Intermediary (first beneficiary) presents documents to the negotiating bank.

②Negotiating bank pays intermediary any funds not assigned to the seller (second beneficiary).

③Negotiating bank pays transferring bank who then in turn pays the seller (second beneficiary) the assigned funds.

④Negotiating bank presents documents to the issuing bank.

⑤Issuing bank pays/reimburses the negotiating bank in accordance with the terms of the credit.

⑥Issuing bank presents to the buyer.

⑦Buyer pays/reimburses the issuing bank in accordance with the terms of the credit.

3. 2. 10   Back-to-back Documentary Credit

It may happen that the documentary credit in favor of the beneficiary is not transferable, or although transferable, can not meet the commercial requirements of transfer in accordance with UCP500 Article 48 conditions. The beneficiary himself, however, may be unable to supply the goods and may need to purchase them from and make payment to another supplier. In this case, it may sometimes be possible to use a back-to-back documentary credit.

The benefit of an irrevocable documentary credit (the primary credit) may be made available to a third party where the primary beneficiary uses the documentary credit as security/collateral to obtain another documentary credit (the secondary credit) in favor of the actual supplier.

This type of documentary credit is essential when the terms and conditions of a transferable documentary credit can not be applied to the transaction.

A back-to-back documentary credit involves two separate documentary credits:

a. one opened in favor of the first or primary Beneficiary, and

b. one opened for the account of the first or primary beneficiary in favor of a secondary Beneficiary who is supplying the goods. The first/primary beneficiary of the first documentary credit becomes the applicant for the second documentary credit. Under this arrangement, the beneficiary of the secondary credit obtains greater protection than he would under an assignment of proceeds.

With the back-to-back documentary credit, the secondary credit should be worded so as to produce the documents (apart from the commercial invoice) required by the primary credit, and to produce them within the time limits set by the primary credit, in order that the primary beneficiary under the primary credit may be able to present his documents within the limits of the primary credit.

The whole procedure of back-to-back documentary credit is shown by Figure 6. 10. meanwhile, back-to-back L/C utilization is shown by Figure 6. 11.

Explanations:

①Buyer and Seller negotiate a contract. Seller places an order with supplier.

②Buyer applies for issuing a documentary credit to issuing bank

③Issuing bank opens a documentary credit and forwards it to advising bank.

④Advising bank notifies the seller of documentary credit.

⑤Seller orders assignment of credit to supplier.

⑥Advising bank assigns credit to supplier.

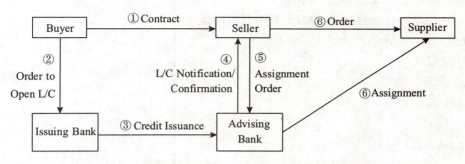

Figure 6.10　Procedure of Transferable Assignment of Proceeds

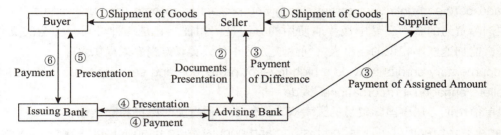

Figure 6.11　Procedure of Transferable Assignment of Proceeds

Explanations:

①Ultimate supplier effects the shipment and invoices to seller who in turn ships the goods to the buyer.

②Seller forwards documents to advising bank.

③Advising bank pays the supplier the amount of designated in seller's assignment order. In the meantime, advising bank pays the seller the difference between the original credit amount and the amount assigned to the supplier.

④Advising bank presents documents for negotiation and issuing bank pays advising bank.

⑤Issuing bank presents documents to buyer.

⑥Buyer effects the payment.

📖 **Words & Expressions**

1. Irrevocable straight documentary credit 不可撤销直接信用证
2. Irrevocable negotiation documentary credit 不可撤销议付信用证
3. Irrevocable confirmed documentary credit 不可撤销保兑信用证
4. Revolving documentary credit 循环跟单信用证
5. Red clause documentary credit 红条款跟单信用证
6. Standby credit 备用信用证
7. Transferable documentary credit 可转让跟单信用证

8. Assignment of proceeds 款项让渡
9. Back to back documentary credit 背对背信用证
10. Confirming bank 保兑行
11. obligor 债务人
12. onus 义务，责任
13. hedge 套头交易

📖 Notes

1. The most commonly used method of payment in the financial business of international trade is the letter of credit which is a reliable and saft method of payment, facilitating trade between unknown parties and giving protection to both the buyer and the seller.
在国际贸易的金融交易中最普通使用的方法是信用证。它是一种可靠、安全的支付方法，能加速互不相识的当事人之间达成贸易并对买卖双方当事人提供保障。

2. Documentary credits provide a high level of protection and security to both buyers and sellers engaged in international trade.
跟单信用证为从事国际贸易的买卖双方提供了一种高度的保护和安全性。

3. Letters of Credit（L/C）is the historic and popular term used for a documentary credit because such credits were and are transmitted in the form of a letter from the buyer's bank.
信用证是一种历史悠久、家喻户晓的术语，用于表示跟单信用证。因为这样一些信用证过去及现在均是买方银行以信函形式而传递。

4. The feature common to all kinds of L/C is that the buyer arranges with a bank to provide finance for the exporter in the country of the latter on delivery of shipping documents.
所有信用证的共同特征就是买方与一家银行安排并为另一国卖方提供融资。要求后者交付装运单据。

5. On presentation of the shipping documents, the bank will pay the purchase price, normally by paying a sigh draft or by accepting a time draft drawn on the buyer.
一经提示装运单据，银行将支付所购商品价格。正常情况下是通过支付一份开具给买方的即期汇票中承兑一份远期汇票。

6. They do not, for example, ensure that the goods actually shipped are as ordered, nor do they insulate buyers and sellers from other disagreements or complaints arising from their relationship.
例如，它们不能确保实际运送的货物就是所订售的货物。它们也不能阻止买卖双方来自其他方面的分歧或双方关系所引发的各种抱怨。

7. The Uniform Customs and Practice for Documentary Credits（UCP）is the internationally recognized codification of rules unifying banking practice regarding documentary credits.

《跟单信用证统一惯例规则》是一个国际上公认的法典编纂，涉及关于跟单信用证统一银行实践的各种规则。

8. In addition, such procedure would be changed when discrepancies are checked out by banks and correspondences take place several rounds between parties involved.

此外，这样的流程就会改变。如当若干不符点被银行审核出所涉及当事人之间会引发多轮通信联系。

9. Issuance describes the process of the buyer's applying for and issuing a documentary credit at the issuing bank and the issuing bank's formal notification of the seller through the advising bank.

信用证的开立描述了买方向开证行申请和开证行开立一份跟单信用证以及开证行通过通知行给予卖方一个正式通知的过程。

10. Amendment describes the process whereby the terms and conditions of a documentary credit may be modified after the credit has been issued.

信用证的改证描述了这样一个过程，是当信用证已经开立后，信用证的一些条款和条件可能会被更改。

11. Utilization describes the procedure for the seller's shipping of goods, the transfer of document from the seller to the buyer to the seller through the bank.

信用证的运用描述了一个程序即卖方发运货物，单据从卖方向买方通过银行的传递和银行付款从买方向卖方的转移。

12. Settlement refers to the process of payment of the beneficiary to the credit after presentation of documents under the credit.

信用证的结算指的是这样一个过程即当信用证项下单据提示后，受益人获得支付的过程。

⟫ Exercises

I. True or False

1. A transferable credit is a credit instrument which authorizes the beneficiary to transfer part of the rights of the credit to a third party or parties.

2. A back-to-back credit is mainly used by a middleman to get from a supplier goods which are sold or resold to a third party or parties.

3. An irrevocable credit can be amended, revoked or cancelled without the beneficiary's consent.

4. A revocable credit can not be amended.

5. An irrevocable confirmed documentary credit gives the beneficiary a double assurance of payment.

6. A credit can be transferred only if it is expressly designated as "transferable" by the issuing bank.

7. Unless otherwise stated in the credit, a transferable credit can be transferred once only.

8. Under the assignment, the beneficiary assigns his right to perform under the credit to a third party.

9. A standby credit is subject to UCP500.

10. A bank runs greater risks when it opens a revolving credit. This is why it will specify a total amount available in the credit.

II. Multiple Choice

1. A revocable credit can not be amended or canceled only after _____.

    A. the documents under it have been honored

    B. it has been amended once

    C. the advising bank has notified the beneficiary of its opening

    D. it has been confirmed by a correspondent bank.

2. Back-to-back credits are advantageous to _____.

    A. all consumers　　　　　　　B. all manufacturers

    C. all customers　　　　　　　D. all traders

3. According to the beneficiary's instructions, a transferable credit may be made available to _____.

    A. one party　　　　　　　　　B. two parties

    C. more parties　　　　　　　　D. an of above

4. A credit can be transferred by _____.

    A. the first beneficiary　　　　B. the second beneficiary

    C. the third beneficiary　　　　D. any person

5. A bank is obligated to transfer the credit only after _____.

    A. being instructed　　　　　　B. being instructed as well as paid

    C. receiving the credit　　　　　D. the credit is confirmed

6. Under _____, the obligation of the issuing bank is extended only to the beneficiary in honoring drafts or documents and usually expires at the counters of the issuing bank.

    A. the revocable credit　　　　　B. the irrevocable credit

    C. the irrevocable straight credit　D. the confirmed credit

7. _____ gives the beneficiary a double assurance of payment.

    A. An irrevocable credit　　　　B. A revocable credit

    C. A confirmed credit　　　　　D. An irrevocable confirmed credit

8. The credit may only be confirmed if it is so authorized or requested by _____.

    A. the issuing bank　　　　　　B. the advising bank

    C. the applicant　　　　　　　D. the beneficiary

9. The revolving credit may revolve in relation to _____.

    A. time　　　　　　　　　　　B. value

C. time and value   D. time or value

10. The red clause documentary credit is often used as a method of _____.

   A. providing the seller with funds prior to shipment

   B. providing the buyer with funds prior to shipment

   C. providing the seller with funds after shipment

   D. providing the buyer with funds after shipment

III. Answer Questions

1. Please describe the process of documentary credit with the help of diagram or flow-chart.

2. What is the relationship between the underlying contract and the documentary credit?

3. What are the final serious outcomes if there are some fundamental discrepancies between the documents and L/C?

Chapter 7   Other Payment Methods

This chapter introduces other payment methods besides documentary collection and credit and tries to tell us that payment in advance is favorable for exporters, while importers will suffer from the biggest risk. Open account is favorable for importers, however, if the buyers are not in good credit standing, it is better for exporters to use it together with export insurance, or factoring, or forfaiting.

In international trade, besides the documentary collections and credits, people also create many other effective methods which are feasible to examine fulfillment of the seller and the buyer. Some are commonly used for international payment in today's international society, namely, payment in advance, open account, factoring and forfaiting, etc.

1. Payment in Advance

Nowadays, the commonly used payment methods are thoroughly studied. How to choose a certain payment method among them is the result through analysis and comparison, and a contest for both the buyer and the seller. Therefore, it is hard to say that in particular situation there is only one method matched, there should always be alternatives. People have to learn how to make possible compromise to ensure successful transaction.

Actually, payment in advance is the worst thing for the buyer to do unless he does not have other choice. However, the buyer may change his situation by combining payment in advance with bank guarantee or standby credit so as to minimize his risks.

Payment in advance refers to that the buyer places the funds at the disposal of the seller prior to shipment of the goods or provision of services.

While this method of payment is expensive and contains degrees of risks, it is not uncommon when the manufacturing process or services delivered are specialized and capital intensive. In such circumstances the parties may agree to fund the operation by partial payment in advance or by progress payment.

This method of payment is used for following situations:

(1) when the buyer's credit is doubtful

(2) when there is an unstable political or economic environment in the buyer's country,

and/or

(3) if there is a potential delay in the receipt of funds from the buyer, perhaps due to events beyond his control.

Generally, there are some advantages to the seller when payment in advance is used for a transaction between the buyer and the seller. Firstly, the seller can immediately use the fund to run the operation. Secondly, this method of payment helps the seller with the shortage of funds. Finally, when payment in advance is used, the seller has no any financial risk. In other words, this method of payment perhaps is the safest one for the seller to fulfill his obligation under a specific transaction.

On the other hand, there are two disadvantages to the buyer. One is that the buyer pays in advance, tying up his capital prior to receipt of the goods or services. The other is that the buyer has no assurance that what he contracted for will be; supplied; received; received in a timely fashion, and/or, received in the quality or quantity ordered.

In reality the buyer seldom makes full payment in advance prior to the shipment; normally he only pays a certain percentage of the goods value, that is down payment. Thanks to taking the greatest risks under payment in advance, the buyer has to consider some key points mentioned below:

(1) The credit standing of the seller must be exceedingly good, and the buyer trusts that the seller will deliver the order in due time.

(2) The potential and economic environment in the seller's country should be stable enough that the government of such country will not prohibit exportation of the commodity contracted after payment has been effected.

(3) The buyer should have sufficient balance sheet liquidity or he is confident of obtaining working capital, in any way, to support him paying in advance;

The buyer should make certain if the foreign exchange control authority in his country (if any) will permit advance payment to be effected.

2. Open Account

In contrast with payment in advance, open account business, called also sale on credit, means an arrangement made between the buyer and the seller whereby the goods are manufactured and delivered before payment is required.

Open account provides for payment at some stated specific future date and without the buyer issuing any negotiable instrument evidencing his legal commitment. The seller must have absolute trust that he will be paid at the agreed date. The seller should recognize that in certain instances it is possible to discount open accounts receivables with a financial institution.

The main advantages to the buyer are as follows:

(1) The buyer pays for the goods or services only when they are received and/or inspected.

(2) The payment is conditioned on such issues as political, legal, and economic issues.

On the other hand, there are some disadvantages to the seller.

(1) The seller releases the title to the goods without having assurance of payment.

(2) There is a possibility that political events will impose regulations which defer or block the movement of funds to seller.

(3) Seller's capital is tied up until the goods are received and/or inspected by the buyer or until the services are found to be acceptable and payment is effected.

Initially, payment under open account may be effected immediately after the buyer is satisfied with the goods or at a predetermined later time, say, at end of month, etc. In other words, the seller is selling on credit without any particular measure to force the buyer to settle his debts on the agreed date. That is to say, in such case, the seller losses control both over the goods and their legal title, while the buyer can take delivery of the goods and dispose of them as he wants. Obviously, allowing the buyer to access the goods prior to payment would only be considered if the seller was satisfied with the good credit standing of the buyer. Under open account, it is clear that the seller has to make sure that:

(1) His own financial standing must be good enough to support the whole performing procedure including producing, shipping, insuring or even customs clearing and so on;

(2) The buyer will effect payment at the agreed date;

(3) The authority of the buyer's country will not impose regulations deferring or blocking the funds transfer.

3. Factoring

Factoring is an agreement between a supplier and a special kind of finance house called a factor or factoring company by which the supplier sells to the factor the right to collect accounts receivables at some future date. It is a form of trade financing service aimed mainly at open account sales, both domestic and international.

3. 1   Essence of Factoring

The essence of factoring is the discounting of acceptable accounts receivables on a non-recourse notification basis.

At first, the factor who buys the accounts receivables without recourse to the supplier, takes the whole trade transaction and must bear the loss if the buyer does not pay. On the other hand, the buyer of goods is notified of the transfer and makes the payment directly to the factor.

On the contrary, in a documentary credit arrangement, the bank usually purchases or discounts a bill of exchange drawn on the buyer on a recourse basis. If the buyer does not pay the bill, the bank may turn to the supplier to obtain payment. Also the buyer is not ordinarily notified about the pledge of debts.

3. 2　Versatile Services

Factors not only take over the account receivables of their clients (the suppliers) but also provide other additional services, among them credit checking, risk bearing, and lending being the major ones. Thus, factors perform the middle-agent role and that of a professional risk manager. Versatile factoring services may make clients have more time to concentrate on running their businesses without worrying about the collection of debts and account receivables.

Factors can offer one or combination of the above services to third clients, depending on their needs. A factor usually provides the following financial management services.

(1) Credit checking

The factor makes an appraisal of credit worthiness of each customer (the buyer) of the supplier and set a credit limit for each of these customers.

(2) Credit risk bearing

On approved transactions, the factor purchases the account receivables, and thereby assumes the risk of the buyer's non-payment due to financial inability. It must be pointed out that the factor only evaluates and assumes the buyer's credit risk.

(3) Accounts managing

After taking over the accounts receivables, the factor sends the invoices to the buyer, makes collections and keeps up the cash position of the supplier's operations.

(4) Advance funds

Usually, the factor pays his client ahead of the maturity date of the accounts receivables, and the amount is usually up to a maximum of 80 percent of factored sales. Typically, the supplier can get paid in cash immediately after selling the accounts receivables to the factor.

3. 3　Types of Factoring

3. 3. 1　Maturity Factoring

This is the most original form of factoring business. The supplier sells the acceptable accounts receivables to the factor, who assumes the responsibility for collection as well as the risk of credit losses and undertakes to pay the supplier at maturity without recourse to him. After handing over the accounts receivables, the supplier only needs to wait for some time for payment. Also the supplier may borrow from a bank in the meantime at a lower interest rate if necessary.

3. 3. 2   Advance Factoring

Advance factoring is also called standard factoring. Under this condition, factored clients are usually given the facility to borrow against the proceeds of the factored receivables prior to their due date.

Advance factoring is especially important to the supplier who is short of working capital, because it turns credit sales into cash sales which accelerate the supplier's cash flow. That is to say, the supplier sells his goods for cash by selling his invoices to the factor. Furthermore, he is in a better position to pay his creditors immediately and receive any discounts that are offered for prompt payment.

However, the advance factoring is a more costly method because under this method the factoring company asks for higher interest charges. The reason for the higher interest charges is that if it pays over cash immediately upon receipt of accounts receivables, the factoring company may have to borrow from other sources or use its own funds that could be gainful employed elsewhere, i. e. opportunity cost.

3. 4   A Normal Transaction of a Maturity Factoring

The procedure for a normal transaction of a maturity factoring can be shown by Figure 7. 1

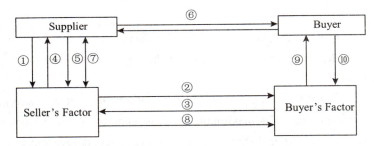

Figure 7. 1   Procedure for a Normal Transaction of Factoring

Explanations:

①The supplier applies for a certain amount credit line of factoring for the goods under open account.

②Supplier's (seller) factor transmits relevant information to the buyer's factor.

③Based on evaluation of the buyer's credit standing, buyer's factor will answer the seller's factor about the amount of credit line and the bank fees charged.

④Supplier's factor will inform the supplier about the results.

⑤Upon agreement of the results, supplier can sign a "Factoring Agreement" with his factor.

⑥Supplier effects the shipment to the buyer in accordance with the contract.

⑦Supplier's factor becomes the creditor after he buys the documents from the supplier.

⑧Buyer's factor becomes the creditor after he buys the documents from the seller's factor.

⑨Buyer's factor will present buyer for making payment.

⑩After receiving proceeds from the buyer's factor, supplier's factor will pay to the supplier.

Generally speaking, factoring is mainly used for the commodities in relative small sum and short term, while for long term capital goods associated with large amount of proceeds, another payment method, namely forfaiting, could be used.

3.5 Development of Factoring

Factoring has its seeds in the Industrial Revolution. In the north of England, when exporting to North America the textile mills appointed agents, or "factor's" to sell their products and to get the money for then and send it back. Gradually, these "factors" expanded the range of their clients and their services.

Although the development of the factoring was primarily in textiles and related trades, there has been a great change and a growing volume of industries in using the factoring services during the last three decades. At present, factoring is mainly used for products or services sold on a short-term (less than one year), normally 30 to 90 days repeated basis to a diverse customer group generally more than a dozen.

Today, the majority of factoring services provided in the world are mainly for international trade purpose. Now take Hong Kong for example. In 2015, the total amount of factoring services in Hong Kong was USD115 million including USD 1,000 million international factoring and USD150 million domestic factoring. It is clear that international factoring is more important.

4. Forfaiting

Essentially, Forfaiting is a non-recourse sole of promissory note, bills of exchange guaranteed by bank and similar documents provided by the buyer. The seller receives cashes in time by selling the notes or bills at a discount from their face value to a specialized financial organization called forfeiter. The forfeiter should arrange the entire operation prior to the beginning of actual transaction. The exporting firm receives a clear and unconditional cash payment at the time of financial transaction, not carrying political and commercial risk of non-payment by the buyer (importer) any more, which is assumed by the guaranteeing bank.

4. 1 Basic Concepts of Forfaiting

Sometimes, "forfaiting" is written as "forfeiting". The word "forfait" comes from the French "a forfait" and thus conveys the idea of "surrendering rights", which is of fundamental feature in forfaiting.

Forfaiting is a method of international trade finance, normally used in the trade of capital equipment by deferred payment. In a forfaiting the forfaiter discounts a series of guaranteed instruments at a fixed interest rate without recourse.

To be more clear about the definition of forfaiting, please pay attention to the following questions:

4. 1. 1 The Forfaiter

The forfeiter is a financial institution specialized in the discounting of a forfeit paper and is usually a bank or a big financial company in the exporter's country. After buying the series of instruments the forfaiter gives the seller an immediate cash payment, of course, with discount interest rate and other charges deducted. Thus, the forfaiter loses his right of recourse to any previous holder of the obligation. This is non-recourse buying of instruments.

4. 1. 2 The Seller of the Instruments

Usually the seller is an exporter who has provided capital goods or services and wishes to pass all risks and responsibilities for collection to the forfaiter in exchange for immediate cash payment.

4. 1. 3 A Series of Instruments

Usually the series of instruments take the form of trade drafts (bills of exchange) or promissory notes, although any form of debt could, in theory, be forfaited. The drafts or notes are usually structured to produce a series of maturities at six monthly intervals and normally cover a medium-term business, of which the maturities of which the maturity is from six months to five or six years.

4. 1. 4 Without Recourse

When selling his obligations, the exporter protects himself from any recourse by including the words "without recourse" in the endorsement. Thus the exporter virtually converts his credit-based sale into a cash transaction. His sole responsibility lies in the satisfactory manufacture and delivery of the goods as well as the correct drawing up of the obligation. He assumes no liability for future payment on the bills or notes and thus in effect receives the discounted proceeds free of any further payment difficulties.

4.1.5 Bank Guarantee

Unless the importer is a first-class obligor of undoubted standing, any forfait debt must carry a security. The series of debts are usually guaranteed by the importer's bank, which is known to the forfaiter and well acquainted with the credit standing of the importer. Instead of issuing a letter of guarantee separately, the guarantor bank may write on the face of the bills or notes "per aval" and put its signs thereunder.

The fulfillment of this condition is of utmost importance in views of the non-recourse aspect of the business, for the forfaiter can only rely on this form of bank guarantee as his sole security in the event of non-payment of the obligor. Bills or notes guaranteed by a bank not only alleviate the risks of the forfeiter, but also enable him to have the bills or notes re-discounted in a secondary market.

4.2 Procedure of a Typical Forfaiting Transaction

Since forfaiting is a main tool to be used for encourage the export of capital goods, those developing countries are quite welcome such financing method. The reason is that the buyer can take fully use of the seller credit to solve his capital shortage problems. However, the buyer should get the permission of his bank to provide payment guarantee either in seller's draft or his own promissory note

A typical forfaiting transaction involves five parties, as shown by Figure 7.2. the steps in the process are as follows:

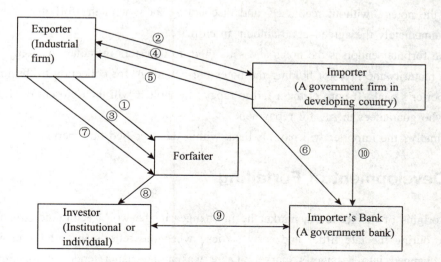

Figure 7.2   Procedure of a Typical Forfaiting Transaction

①The exporter contacts a forfeiter and comes to a preliminary agreement on the amount, maturity of the paper and discount rate, because the exporter will add the discount interest and other charges in his selling price and the importer needs to calculate the cost of funding.

②The exporter negotiates with the importer over the maturity of the instruments, the guaranteeing bank, and the interest rate upon which discount interest is calculated during the period of deferred payment.

③The exporter concludes a forfaiting agreement with the forfeiter, which states states the details of the forfaiting transaction, the discount rate, the fees to be charged, the latest date of transfer and delivery of the instruments.

④The exporter and the importer conclude a commercial contract on a series of transactions. The importer will pay periodically over an intermediate (two-to-five-year) period against progress sin delivery or completion of the project.

⑤The importer issues a series of promissory notes, usually maturing every six or twelve months against progress in delivery or completion of the project. Then the importer delivers the notes to a bank operating in the place where he resides, i. e. the importer's bank.

⑥The importer's bank guarantees the notes by writing the word "per aval" on the face of the notes and putting its signature thereunder. At this point the importer's bank becomes the primary obligor in the eyes of all subsequent holders of the notes. Then the bank forwards the guaranteed promissory notes to the exporter.

⑦Within the commitment period, which is about six months beginning on the date of signature of the forfaiting agreement and ending on the date of signature of the forfaiting agreement and ending on the date of the actual transfer and delivery of the guaranteed notes, the exporter must transfer and deliver the guaranteed notes, and the forfaiter must carry out his obligation of discounting the notes in accordance with the terms of the agreement. After endorsing the notes "without recourse" and discounting them with the forfaiter, the exporter receives immediately the agreed-upon amount in cash.

⑧The forfaiter endorses the notes and sells them to investors in money market.

⑨At maturity the investor holding the notes presents them for collection to the importer or to the importer's bank. If both of them fail to repay, the holder will then present the notes to the forfaiter who guarantees them, for repayment.

⑩ Finally, the importer will pay his bank within the specified time period.

4.3   Development of Forfaiting

The origins of the forfaiting market lie in changes in the world economic structure which took place during the late fifties and early sixties, when the seller's market for capital goods gradually changed into a buyer's market. There was a increasing tendency for importers to demand periods of credit extending beyond the traditional 90 or 180 days. However, the exporting firms could not finance such medium-term credits out of their own funds, and the existing banks were unable to offer the services the exporter desired. Forfait finance was thus created to satisfy growing demands in international trade finance.

West German capital goods exports were the foundation of the forfaiting market. In the early 1960's, West German exporters were keen to sell capital goods into Eastern Europe. However, West German banks wanted to get rid of some of the risks attached to supplier's credits and did not want to provide supplier's credits to its exporter. On the contrary, Swiss bank were willing to take the obligations arising from the transactions between West Germany and Eastern Europe off the German bank's hands on a forfait basis.

The Swiss dominated the forfaiting market for the first 10 years or so. Then the Germans, worried that their customers were getting a better service elsewhere, entered the competition. As the 1970's progressed, more and more banks in Europe saw forfaiting as a lucrative market where margins looked mouthwatering by the side of traditional international rollover credit market. Over the last couple of years, the forfaiting market has taken off by leaps and bounds. In some countries, finance by forfaiting has become an alternative to officially supported export credits and term loans.

4. 4 Difference Between Factoring and Forfaiting

(1) Although both factoring and forfaiting are the discounting of accounts receivables on a non-recourse basis, they have the following differences:

(2) Factoring is suitable for the financing of the export of consumer goods sold on a short-term (usually less than one year) and involving smaller amount of money. Forfaiting is used for the financing of capital goods exports sold on a medium-term (usually two to five years) and involving larger amount of money.

(3) Factoring does not need the guarantee of the importer's bank while forfaiting must be guaranteed by the words "per aval" or the letter of guarantee made by the importer's bank.

(4) In factoring, the exporter need not negotiate with the importer beforehand; however, prior to reaching a forfaiting agreement the exporter must negotiate with the importer to reach an agreement.

(5) Factoring usually does not cover the political and transfer risks while a forfaiter must bear these risks:

(6) A factor provides versatile services to his clients while a forfaiter focuses on discounting business.

📖 Words & Expressions
1. payment in advance 预付货款
2. open account 赊销(寄售)

3. factoring 保理业务

4. forfaiting 福费廷业务

5. credit standing 信用状况

6. balance sheet 资产负债表

7. liquidity 流动性

8. working capital 流动资金

9. foreign exchange control authority 外汇管理局

10. legal commitment 法律业务

11. accounts receivables 应收款项

12. assurance of payment 付款保证

13. financial standing 财务状况

14. customs clearing 清关，报关

15. factor 保理商

16. discount 贴现业务

17. non-recourse 无追索权

18. versatile services 多样化服务

19. credit checking 调查资信

20. lending 提供贷款

21. credit risk bearing 承担信用风险

22. account managing 财务管理

23. advance funds 预支贷款

24. maturity factoring 到期保理业务

25. advance factoring 预支保理业务

26. surrendering rights 放弃权利

27. international trade finance 国际贸易融资

28. forfaiter 包买机构

29. per aval 担保

30. line of credit 信贷限额

31. lucrative market 有利可图市场

32. rollover credit market 滚转信贷市场

33. taken off by leaps and bounds 迅猛腾飞

Notes

1. Payment in advance is the worst thing for the buyer to do unless he does not have other choice.

   除非买方没有其他选择，预付货款对买方而言是能做的最糟糕的事情。

2. Payment in advance refers to that the buyer places the funds at the disposal of the seller prior to shipment of the goods or provision of services.

预付货款指的是：卖方在货物发运前或提供服务前将资金交由卖方处理。

3. In reality, the buyer seldom makes full payment in advance prior to the shipment; normally he only pays a certain percentage of the goods value, that is down payment.

在现实中，买方很少在发运货物前支付全额预付货款。正常情况下买方仅支付全部货值的一定比例(百分率)的预付款即定金。

4. In contrast with payment in advance, open account business, called also sale on credit, means an arrangement made between the buyer and the seller whereby the goods are manufactured and delivered before payment is required.

与预付货款相反，寄售贸易业务，也称为赊购指的是买卖双方之间的一种约定，即商品(货物)的生产及交付发生在支付之前。

5. Open account provides for payment at some stated specific future date and without the buyer issuing any negotiable instrument evidencing his legal commitment.

寄售是按照所说明的某个特定未来日期支付货款而没有买方签署的任何流通票据以证明他的合法付款承诺。

6. Factoring is an agreement between a supplier and a special kind of finance house called a factor or factoring company by which the supplier sells to the factor the right to collect accounts receivables at some future date.

保理业务是供货商与一个特殊种类的金融机构称为保理商或保理公司之间的约定。即供货商将自己在未来某个日期应收款项的权利转卖给保理商。

7. Forfaiting is a non-recourse sale of promissory notes, bills of exchange guaranteed by bank and similar documents provided by the buyer.

福费廷是由银行所担保的本票、汇票以及相类似的由卖方提供的单据的一种无追索权的销售。

8. The forfaiter should arrange the entire operation prior to the beginning of actual transaction.

包买机构必须在实际交易开始前安排好全部的运作。

9. Forfaiting is a method of international trade finance, normally used in the trade of capital equipment by deferred payment.

福费廷是一种国际贸易融资的方式，大多用于追期付款的资本设备的贸易方式。

10. In a forfaiting, the forfaiter discounts a series of guaranteed instruments at a fixed interest rate without recourse.

在一笔福费廷业务中，包买机构无追索权也按照固定贴现率对一系列担保的票据进行贴现办理。

11. The forfaiter is a financial institution specialized in the discounting of a forfait paper and is usually a bank or a big financial company in the exporter's country.

包买机构是一种专营福费廷票据贴现业务的金融机构。通常是出口商所在国的一家银行或大型财务公司。

12. When selling his obligations, the exporter protects himself from any recourse by

including the words "without recourse" in the endorsement.

当卖出自己的权利义务时，出口商为使自己免受任何追索，在背书时加上这样的文字"无追索权"。

>>> **Exercises**

I. True or False

1. Payment in advance, open account, collection and documentary credit are the usual methods of payment to settle international trade transactions.

2. To the export of goods, the most satisfactory arrangement as far as payment is concerned is to receive payment in advance.

3. Trade on open account arrangement usually satisfies the seller's desire for cash and the importer's desire for credit.

4. In reality, the importer usually makes full payment in advance prior to the shipment.

5. Obviously, allowing the buyer to access the goods prior to payment would only be considered if the seller was satisfied with the good credit standing of the buyer.

6. The essence of factoring is the discounting of acceptable accounts receivables on a recourse basis.

7. Advance factoring is also called standard factoring.

8. Forfaiting is a method of international trade finance, seldom used in the trade of capital equipment by deferred payment.

9. In a forfaiting, the forfaiter purchases in advance a series of guaranteed instruments at a fixed interest rate with recourse.

10. Factoring does not need the guarantee of the importer's bank while forfaiting must be guaranteed by the words "per aval" or the letter of guarantee made by the importer's bank.

II. Multiple Choice

1. To the exporter, the fastest and safest method of settlement is _____.
   A. L/C   B. payment in advance   C. open account   D. draft

2. To the importer, the fastest and safest method of settlement is _____.
   A. letter of credit   B. payment in advance
   C. open account   D. bank's draft

3. When the payment in advance is used, the buyer places the _____ at the disposal of the seller prior to shipment of goods.
   A. credit standing   B. funds   C. guarantee   D. insurance

4. Open account means that an _____ between the buyer and seller whereby the goods are manufactured and delivered before payment is required.

A. appointment B. contract C. arrangement D. desire

5. Open account provides for payment at some stated specific future date and _____ any negotiable instrument evidencing his legal commitment.

A. without the buyer B. without the seller

C. with the buyer D. with the seller

6. The essence of factoring is the discounting of acceptable accounts receivables on a _____ basis.

A. recourse notification B. non-recourse notification

C. beneficial notification D. B and C

7. Advance factoring is especially important to the supplier who is short of _____, because it turns credit sales into cash sales which accelerate the supplier's cash flow.

A. finance B. proceeds C. capital D. working capital

8. The forfaiter is a _____ specialized in the discounting of a forfait paper and is usually a bank or a big financial company in the exporter's country.

A. financial investor B. financial institution

C. financial person D. financial individual

9. Usually the series of instruments take the form of _____, although any form of debt could, in theory, be forfeited.

A. bills of exchange B. promissory notes

C. cheques D. bills of exchange or promissory notes

10. Unless the importer is a first-class obligor of undoubted standing, any forfaited debt must carry a _____.

A protection B. assurance C. service D. security

Chapter 8 Documents

This chapter introduces the importance and key elements of various documents used in international trade. It is evident that documents which stand for the goods, certify performance of the traders, become the basis for making payment in international trade payment. Meanwhile, it is essential for the traders to make sure that documents are exactly in conformity with the terms and conditions of L/C.

Documents refer to a set of certificates or papers used in merchandise transaction. In international trade settlement or payment, documents play an important role in safe exchange between the goods and proceeds. Each document will be defined, key elements listed, and cautions offered concerning important issues and common problems associated with each.

It is important to note that the technical name for letters of credit is documentary credits and, along with documentary collections, that documents are at the heart of all forms of international trade payment.

As with all matters involving money and payments, the form and content of these documents is of great importance to all parties to the transaction. Subtle differences between forms and subtle changes in wording can mean the difference between a successful and an unsuccessful transaction.

Before specifying the required documents the buyer should ensure that the seller is willing and able to provide the documents called for and that they can be provided in the form and with the details stipulated.

Normally, documents can be classified into 4 groups by different issuers:

Business documents issued by business people;

Transport documents issued by carriers;

Insurance documents issued by the insurers;

Official documents issued by state authorities.

Importance of various documents in international trade payment are different, some is indispensable in all transactions, namely, key documents, such as commercial invoices, transport documents and insurance documents; some are called complementary documents, which are occasionally called for according to the nature of goods and the foreign trade regulations of nations.

Under documentary credits, documents are the unique basis for banks to make payment.

Therefore, requirements to the key documents have been set clearly in detail in UCP600.

1. Business Documents

Business documents refer to the documents which are issued by sellers, buyers or other traders, for facilitating trade and payment. Among business documents, the most important one is commercial invoice. Consular invoice and customs invoice function similarly as commercial invoice. Packing list and the third party certificate of inspection are also commonly used documents in international trade payment. Financial documents, which are closely associated with international trade payment, also partially belong to business documents.

1.1 Commercial Invoice

The commercial invoice is the key accounting document describing the commercial transaction between the buyer and the seller. Generally, a commercial invoice gives details of the goods, details of the payment and delivery terms, and a detailed breakdown of the monetary amount due. Normally, invoices are prepared by the seller.

1.1.1 Key Elements of Commercial Invoice

The commercial invoice includes the following elements:
Name and address of seller;
Name and address of buyer;
Date of issuance;
Invoice number;
Order or contract number;
Quantity and description of the goods;
Unit price, total price, other agreed upon charges and total invoice amount stated in the currency of the documentary credit;
Shipping details including weight of goods, number of packages, and shipping marks and numbers;
Terms of delivery and payment;
Any other information required in a specific documentary credit;
Signature of the exporter (seller).

1.1.2 Cautions and Notes

In transaction involving a documentary credit it is vitally important that the description of the goods in the commercial invoice correspond precisely with the description of goods in the documentary credit.

The invoice amount should match exactly (or at least should not exceed) the amount specified in the credit. Banks have the right to refuse invoices issued for amounts in excess of the amount stated in the credit. For this, as well as other reasons, the invoice should be made out in the same currency as the credit amount.

Unless otherwise stipulated in the documentary credit, the commercial invoice must be made out in the name of the applicant (buyer). However in a transferable documentary credit the invoice may be made out to the intermediary.

The buyer, seller, and bank should all carefully check for discrepancies in the invoice. The details specified therein should not be inconsistent with those of any other documents, and should exactly conform to the specifications of the documentary credit.

The specimen of commercial invoice is shown by Figure 8. 1.

湖北金士达医用产品有限公司
KINGSTAR MEDICAL PRODUCTS CO.,LTD.

INVOICE

TO: MANSFIELD MEDICAL DISTRIBUTORS LTD.

Date: Dec. 25, 2002
P.O.No.: # 021029
Invoice No.: K02255

Terms of Payment: T/T
Delivery from Shanghai, China to Montreal, Canada by sea freight
Price Condition: FOB Shanghai

Art. No.	Quantity		Price (@USD/pc)	Amount USD
TRIANGULAR BANDAGE				
100% pure cotton, 40'sx40's, 50x50, 40"x56"x40"				
	14 ctns	8,500 pcs	0.130	1,105.00
TOTAL:	14 ctns	8,500 pcs		1,105.00

SHIPPING MARKS:

M.M.D.
CODE: BLK-TRIAD
TRIANGLE BANDAGE
40"X56"X40"
QUANTITY: 600PCS
FABRIQUE EN CHINE MADE IN CHINA
GROSS WEIGHT: 22KGS NET WEIGHT: 20KGS

PAYMENT NOTICE:

KINGSTAR MEDICAL PRODUCTS CO.,LTD.

TÜV ISO 9002 EN 46002

办公地址：湖北省武汉市建设大道709号建银大厦2718室
Office Address: Unit 2718, Jianyin Building, 709 Jianshe Avenue, Wuhan, Hubei Province, China
邮政编码：430015 电话：+86-27-85486669 传真：+86-27-85486661
Postal Code: 430015 Tel: +86-27-85486669 Fax: +86-27-85486661
工厂地址：湖北省仙桃市张沟镇文卫路2号
Factory Address: 2 Wenwei Road, Zhanggou Town, Xiantao City, Hubei Province, China
邮政编码：433012 电话：+86-728-2721666, 2722453 传真：+86-728-2724231
Postal Code: 433012 Tel: +86-728-2721666, 2722453 Fax: +86-728-2724231
Email:mliu@public.wh.hb.cn ; kingmed@public.wh.hb.cn

Figure 8. 1 Commercial Invoice

1. 2 Other Invoices

In order to abide by regulations of control on foreign trade and foreign exchange, importers of some countries probably call for other forms of invoices as follows:

1. 2. 1 Origin Invoice

Origin invoice is a combination of commercial invoice and origin, sometimes required for differing tariffs and customs duty based on the country of origin. Normally, some countries' customs offices require such kind of invoice to certify the origin of exported commodities.

1. 2. 2 Consular Invoice

Consular invoices are ones attested, in the country of dispatch, by the consulate of the importing country. Such invoices, mostly required by the Latin American countries, are used by customs official of the entry country to verify the value, quantity, country of origin, and nature of the merchandise. The certification and legalization of such invoices made by the consulate take more time than the normal commercial invoice. Accordingly, seller and buyer have to think over such invoices are really needed.

1. 2. 3 Certificate Invoice

Certificate invoice is sealed by a Chamber of Commerce or Chamber of Manufacturers on the commercial invoice. This kind of special invoice is normally asked for by the customs or laws of the trading nations. Forms and contents of such invoices vary from country to country, and even from product to product.

1. 2. 4 Customs Invoice

Customs invoice is made by the exporter by filling out a given invoice form specified by the customs of importing country, is a necessary evidence for the goods entry with a levy of lower import duty or even free of duty. The same as the consular document, it determines the basis of calculating import duty and serves to prevent dumping of imports at low prices (lower than its domestic price). The custom of importing country use it also for statistical purposes and checking origin of goods.

Generally, both consular invoices and customs invoice may have the similar function in international trade. First of all, they can be used for anti-dumping purpose, since the exported commodities' prices should be higher than the regulated price mentioned in those invoices. Then, when the exporters have got such invoices, the commodities can enjoy the preferential treatment in tariff imposition when declaring for importation.

1.2.5 Proforma Invoice

Proforma invoice is made by the exporter prior to shipment of goods and marked the wording "Proforma" on the invoice. Actually, it is a form of "offer" or "quotation" to the buyer which shows the intention of the exporter to conclude the contract with the buyer. In the meantime, proforma invoice is often used for application of import license or foreign exchange. Once the proforma invoice is accepted by the buyer wholly, it will become a formal contract between the buyer and the seller. In such case, a commercial invoice will be made out for payment.

The customs invoice and proforma invoice are shown by Figure 8.2 and Figure 8.3 respectively.

Customs Invoice
(海关发票样本)

海关发票是出口商应进口国海关要求出具的一种单据，基本内容同普通的商业发票类似，其格式一般由进口国海关统一制定并提供，主要是用于进口国海关统计、核实原产地、查核进口商品价格的构成等。

由于各国各地区的海关发票格式不一，加之是用外文印制的，所以在这里不能一一附录如下。

××国海关发票

发票号：　　　　　　　　　　发票日期：

1. 卖方 _____

2. 随附单据 _____

3. 装运时间，转运和运输情况 _____

4. 收货人 _____

2. 买方 _____

3. 原产地 _____

7. 贸易和付款条件 _____

8. 使用货币 _____

9. 货物描述及规格 _____

10. 数量 _____

11. 单价 _____

12. 发票总额 _____

13. 费用项目：

    （1）包装费 _____　　　（2）海运或国际运费 _____

    （3）保险费 _____　　　（4）国内运输费用 _____

    （5）其他费用 _____

14. 签字：

Figure 8.2　Customs Invoice

Hubei Zhongyuan International Trade Corporation

54 Wuchang Road, Wuhan, Hubei, P. R. China

To: Philippines Trading Co.

22, Commercial Building

Manila, Philippines

Invoice No. ZYE-008

Date: June 18, 2016

Proforma Invoice

Descriptions of Goods	Unit Price	Amount
"Forever" 26 Inch Men's Bicycle 5.000 PCS Made in Shanghai	USD 115/PC CIF Manila	USD 575,000.00
This offer is subject to our final confirmation if your import license and foreign exchange are available.		

Figure 8. 3   Proforma Invoice

2. Packing List

A packing list contains some or all of the following information: name of shipping company, address of origin, ports of exit and entry, destination information, weight and measurements of the contents, number of items in the package, product's item number, product description and cost, invoice number, import number if being shipped from outside the country, marks from customs or the shipper's signature, and shipping date.

On the other hand, a packing list is a document prepared by the shipper listing the kinds and quantities of merchandise in a particular shipment.

It is clear that a packing list is also a type of certificate of fulfillment, presenting that the shipper have packed the goods in accordance with the terms of contract or suitable for the transport mode, so that the goods can arrive the destination with perfect condition. On the other hand, packing list is necessary for carrier to arrange loading, unloading and transshipment during transportation.

When it comes to the function of packing list, the packing list serves as a backup to the package's invoice and as a checklist for customs officers if the package is imported. The packing list is also important in helping the hauler determine how much space a package will take on a ship or truck.

A packing list is shown by Figure 8. 4.

A Sample of Packing List

ISSUER SHANGHAI HERO IMP&EXP CORP. ROOM 4413, 47, JIANG NING RD. SHANGHAI CHINA	PACKING LIST				
TO AL ABRA HOME APPLIANCES TRADING EST P. O. BOX 21352 DUBAI, UAE	INVOICE NO. 96RE232		DATE 5—JAN—1997		

Marks and Numbers	Number and Description of Goods	Quantity	Package	G. W.	N. W.	Meas.
AL ABRA/DUBAI/ TEL: 266632	POR TABLE TYPERWRITER ART. NO. TP200 ART. NO. TP900	1160SETS 1200SETS	CTNS CTNS	21KG 22KG	23KG 24KG	60 * 40 * 40CM 60 * 40 * 40CM
TOTAL: 2360SETS				43KG	47KG	
SAY TOTAL	SAY EIGHTY THOUSANDS AND THREE HUNDREDS EIGHTEEN AND FOUR POING ONLY					

THE NAME AND ADDRESS OF THE MANUFACTURER: SHANGHAI HERO CO. Ltd.

SIGNATURE: SHANGHAI HERO IMP&EXP CORP.

ROOM 4413, 47, JIANG NING RD.

SHANGHAI, CHINA

SIGNITURE: ANDYLVKING

Figure 8.4   Packing List

2.1   Key Elements of Packing List

Generally, the packing list should include the following elements:

(1) Name and address of seller.

(2) Name and address of buyer.

(3) Date of issuance.

(4) Invoice number.

(5) Order or contract number.

(6) Quantity and description of the goods.

(7) Shipping details including: weight of goods, number of package, and shipping markets and numbers.

(8) Quantity and description of contents of each package, carton, crate or container.

(9) Any other information as required in the documentary credit (e. g. country of origin).

(10) Signature of the seller.

Usually, the ten key elements above-mentioned are essential parts for all packing list used in international trade.

2. 2 Cautions and Notes

The packing list is a more detailed version of the commercial invoice but without price information. The type of each container is identified, as well as its individual weight and measurements. The packing list is attached to the outside of its respective container in a waterproof envelope marked "packing list enclosed", and is immediately available to authorities in both the countries of export and import.

Although packing list may not be required in some specific transactions, it is required by most countries and buyers.

Bear in mind, the contents of packing list should be consistent with those stated in other documents, especially with the related invoice as well as with the actual packing conditions.

2. 3 Non-official Certificate of Inspection

Non-official certificate of inspection refers to the inspection certificate made by non-official institutions such as one of two parties or a third party, most likely, issued by exporter himself or trade association or other non-official certifying organizations. And it is also very often used in international trade to manifest the exporter's fulfilling of contract. It is not difficult for the exporter to obtain such inspections. In export trade, inspection certificate issued by importer is also not seldom used as payment document. For example, on early 1990's of the 20th century, by exporting scallop from coastal area of Shandong Province to Japan, the certificate issued by the Japanese importer must be presented for payment. of course, from the point of view of importers, it is reasonable to ensure the quality of the goods by such certificate. However, the exporters have to consider whether or not they can meet such requirement, otherwise, there would be potential problems for them to receive the payment smoothly.

3. Transport Documents

Transport documents are ones, issued by the carriers, certifying that the goods have been loaded on board or dispatched or taken in charge. Transport document is one of the key documents in international trade payment. According to the transport model, there are four categories of transport documents, i. e. Marine Bill of Lading issued by the ship company or its agent. Air Waybill issued by the airline company or its agent. Multimodal Transport Document issued by the multimodal operator as well as Road Waybill issued by a motor firm and Rail Waybill issued by railroad organization or Railway Cargo Receipt issued by forwarders.

3. 1   Marine Bill of Lading (B/L)

A marine bill of lading, named sometimes ocean bill of lading or port-to-port bill of lading, is a document issued by a carrier or its authorized agents, to a shipper.

Its importance lies in three characteristics. First, it is a contract of carriage. Second, it is a receipt for goods and, third, it is a transferable document of title. Just this third characteristic makes the exporters be willing to ship goods before obtaining payment, because they can continually control goods through holding the bill of lading until payment is received or a promise to pay is obtained.

Only against original bills of lading, as a document of title to the goods, the merchandise after arrival can be released and can be transferred from one person to another. Bills of lading normally are issued in three or more originals to prevent from loss through mail or courier services. One of the full set of original bills of lading is used for picking up the goods, the other will be automatically null and void.

There are number of types of bills of lading in light of different points of view, as far as international trade payment is concerned, differences of some types of bills of lading will be illustrated as follows:

3. 1. 1   Shipped on Board B/L Versus Received for Shipment B/L

A shipped on board B/L is one evidencing that the goods have been actually shipped on a named vessel, while the received for shipment B/L just mean that the goods have been handed over to the ship owner and are in his custody, not yet been shipped on a vessel. Most of bills of lading are shipped on board B/L by pre-printed wording "shipped on board in apparent good order and condition", which confirms the goods actually on board the vessel. Date of issuance of a bill of lading will be deemed to the date of loading on board and the date of shipment. A received for shipment B/L indicated by wording "received in apparent good order and condition" is just a receipt, not a document of title to the goods, so it is normally not accepted or bought by the banks under L/C. however, it can be converted into an on board bill of lading by adding a proper annotation thereon by the shipping company, such as stamping the words "on board" plus the name of vessel, the date of annotation as well. After that, banks involved under L/C should accept the bill of lading.

3.1.2 Clean B/L Versus Unclean B/L

A clean B/L is one where the carrier has noted — mostly pre-printed on a bill of lading — that the merchandise has been shipped or received in apparent good condition (no apparent damage, loss etc.) and does not bear such notations as "shipper's load and counts". On the contrary, an unclean B/L refers to that carrier adds clauses specifically stating unusual conditions of the goods and related packages, such as inadequate packaging, wet, or stained cartons, carton missing etc. Most of L/C require a clean B/L in order for the seller to obtain payment under a documentary credit. There are, however, particular circumstances in some trades, in which transport documents with special clauses are acceptable. For example, on steel trade, such notation are the rule rather than the exception.

3.1.3 Straight B/L Versus Transshipment B/L

A straight B/L is issued when goods are shipped by one vessel direct from the loading port to the destination port without transshipment on the route, while transshipment B/L is one when carrier is preparing to transship the cargo from one vessel to another at a named transshipment port at his expense. On the form of L/C, it must be given that the transshipment is allowed or not, if you present a transshipment B/L to bank for payment instead of straight B/L are stated in the L/C, the bank has right to refuse to effect the payment because a transshipment B/L bears more risks than a straight one.

3.1.4 Named Consignee B/L Versus Order B/L

A named consignee B/L, called also non-negotiable B/L, indicates consigned to a named consignee. The name of a specific person or business appears on the consignee column of a bill of lading, so that no one except the named consignee can take delivery of the goods, that is to say, this kind of B/L can not be transferred from one to another. Conversely, an order B/L, called also negotiable B/L, directs the carrier to deliver goods to anyone whom the last endorser orders (the first endorser is normally the shipper). This negotiable bill of lading enables the order to transfer the title to the goods to any one else by endorsement. The wording on the consignee column of such bills of lading could be "order of (name)", which might be the order of shipper himself, or the order of issuing bank or the order of negotiating bank as well.

Due to its negotiability, the order B/L is broadly used under L/C, where the shipper, i. e. the exporter, can transfer the title of the goods by endorsement to, say, the issuing bank for payment, and the latter in turn can endorse the B/L to the importer after his payment. The arrangement of the institution facilitates not only controlling the title to the goods against payment, but also simplifying the transfer procedure just through a signature and more importantly, decreasing the transaction cost, that is the reason why the order B/L is mostly used in the international trade.

Under L/C, normally, banks pay money to the exporter prior to importer's payment. as a collateral, bill of lading is a vital voucher of obtaining compensation in case that imbursement does not succeed and the exporter is unable to make payment to the bank. Banks attempt to know through the notations on the B/L whether the goods do have been shipped on board the named ship in perfect conditions, and will arrive agreed destination straightly. If the goods are damaged or even lost, according to regulations of international cargo transportation, such as "The Hague Rules" and "Hamburg Rules", the losses should be indemnified perhaps by the carrier or related issuance company. In addition, bills of lading are transferable, so that banks can transfer them legally to the new purchaser when bank sells off the goods because of failing to obtain proceeds from the importer. In order to assume no risk in any circumstances, banks are willing to accept shipped on board, clean, straight and order bills of lading.

Normally, marine bills of lading contain the key elements as follows:

(1) Name of carrier with a signature identified as that of carrier, or ship's master, or agent on behalf of either the carrier or ship's master.

(2) Indication that the goods have been loaded on board or shipped on a named vessel

(3) Date of issuance or date of loading.

(4) Indication of the port of loading and the port of discharge.

(5) Number of originals issued.

(6) Consignee, either a specific person, or the order of a specific person.

(7) Description of the goods including name, shipment marks, weight, measurements etc.

(8) Name of shipper.

(9) Name of vessel and voyage.

(10) Number of originals.

Also, both indication of freight paid or collected and indication of transshipment and partial shipment allowed or prohibited should be clearly demonstrated on the surface of ocean bill of lading.

If a bill of lading indicates a place where the goods were received by the carrier different from the port of loading, the B/L must also contain an "on board" notation indicating the port of loading as specified in the L/C and named vessel, along with the date.

If the bills of lading are made out "to the order of the exporter" or "to order", they must be endorsed by the exporter.

The ocean B/L is shown by Figure 8. 5

A Sample of Bill of Lading

1. SHIPPER		B/L NO.
2. CONSIGNEE		COSCO
3. NOTIFY PARTY		**CHINA OCEAN SHIPPING（GROUP）CO.**
4. PR-CARRIAGE BY	5. PLACE OF RECEIPT	ORIGINAL
6. OCEAN VESSEL VOY. NO.	7.PORT OF LOADING	Combined Transport Bill of Lading
8.PORT OF DISCHARGE	9.PLACE OF DELIVERY	10.FINAL DESTINATION FOR THE MERCHANT'S REFERENCE

11. MARKS	12. NOS. & KINDS OF PKGS	13.DESCRIPTION OF GOODS	14.G. W.（KG）	15.MEAS（M³）
16. TOTAL NUMBER OF CONTAINERS OR PACKAGES(IN WORDS)				

17.FREIGHT & CHARGES	REVENUE TONS	RATE	PER	PREPAID	COLLECT
PREPAID AT	PAYABLE AT	18.PLACE AND DATE OF ISSUE			
TOTAL PREPAID	19.NUMBER OF ORIGINAL B(S)L	22.SIGNED FOR THE CARRIER CHINA OCEAN SHIPPING（GROUP）CO. ×××			
20.DATE	21.LOADING ON BOARD THE VESSEL BY				

Figure 8. 5　Ocean B/L

3. 2　Multi-modal（Combined）Transport Document

In practice of international trade, the marine B/L is often combined with the multi-modal transport bill of lading or combined transport bill of lading, which, as defined in UCP500, covers at least two different modes of transport of goods from the point of departure to the point of final destination by sea, inland waterway, air, rail or road.

A multi-modal transport document contains the following elements:

（1）Name of carrier or multi-modal transport operator or agent with a signature.

（2）An indication that shipment has been "dispatched", "taken in charge", or "loaded on board" along with the date of issuance.

（3）Indication of the place of delivery of the goods.

（4）Number of originals of bills of lading.

In multi-modal situation, the contract of carriage and liability is from the place of dispatch to place of delivery, thus, the document evidences receipt of goods and not shipment on board.

Even if a L/C prohibits transshipment, banks will accept a multi-modal transport document which indicates that transshipment will or may take place, provided that the entire carriage is covered by one transport document.

A multi-modal transport document issued by a freight forwarder is acceptable unless the L/C stipulated otherwise or unless L/C specifically calls for a "marine bill of lading". The issuing freight forwarder undertakes responsibility for performance of the entire contract of carriage and liability for loss or damage wherever and however it occurs.

As described previously, a bill of lading is semi-negotiable instrument against which the goods will be delivered to the holder of originals. That is good for controlling the title to the goods, meanwhile, it is also inconvenient for some cases, for example, mobility of semi-finished products or parts between subsidiaries located in different countries of transactional companies does not need to deliver the goods against payment; perishable goods may become putrid in waiting for the B/L being transferred from the bank to the importer. That is the important reason why so-called non-negotiable Sea Waybill is getting on more and more popular in foreign trade.

Multi-modal transport document is shown by Figure 8. 6.

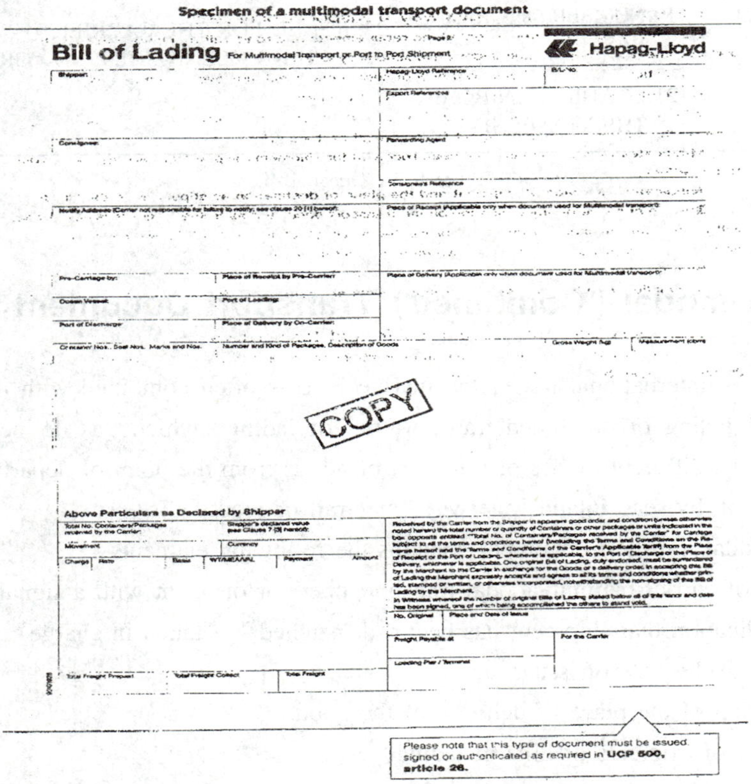
Specimen of a multimodal transport document

Bill of Lading For Multimodal Transport or Port to Port Shipment

Hapag-Lloyd

Shipper: | Hapag-Lloyd Reference | B/L-No.

Export References

Consignee: | Forwarding Agent

Consignee's Reference

Notify Address (Carrier not responsible for failure to notify; see clause 20 (1) hereof) | Place of Receipt (Applicable only when document used for Multimodal transport)

Pre-Carriage by: | Place of Receipt by Pre-Carrier | Place of Delivery (Applicable only when document used for Multimodal transport)

Ocean Vessel | Port of Loading

Port of Discharge | Place of Delivery by On-Carrier

Container Nos., Seal Nos. Marks and Nos. | Number and Kind of Packages, Description of Goods | Gross Weight (kg) | Measurement (cbm)

COPY

Above Particulars as Declared by Shipper

Total No. Containers/Packages received by the Carrier | Shipper's declared value (see Clause 7 (3) hereof)

Movement | Currency

Charge | Rate | Basis | WT/MEA/VAL | Payment | Amount

Total Freight Prepaid | Total Freight Collect | Total Freight

Received by the Carrier from the Shipper in apparent good order and condition (unless otherwise noted herein) the total number or quantity of Containers or other packages or units indicated in the box opposite entitled "Total No. of Containers/Packages received by the Carrier" for Carriage subject to all the terms and conditions hereof (including the Terms and Conditions on the Reverse hereof and the Terms and Conditions of the Carrier's Applicable Tariff) from the Place of Receipt or the Port of Loading, whichever is applicable, to the Port of Discharge or the Place of Delivery, whichever is applicable. One original Bill of Lading, duly endorsed, must be surrendered by the Merchant to the Carrier in exchange for the Goods or a delivery order. In accepting this Bill of Lading the Merchant expressly accepts and agrees to all its terms and conditions whether printed, stamped or written, or otherwise incorporated, notwithstanding the non-signing of this Bill of Lading by the Merchant.

In Witness whereof the number of original Bills of Lading stated below all of this tenor and date has been signed, one of which being accomplished the others to stand void.

No. Original | Place and Date of Issue

Freight Payable at | For the Carrier

Loading Pier / Terminal

Please note that this type of document must be issued signed or authenticated as required in **UCP 500, article 26.**

Figure 8. 6 Multi-modal Transport Document

3. 3　Sea Waybill

A sea waybill is a transport document covering port-to-port shipment. It is not a title document, not negotiable and can not be endorsed, the carrier is allowed to deliver the goods merely to the consignee identified in the bill, no matter whether the consignee holds the originals or not, unlike the situation in the bill of lading.

In principle, the key elements on a non-negotiable sea waybill are the same as stated on the section of marine bill of lading except the consignee must be a specific person, and on the surface, a sea waybill looks very like a marine bill of lading except for with words "not negotiable" and without the words "bill of lading".

If a L/C calls for a port-to-port shipment but does not call specifically for a marine bill of lading, the bank will accept a transport document, however named, that contains the above information. That is to say, a sea waybill can also satisfy the requirement of port-to-port.

Because sea waybills are not title documents, they eliminate many of the inconvenience of a bill of lading, and furthermore, they reduce the opportunity for fraud and remove troubles of goods arriving ahead of documents. Shipments stated in a sea waybill can be delivered by the carrier directly to the specified consignee without having to present originals. Indeed, it is convenient for the consignee to pick goods up, but no way for the exporters and banks to force importer to pay against original transport documents. Therefore, sea waybills are appropriate for shipments between associated companies, for shipments to an agent for sale at destination on an open account basis, and for organizations that have established mutual trust.

3. 4　Air Waybill (Air Consignment Note)

In case of an air shipment, an air waybill will be required. Generally, air waybills are issued by the carrier or airline when the goods need to be sent by air freight. There is no such thing as a bill of lading with air transport document. Therefore, the definition of air waybill refers to a document issued by carrier or airline acknowledging receipt of the goods.

Similar to a sea waybill, an air waybill does not convey title to the goods, instead of that, the shipment is consigned to a particular party. The consignee may obtain access to the goods without presentation of an air waybill.

Normally, the consignee takes delivery at the port of destination as per the shipment advice which is issued by destination airport evidencing arrival of goods.

As the shipper can not control over the goods when he hands over them to the airline, even though a bill of exchange is attached to the shipping documents under collections, the exporter still probably suffers from losses of both goods and proceeds. To overcome this, the goods can be consigned by the shipper to a trusted third party (if he agrees) who will release the goods after receiving payment or a promise of payment made by importer. An air waybill usually contains the following items:

(1) Place and date of issue.

(2) Name of departure and destination airports.

(3) Name and address of consignor, consignee and carrier (the airline or shipping company).

(4) Description if goods.

(5) Number of packages with marks, weights, quantity and dimensions.

(6) Freight charges prepaid or to collect.

(7) Date of flight. If the document does not contain a flight date, the date of issue will be deemed to be date of shipment.

(8) Signature of shipper or his agent.

(9) Signature of issuing carrier or his agent.

A sample air waybill is shown by Figure 8. 7.

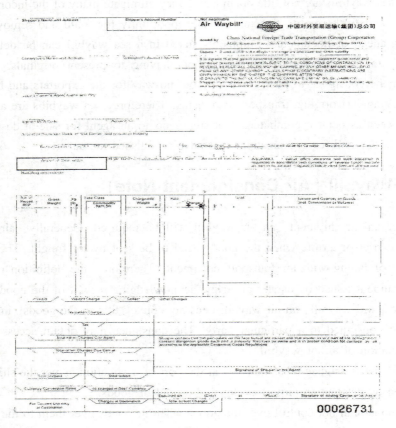

Figure 8. 7   Air Waybill

3.5   Road Waybill, Rail Waybill and Railway Cargo Receipt

Road waybill and rail waybill are transport documents covering transport of cargo from named points via road or rail modals of transport. The contents of a road waybill or a rail waybill are similar as follows:

（1）Name of carrier with a signature or authentication identified as that of carrier or its authorized agent.

（2）Name and address of sender and consignee.

（3）An indication of the place of shipment and place of destination.

Ordinary description of goods including item name, weight, packing, quantity（if any）like air waybill and sea waybill, road waybill and rail waybill are not title documents either.

It should be emphasized that railway cargo receipt is a transport document issued by branches of Sino-trans, specifying the shipment from mainland of China to Hong Kong and Macau areas via railway transportation. Unlike sea waybill, road waybill and rail waybill, the consignee must present cargo receipt for taking delivery.

A sample of railway cargo receipt is shown by Figure 8.8.

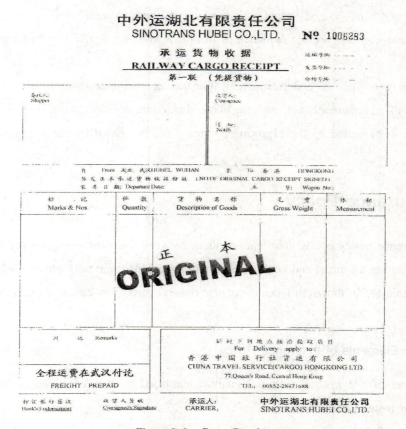

Figure 8.8   Cargo Receipt

4. Insurance Documents

Owing to long distance transportation, goods under international trade could be damaged by various accidents. Additionally, by loading and warehousing there are also some risks. In order to be indemnified in event of damage, seller or buyer, depending on the trade terms, effects insurance prior to the shipment.

Insurance documents are ones, issued by insurance companies, indicating the type and amount of insurance coverage in force on a particular shipment. Used to assure the consignee that insurance is provided to cover loss of or damage to cargo while in transit.

As a title document, insurance document can be transferred. The same as the bill of lading transfer can be made by endorsing and delivering the full set of originals. Under term of CIF, the seller effects the insurance, the risk, however, will be undertaken by the buyer as soon as the goods crossed side of ship. Accordingly, the seller should transfer insurance document together with the bills of lading, i. e. the right of indemnity will be also transferred.

Insurance documents are the evidence of insurance contract signed between the insurer and the insured.

There are two types of endorsement by transferring insurance documents, i. e. blank and named. Most of endorsements are made in blank. Insurance documents made of in the name of exporter have to be sealed by the exporting company and be signed by the authorized person by endorsing.

4. 1   Insurance Policy

An insurance policy is a written legal contract between the insurance company and the party insured, containing all terms and conditions of the agreement (normally pre-printed on the back side of the policy). It shows full details of the risks covered, so called also formal insurance document.

4. 1. 1   Key Elements of Insurance Policy

(1) Name of the insurer with a signature identified as that of insurance company, or underwriter or insurance agent.

(2) Name of the insured, both the seller and the buyer might be the insured provided that.

(3) They have insured interest and with good faith.

(4) The insured goods.

(5) Type of risks covered, which should be one of three basic risks, i. e. Free From Particular Average (F. P. A.), With Particular Average (W. P. A.) and All Risks, added by some supplementary special risks such as War Risk and Strike Risk.

(6) Name of the insurer with a signature identified as that of insurance company, or

(7) Insurance provisions

(8) Amount and currency insured

(9) Place of claim payable

(10) Transport model and vessel's name

Finally, loading port and destination port, if transshipment is required, the goods should cover transshipment risks, such as warehouse to warehouse including transshipment risk. Similarly, time and place of issue should also be illustrated on the surface of insurance policy.

4. 1. 2　Claim Against Damage or Loss

The consignee should always note on the delivery document any damage or loss prior to signing for receipt of the goods. The consignee has the responsibility to make reasonable efforts to minimize loss. This includes steps to prevent further damage to the shipment. Expenses incurred in such efforts are almost universally collectible under the insurance policy. Prompt notice of loss is essential.

Copies of documents necessary to support an insurance claim include the insurance policy, bill of lading, invoice, packing list, and a survey report (usually prepared by a claims agent).

4. 2　Insurance Certificate

An insurance certificate is a document issued to the insured certifying that insurance has been effected. It contains the same details as an insurance policy except that the version of provisions is abbreviated. If a documentary credit calls for insurance policy, bank will refuse an insurance certificate for payment because the latter relies on other documents, lack of complete independence.

4. 3　Cover Note

Cover note is a document normally issued to give notice that an insurance has been placed pending the making policy or certificate. Such document is normally applied by the buyer before shipment from the seller's country under the term of FOB by which goods would be on the way after the buyer receives the shipment notice, therefore it does not contain full details of the insurance, such as quantities of the goods to be insured, amount to be insured, vessel's name, and so on. The insurer shall also make claims payable if the goods were damaged or lost after issuing the cover note and prior to issuing formal policy. Normally, documentary credit will not require a cover note as the insurance documents.

4. 4　Open Cover

An open cover is an insurance document by which the underwriter undertakes to issue a specific policy subsequently in conformity to the terms of cover, called also a general insurance for the recurring shipment. The details of the insurance for each shipment may be unknown usually when the insurance is effected. The operation of an open cover for the insured is likewise bound to declare each shipment effected thereunder unless the insurance contract otherwise provided. Upon receipt of declaration, the underwriter issues the policy. Regarding to payment to the seller under an open cover under a credit, UCP500 states "banks will accept a declaration under an open cover pre-signed by insurance companies or underwriters or their agents."

Among insurance documents stated above, insurance policy is the most formal one, which can substitute others if necessary. Exactly speaking, if a L/C specifically calls for an insurance or declaration under an open cover, banks will accept, in lieu thereof, an insurance policy.

Under a letter of credit, the minimum amount of an insurance document should be 110 percent of either the CIF or CIP value of shipment, the amount of the payment specified in the L/C, or the gross amount of the commercial document. Banks will not accept an insurance document which bears a date of insurance later than the date of loading on board or dispatch or taking in charge as indicated in the related transport document.

It is noted that documentary credit transactions indicating CIF or CIP pricing should list an insurance document in their required documentation.

Usually, "cover note" issued by insurance brokers are not accepted in L/C transactions unless authorized specifically by the L/C.

The sample insurance policy is shown by Figure 8. 9.

PICC	The People's Insurance Company of China
	Head Office Beijing Established in 1949

MARINE CARGO TRANSPORTATION INSURANCE POLICY			
INVOICE NO.		POLICY NO.	
CONTRACT NO.			
L/C NO.			
THE INSURED:			

THIS POLICY OF INSURANCE WITNESSES THAT THE PEOPLE'S INSURANCE COMPANY OF CHINA (HEREINAFTER CALLED "THE COMPANY") AT THE REQUEST OF THE INSURED AND IN CONSIDERATION OF THE AGREED PREMIUM PAID TO THE COMPANY BY THE INSURED, UNDERTAKES TO INSURE THE UNDERMENTIONED GOODS IN TRANSPORTATION SUBJECT TO THE CONDITIONS OF THIS OF THIS POLICY AS PER THE CLAUSES PRINTED OVERLEAF AND OTHER SPECIAL CLAUSES ATTACHED HEREON..

MARKS&NOS	QUANTITY	DESCRIPTION OF GOODS	AMOUNT INSURED
TOTAL AMOUNT INSURED:			
PERMIUM:	DATE OF COMMENCEMENT:		PER CONVEYANCE:
FROM:	VIA	TO	
CONDITIONS:			

IN THE EVENT OF LOSS OR DAMAGE WITCH MAY RESULT IN A CLAIM UNDER THIS POLICY, IMMEDIATE NOTICE MUST BE GIVEN TO THE COMPANY'S AGENT AS MENTIONED HEREUNDER. CLAIMS, IF ANY, ONE OF THE ORIGINAL POLICY WHICH HAS BEEN ISSUED IN _____ ORIGINAL(S) TOGETHER WITH THE RELEVANT DOCUMENTS SHALL BE SURRENDERED TO THE COMPANY. IF ONE OF THE ORIGINAL POLICY HAS BEEN ACCOMPLISHED. THE OTHERS TO BE VOID.

CLAIM PAYABLE AT	

Figure 8.9   Insurance Policy

5. Official Documents

A variety of official documents may be required to meet both the exporting and importing countries' customs or foreign exchange regulations. Documents relating to origin, quality, fumigation, health, weight, inspection and export licenses are some examples of official documents. The documentation required to ensure prompt clearance through customs will vary with countries, buyers and goods traded. Traders should, therefore, familiarize themselves with the respective import/export regulations in their countries.

5. 1 Certificate of Origin

A certificate of origin is a document issued by an authority, evidencing the goods originated from a particular country. It could be issued by the Inspection Burear or by the Council of International Trade or by exporter himself. In China a GSP (Generalized System of Preference) certificate of origin is a certificate used to obtain the treatment of preference customs duty imposed by the developed country on the developing countries China began to use it in 1978.

5. 1. 1 Key Elements of Certificate of Origin

In documentary credit transactions a certificate of origin should include the following elements:

(1)Key details (typically consignor, consignee, and description of goods) regarding the shipment. Also, such details to be in conformity with other documents (e. g. documentary credit, commercial invoice).

(2)A statement of origin of the goods.

(3)The name, signature and/or stamp or seal of the certifying authority.

The certificate of origin is typically required by the buyer's country as a requirement for import processing. If you are the buyer, your country requires such documentation (in form and content) in the documentary credit as stipulated by related state authority.

5. 1. 2 Cautions and Notes

The certificate of origin can be the key document required for obtaining special (reduced) tariff rates for imports from countries listed as beneficiary to programs such as the GSP. In such a case specific forms (such as the Certificate of Origin Form A — for GSP Certification) must be used.

Buyers should avoid use of such terms as "first class", "well-known", "qualified", "independent", "official", "competent", or "local" when referring to the certifying authority. It is preferable to specifically name the required certifying authority.

Use of vague terminology (as mentioned above) will result in the bank's acceptance of any relevant document that appears "on its face" to be in compliance with the documentary credit, so long as it was not issued (signed) by the beneficiary (seller).

In certain countries the certificate of origin is prepared by the seller (beneficiary to the documentary credit) on a standard form and then certified (with a signature, stamp or seal) by the certifying authority.

Certifying authorities most often used are city and regional chambers of commerce and chambers of commerce and industry. In China, GSP Certificate of Origin Form A is issued by Commodity Inspection Bureau of Import/Export. However, the ordinary Certificate of Origin is issued by the Council for Promotion of Foreign Trade.

The sample GSP Certificate of Origin Form A and Certificate of Origin are shown by Figure 8. 10 and Figure 8. 11 respectively.

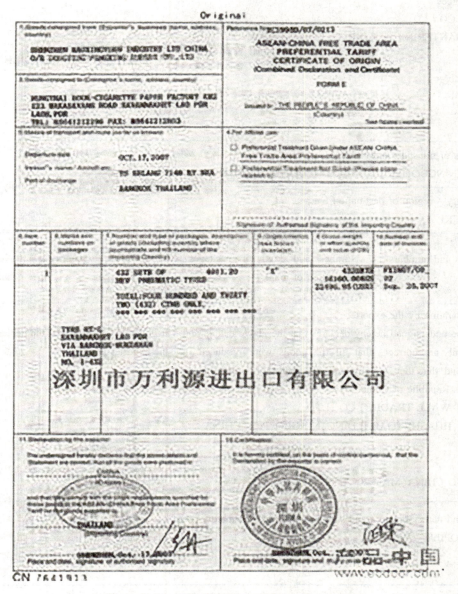

Figure 8. 10　GSP Certificate of Origin Form A

A Sample of Certificate of Origin

1.Exporter GREAT WALL TRADING CO.,LTD. RM201,HUASHENG BUILDING, NINGBO,P. R. CHINA	Certificate No. **CERTIFICATE OF ORIGIN** **OF** **THE PEOPLE'S REPUBLIC OF** **CHINA**
2.Consignee F. T. C. CO. AKEKSANTERINK AUTO P. O. BOX 9,FINLAND	
3.Means of transport and route FROM NINGBO,P.R CHINA TO HELSINKI BY SEA 4.Country / region of destination HELSINKI	5.For certifying authority use only

6.Marks and numbers	7. Number and kind of packages; description of goods	8.H.S.Code	9.Quantity	10.Number and date

11.Declaration by the exporter　The undersigned hereby declares that the above details and statements are correct, that all the goods were produced in China and that they comply with the Rules of Origin of the People's Republic of China. GREAT WALL TRADING CO.,LTD. RM201,HUASHENG BUILDING,NINGBO,P. R. CHINA NINGBO CHINA,MAY 20,2005 --- Place and date, signature and stamp of authorized signatory IN 2 COPIES	12.Certification It is hereby certified that the declaration by the exporter is correct. ANDYLVKING -- ------------------ Place and date, signature and stamp of certifying authority

Figure 8. 11　Certificate of Origin

5. 2   Inspection Certificate

Inspection certificate is a document issued by an authority, indicating that the goods have been inspected prior to shipment and the results of the inspection. The purpose of Inspection Certificate is to ensure that the quality and quantity of merchandise have come up to the standard or specifications mentioned in contract.

Inspection certificate can be, generally, obtained from neutral testing organizations, e.g. government entity or independent service company.

The most commonly used inspection certificate in international trade are as follows:

(1) Inspection Certificate of Quality;

(2) Inspection Certificate of Weight;

(3) Inspection Certificate of Quantity;

(4) Inspection Certificate of Analysis;

(5) Inspection Certificate of Veterinary;

(6) Inspection Certificate of Plant Quarantine.

It is those inspection certificates issued by the authorities to show that the seller has met the requirements specified in the trade contract, as well to help buyer or his issuing bank decide to effect payment or not. Accordingly, under a letter of credit, it is vital to specify types and issuing authorities of certain inspection certificates, so as to reduce the risks relating to each party and cut down the transaction cost as well.

The sample inspection certificate is shown by Figure 8. 12.

5. 2. 1   Key Elements of Inspection Certificate

In documentary credit transactions an inspection certificate should include the following elements.

Key details (typically consignor, consignee and description of goods) regarding the shipment. Also, such details to be in conformity with other documents (e. g. documentary credit, commercial invoice):

(1) Date and place of the inspection.

(2) Statement of sampling methodology.

(3) Statement of the results of the inspection.

(4) The name, signature and/or stamp or seal of the inspecting entity.

5. 2. 2   Cautions and Notes

In the case of certain countries and certain commodities the inspection certificate must be issued by an appropriate government entity.

Buyers should avoid the use of such terms as "first class", "well-known", "qualified", "independent", "official", "competent" or "local" when referring to an acceptable inspection authority. It is preferable to agree beforehand as to a specific inspection organization or entity and for the buyer to name the required certifying organization or entity in the documentary credit.

Use of vague terminology will lead to the banks acceptance of any relevant document that appears "on its face" to be in compliance with the documentary credit, so long as it was not issued by the beneficiary.

The sample of inspection certificate is shown by Figure 8. 12.

ENTRY-EXIT INSPECTION AND QUARANTINE OF THE PEOPLE'S REPUBLIC OF CHINA			
INSPECTION CERTIFICATE OF QUALITY			
Consignor			
Consignee			
Description of Goods			
Quantity / Weight Declared			
Number and Type of Packages			
Place of Origin			
Port of Destination			
Means of Conveyance s.s.		Date of Inspection	
Results of Inspection			
WE HEREBY STATE THE RESULTS OF INSPECTION ARE IN CONFORMITY WITH THE CHINESE STANDARD.			
Place of Issue		Date of Issue	
Authorized Officer		Signature	

Figure 8. 12   Inspection Certificate

5.3　Export License

An export license is a document made by a government authority, granting the right to export a specific quantity of a commodity to a specific country. The export license of each country will have its own form and contents.

This document is often required for the exportation of certain natural resources, national treasures, drugs, strategic commodities, and arms and armaments.

5.3.1　Key Elements of Export License

The export license of each country may have its own forms and countries. However, certain elements are likely to be included in all export licenses as follows:

(1) Name and address of seller.

(2) Name and address of buyer.

(3) Date of issuance.

(4) Validity date.

(5) Description of goods covered by license.

(6) Name of country of origin.

(7) Name of country of ultimate destination.

5.3.2　Cautions and Notes

Some countries require export licenses for virtually all commodities and products. The license is a means of control and taxation. In some cases the lack of an export license can be cited as a reason why the goods can not be shipped, even though payment has been made. Buyers should be especially careful about buying sensitive goods from countries with a demonstrated lack of rule by law.

The export license is typically the responsibility of the seller. However, if the buyer is dealing in sensitive goods, he should research the need for an export license beforehand. Failure to secure such a license can delay or prevent shipment and jeopardize the validity of a documentary credit.

The sample of textile export license and sample of technology export license are shown as Figure 8.13 and Figure 8.14.

纺织品出口许可证 / 商业发票

TEXTILE EXPORT LICENCE/COMMERCIAL INVOICE

正 本
ORIGINAL

1 出口人（代码、名称和地址）
Exporter (EID, name & address)

2 许可证号码
LICENCE No. 2 CN 000000

3 协议年度
Agreement year

4 类别号
Category No.

5 发票号码
Invoice No.

6 收货人（名称和地址）
Consignee (name & address)

7 装运地、装运期及目的地
Place & time of shipment, destination

8 中国港口离岸价值
Value of FOB Chinese port

9 唛头—包装件数—商品名称
Marks & numbers - number of packages - DESCRIPTION OF GOODS

10 数量
Quantity

11 单价
Unit price

12 总值
Amount

样 品

13 生产厂家代码
M. I. D.

14 出口人签章
Exporter's stamp and signature

日期
Date

15 发证当局签章
Issuing authorities' stamp and signature

Figure 8.13 Textile Export License

中华人民共和国敏感物项和技术出口许可证

EXPORT LICENCE FOR SENSITIVE ITEMS AND TECHNOLOGIES OF PRC

No. 4000000

1. 出口商: Exporter		2. 出口许可证号: Export licence No.
3. 出口经营登记证号: Registration number		4. 许可证有效日期至: Export licence expiry date
5. 贸易方式: Terms of trade		6. 付款方式: Payment
7. 进口国（地区）: Country/Region of purchase		8. 最终目的国地区): Destination
9. 合同号: Contract No.		10. 合同签订日期: Date of contract signed
11. 收货人: Consignee		12. 最终用户: End-user
13. 报关口岸: Place of clearance		14. 运输方式: Mode of transport
15. 商品名称: Description of goods		商品编码: Code of goods

16. 规格，等级 Specification	17. 单位 Unit	18. 数量 Quantity	19. 单价（ ） Unit price	20. 总值（ ） Amount	21. 总值折美元 Amount in USD
总　计 Total					

22. 备　注 Supplementary details	23. 发证机关签章 Issuing authority's stamp & signature
	24. 发证日期 Licence date

第一联《正本》出口商办理海关手续

中华人民共和国商务部制（2001）

Figure 8.14　Technology Export License

6. Document Checklists

The following is a series of checklists for document preparation and examination by the buyer, seller, advising bank, negotiating bank and issuing bank. They are not fully comprehensive as there are an almost infinite number of transaction variations possible, some of which require specialized procedures and documentation. Therefore, they should be viewed only as a general guide.

6. 1　Seller/Exporter/Beneficiary

The seller/exporter/beneficiary has the responsibility of preparing and presenting documents in accordance with the terms and conditions of the documentary credit or collection. If the documents are incorrect or inconsistent, there is a risk of having them refused or dishonored, wasting time and money, and possibly imperiling the transaction itself.

6. 2　Issuing Bank

The issuing bank has the responsibility of examining the documents package presented by the seller/beneficiary to make sure that they are in conformity with the terms and conditions of the documentary credit or collection.

6. 3　Advising/Negotiating Bank

The advising or negotiating bank has the responsibility of examining the documents presented by the issuing bank to determine their authentication and if they are consistent with the requirements of the documentary credit or collection.

6. 4　Buyer/Importer/Applicant

The buyer/importer/applicant first has the responsibility of listing documents that are required of the seller in the documentary credit. Upon presentation by the bank the buyer examines documents for consistency and accuracy. Problems with documents often lead to problems securing goods from the shipping company or customs or receiving unwanted or incorrect goods.

7. Documents Examination

Whether has a nominated bank or confirming bank conducted its obligation to pay the beneficiary depends on the documents presented by the beneficiary being in conformity with the requirement specified in the L/C. Whether the issuing bank performing imbursement to the nominated bank which has made payment to the beneficiary depends also on documents received being in compliance with the requirements in the L/C. The buy must check the documents released by the issuing bank to him so as to decide to pay to the issuing bank. Even the seller should also carefully examine the documents after having made out them, all the documents to be submitted to the bank. In a word, one issue in common to all parties involved in a documentary L/C is to examine documents required in the L/C. Once again, to be handled, to be presented, to be transacted, to be examined in the L/C is documents rather than goods. Examine documents must be considered as an vital step in the whole transaction.

7.1 Principles by Examining Documents

Parties by examining documents should be strictly but with reasonable care. There is no doubt that all parties except the beneficiary have to complete examination within a reasonable period, normally up to seven banking days after receiving documents. The following points should be emphasized:

(1) The documents must comply with terms and conditions of credit.

(2) The documents must be consistent with each other.

(3) The parties involved only check documents clearly identified in the L/C, non-document conditions would be ignored.

7.2 Procedure of Examining Documents

Procedure of examining documents differs from country to country and even from bank to bank. Procedure listed below can be considered as a reference or a recommendation:

(1) To sort and count types and numbers of documents received;

(2) To write a receipt of document package in duplicate, indicating the date of receipt, one of them should be returned to party from which the documents are received.

7.2.1 To Check the L/C and Documents to Make Certain That

First of all, the documentary credit is advised by an advising bank. If the L/C is sent directly to the beneficiary, its authenticity should be verified by any means.

Then, the documentary credit is an irrevocable credit issued by a bank with good credit reputation.

Next, the documentary credit indicates the availability clearly and correctly. Meanwhile, the documentary credit should still be valid.

Finally, the documentary credit is sufficient to cover the value stated in the contract.

7.2.2 The Draft Bears the Correct Documentary Credit Reference Number

(1) The draft has a current date.

(2) The draft has been signed by an authorized person of the beneficiary's company.

(3) The draft is drawn on the proper drawee, i.e. a bank.

(4) The draft indicates amount in figures and in words consistently.

(5) The draft has the amount not exceeding the balance available in the credit.

(6) The draft indicates the tenor as required by the credit.

(7) he draft is endorsed properly (if any).

(8) The draft has no restricted endorsement.

(9) The draft has no notation "without recourse" unless authorized by the credit.

7.2.3 The Invoice Is Issued by the Beneficiary of Credit

(1) The invoice is addressed to the applicant, unless otherwise stated in the credit.

(2) The invoice describes the goods as the same as that given in the credit.

(3) The invoice indicates the details of prices and terms as mentioned in the credit.

(4) The invoice has the currency to be corresponding to that in the draft.

(5) The invoice has the amount not exceeding the balance available in the credit.

7.2.4 Transport Document Indicates the Number of Full Set of Originals

(1) Transport document is not a "charter party" transport, unless is agreed by the credit.

(2) Transport document is not a forwarder's transport document.

(3) Transport document indicates the name of consignee as required in the credit.

(4) Transport document is endorsed appropriately if needed.

(5) Transport document indicates the name and address of the notify party as required in the credit

(6) Transport bears the name of shipper or his agent.

(7) Transport document indicates freight prepaid or freight collected as required in the credit.

(8) Transport has no unclean notation.

7.2.5 Insurance Document Is Issued in the Form Required in the Credit

(1) Insurance document indicates the number of full set of the insurance document.

(2) Insurance document is issued and signed by the insurance company or underwriter or their agents.

(3) Insurance document has the date of issuance or date from when cover is effective, at the latest from the date of loading on board or dispatch or taking in charge of the goods, as the case may be.

(4) Insurance document has the value insured as required by the documentary credit, normally 110% of the invoice value.

(5) Insurance document describes the goods as the same as that in the invoice.

(6) Insurance policy covers the commodity from the designated port of embarkation or point of taking in charge to port of discharge or point of delivery.

(7) Insurance document covers all the risks as stated in the credit.

(8) Insurance document is endorsed correctly and properly, if the name of the insured is other than the paying bank.

7.2.6　To Compare Documents with the Credit

By comparing documents with credit, arranging them in the order of Figure 8.15. the sequence of comparison is firstly in vertical direction and then in horizontal direction. So-called "vertical" means that all documents are to be compared with credit, in detail, items in various documents should be consistent with those stated in the credit. "Horizontal" means that all documents are to be compared with invoice. All discrepancies should be listed out during the comparison, and written down in the column of "discrepancies and action taken" of the list. For some simple credits, only those items that are easy to become discrepancies would be checked, so as to faster the examination.

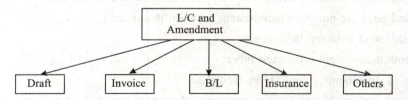

Figure 8.15　Sequence of Checking L/C and Documents

8. Disposal of Discrepancies

Discrepancies refer to documents presented under a credit are missing or/and have one or more points which are not consistent with those in the credit or in any other documents. In the event of discrepancies, the security given by the credit is largely lost, as a documentary credit is undertaking of payment with prerequisite, where terms and conditions in the documents presented are on face consistent with those in the credit.

8. 1   Essential Discrepancies

Discrepancies have different influence on banker's payment. The discrepancies, commonly not acceptable by the bank involved, are listed as follows:

Credit expired.

bill of exchange drawn on the buyer or a wrong party.

bill of exchange payable on an undeterminable time.

Amount on the bill of exchange exceeded that of the credit.

Description of goods on the invoice different from that shown in the credit.

Being an unclean bill of lading.

No notation "shipped on board" in a marine bill of lading.

Place of loading on board/dispatch/taking in charge and destination being inconsistent with those stated in the credit.

Bill of lading not showing the freight paid or not.

Late shipment.

Short shipment

Goods shipped on desk.

Type of insurance document being rather than that required by the credit.

Insurance risks covered not as specified in the credit.

Under-insured

Date of insurance issuance being later than that of transport document.

Marks and package numbers inconsistent between documents.

Weight different between documents.

Documents inconsistent with each other.

Absence of documents called for in the credit.

Instruments such as bill of lading, insurance document and bill of exchange not endorsed correctly.

Absence of signatures required on the documents.

Documents presentation is not in time.

8. 2   Disposal of Discrepant Documents by Banks

Banks concerned have up to seven banking days following the receipt of documents to examine and notify the party, from which it received the documents, of documents being order or not. A bank finding out discrepancies in the documents has several options.

The nominated bank or confirming bank in the interest of the beneficiary can point out the discrepancies and return them to beneficiary. If the beneficiary due to his apparent carelessness introduces discrepancies in creating documents. Such as typing mistakes, spelling mistakes, whatever, he can correct or replace them.

The nominated bank remits the documents with discrepancies continuously to the issuing bank, draws its attention to the discrepancies, informs the latter that it has paid or negotiated under reserve or against an indemnity in respect of such discrepancies. If the issuing bank decides to reject the documents, it must notice to the bank from which it received the documents by telecommunication, not later than the close of the seven banking days following the day of receipt of the documents.

The nominated banks ask for an authorization from the issuing bank to pay, accept or negotiate at the request of the beneficiary.

The nominated bank sends the documents with discrepancy, if not essential, to the issuing bank continuously, which effects his responsibility for payment, or acceptance, or negotiation, but in the meantime, asks for an guarantee from the seller to reimburse the proceeds if the issuing bank does not honor the documents at presentation.

The nominated bank dispatches the documents with discrepancies continuously to the issuing bank without effecting his obligation of payment, or acceptance, or negotiation. That eventually changes a payment under documentary credit to that under documentary collection, which is subject to the Uniform Rules of Documentary Collection No. 522.

The issuing bank, if it feels the discrepancies are not fatal to the transaction, can confer with the buyer on a waiver for the specific discrepancies, but must do so within seven banking days.

The bank, which received the documents and found discrepancy, refuses to accept them.

Note, if the nominated bank, or confirming bank, or the issuing bank refuses to take over the documents owing to the discrepancies, i. e. refuses to fulfill its obligation under a credit, it has to notify the party, from which it received the documents, its decision by telecommunication or by other expeditions means, not later than the close of the seventh banking day following the day of receipt of the documents, otherwise, it has no right to refuse to effect its obligation, point out all the discrepancies in respect of which it refuses the documents at one time, state keeping documents at the disposal of presenter or send all documents directly back to the presenter.

Generally speaking, problem of dishonor by the paying bank due to the discrepancy, if not fraudulent, can be solved in compromise by the seller or the buyer, for example, waiving discrepancies, cutting down price, change to by means of payment of collection, and so on.

 ## Words & Expressions

1.consular invoice 领事发票

2.customs invoice 海关发票

3.certificate invoice 产地证发票

4.proforma invoice 形式发票

5.packing list 装箱单

6.non-official certificate of inspection 非官方检验证书

7.transport document 运输单据

8.marine B/L 海运提单

9.shipped on board B/L 已装船提单

10.received for shipment B/L 备运提单

11.clean B/L 清洁提单

12.unclean B/L 肮脏提单,不清洁提单

13.straight B/L 直运提单

14.transshipment B/L 转运提单

15.named consignee B/L 记名提单

16.order B/L 指示提单

17.multi-modal（combined）transport document 多式联运单据

18.sea waybill 海运单

19.air waybill 空运提单

20.road waybill 公路运单

21.rail waybill 铁路运单

22.railway cargo receipt 铁路承运收据

23.insurance document 保险单据

24.insurance policy 保险单

25.insurance certificate 保险凭证

26.cover note 暂保单

27.open cover 预约保险单

28.certificate of origin 原产地证

29.inspection certificate 商检证书

30.inspection certificate of veterinary 兽医检验证书

31.inspection certificate of plant quarantine 植物检疫证书

32.export license 出口许可证

33.document checklists 单据校对清单

34.document examination 单据审核

35.charter party 租船合约

36.discrepancy 不符点

37.waiving discrepancies 放弃不符点

📖 Notes

1. Documents refer to a set of certificates or papers used in merchandise transaction.
   单据指的是一系列用于商品货物交易的凭证或文件。

2. Normally, documents can be classified into 4 groups by different issuers: Business documents issued by business-people; Transport documents issued by carriers; Insurance documents issued by the insurers; Official documents issued by state authorities.
   正常情况下,单据可根据签发人分为四类:由商人签署的商业票据;由承运人签署的运输单据;由保险商签署的保险单据;由国家权威机构签署的官方单据。

3. Business documents refer to the documents which are issued by sellers, buyers or other traders, for facilitating the trade and payment.
   商业单据指的是由卖方、买方或其他人签发的单据,以促进贸易和支付。

4. Transport documents are ones, issued by the carriers, certifying that the goods have been loaded on board or dispatch or taken in charge.
   运输单据是指那些由承运人签发的单据它们证明货物已装上船、或货物运输或接管货物。

5. A multi-modal transport document issued by a freight forwarder is acceptable unless the L/C stipulated otherwise, or unless L/C specifically calls for a "marine bill of lading".
   除非信用证另有规定或除非信用证特别规定要求"海运提单",否则多式联运运输单据是可以接受的。

   As described previously, a bill of lading is a semi-negotiable instrument against which the goods will be delivered to the holder of originals.
   正如先前所描述那样,海运提单是一份准流通票据,凭此货物将被运输给提单原件的持票人。

6. Generally, air waybills are issued by the carrier or airline when the goods need to be sent by air freight. There is no such thing as a bill of lading with air transport document.
   一般地说,当货物需要用空运方式发运时,空运单是由承运人或航空公司签发的。

7. The consignee may obtain access to the goods without presentation of an air waybill.
   收货人可能提取货物而无需出示一份空运单。

8. Cargo receipt is a transport document issued by Branches of Sino-trans, specifying the shipment from mainland of China to HongKong and Macau via railway transportation.
   铁路货运收据是由中国外贸总公司各分公司所签发的运输单据,它特定货物通过铁路运输方式从中国大陆运至香港和澳门地区。

9. Insurance documents are ones, issued by insurance companies, indicating the type and amount of insurance coverage in force on a particular shipment.
   保险单据是由保险公司签发的,表明某一特定货物运输生效的保险险种的类型和保险金额。

10. Cover note is a document normally issued to give notice that an insurance has been

placed pending the making policy or certificate.

暂保单是证明业已投保尚未制作正式保险单或是保险凭证的文件。

11. An open cover is an insurance document by which the underwriter undertakes to issue a specific policy subsequently in conformity to the terms of cover, called also a general insurance for the recurring shipment.

预约保险单又称统保单,是为了对长期连续装运的货物投保事先签订的"一揽子"保险合同。

12. A variety of official documents may be required to meet both the exporting and importing country's customs or foreign exchange regulations. Documents relating to origin, quality, fumigation, health, weight, inspection and import and export licences are some examples of official documents.

许多官方单据需要满足进口国、出口国家海关或外汇管理需要。原产地证、质量检验证、熏蒸检验证书、健康检疫证书、重量证书、进口许可证、出口许可证等都是可能需要的官方单据。

13. Inspection certificate is a document issued by an authority, indicating that the goods have been inspected prior to shipment and the results of the inspection.

商检证书是由权威机构签发的单据,表明货物在发运前已被检验以及检验的结果。

14. Discrepancies refer to documents presented under a credit are missing or/and have one or more points which are not consistent with those in the credit or in any other documents.

不符点是指信用证项不提示的单据不全,或者是单据上有一处甚至多处与信用证或其他单据的提法不一致。

15. Generally speaking, problems of dishonor by the paying bank due to the discrepancy, if not fraudulent, can be solved in compromise by the seller or the buyer, for example, waiving discrepancies, cutting down price, change to be means of payment of collections, and so on.

一般说来,不符点导致的拒付问题,如果不是有欺诈行为,买卖双方完全可以通过协商妥善解决,如放弃不符点,降价,改为托收方式等。

 **Exercises**

I. True or False

1. The description of the goods in the invoice must correspond with description in the credit, whereas in other documents the goods may be described in general terms.

2. A certificate of quantity is simply a certificate to the effect that the goods dispatched are of the quality specified in the contract.

3. Cover notes issued by brokers are not acceptable unless specifically authorized in the credit.

4. Unless otherwise specified, the insurance document must be expressed in the same currency as the credit.
5. A packing list is a document issued by the exporter declaring the weight and measurement of the goods in the consignment.
6. A sea waybill is a negotiable instrument.
7. Bill of lading is issued when the goods are sent by air freight.
8. A bill of lading may be a stale one when it is presented after the expiry of the credit or it is dated after the shipment date stipulated in the credit.
9. Railway cargo receipt cannot be used for taking delivery in Hong Kong and Macau areas.
10. Export license is issued by government department for restricting import.

II. Multiple Choices

1. A railway receipt _____ an air consignment note is a document of title to goods in the same way that a bill of lading is.
   A. Neither... nor　　B. Either... or　　C. Not only... but also　D. Both... and
2. _____ certifies that the goods were produced in a particular country.
   A. A weight list　　　　　　　B. An insurance policy
   C. A certificate of origin　　　D. An inspection certificate
3. A consular invoice is an invoice signed by _____.
   A. a consul of the importing country in the country from which the goods are consigned
   B. a consul of the exporting country in the country from which the goods are consigned
   C. a manufacture in the importing country
   D. a manufacturer in the exporting country
4. Where the contract between the exporter and the foreign importer is a CIF contract, it is the _____ responsibility to insure the goods.
   A. importer's　　B. exporter's　　C. issuing bank's　　D. negotiating bank's
5. Banks may refuse insurance documents if they bear a date _____.
   A. earlier than the date of shipment
   B. later than the date of shipment
   C. just the same as that of shipment
   D. B and C
6. _____ is the person or company that holds himself or itself liable to compensate the assured in the event of a loss to the insured property approximately caused by a peril insured against.
   A, The insured　　B. The insurer　　C. The carrier　　D. Claimant
7. A bill of lading acts as a receipt for the goods _____.
   A. from the exporter to the importer
   B. from the shipping company to the exporter

    C from the shipping company to the importer

    D. from the importer to the exporter.

8. When there is no indication of damage to the goods, a bill of lading is said to be _____ .

    A. clean   B. good   C. qualified   D. dirty

9. _____ is a quasi negotiable document.

    A. A draft   B. An invoice   C. A bill of lading   D. A check

10. _____ can not be transferred.

    A. An on board B/L   B. A transshipment B/L

    C. A clean B/L   D. A straight B/L

III. Answer Questions

1. What are the functions of an Ocean Bill of Lading?

2. What will the bank do if the bill of lading presented is a dirty one?

3. What are the main differences between the insurance policy and the insurance certificate?

Chapter 9 Trade Forms

In this chapter students need to familiarize with different trade forms besides the normal import and export. Therefore, they can easily deal with some special trade forms encountered with various trade partners. Also, it is clear that students may need to know the content and functions of various trade forms. Lastly, it is advisable to utilize suitable trade forms as per the actual circumstance

1. Distribution and Agency

Generally speaking, distribution and agency are widely used in international trade and settlement. It is important for traders to familiarize with such concepts in order to make international trade and settlement conduct smoothly and effectively.

1. 1   Distribution of Commodities

Product distribution is one of the four elements of the marketing mix. Distribution is the process of making a product or service available for use or consumption by a consumer or business user, using direct means, or using indirect means with intermediaries. The other three parts of the marketing mix are product, pricing and promotion.

Distribution of products takes place by means of channels. Channels are sets of interdependent organizations (called intermediaries) involved in making the product available for consumption. Merchants are intermediaries that buy and resell products. Agents and brokers are intermediaries that act on behalf of the producer, but do not take title to the products.

In practice, many organizations use a mix of different channels; in particular, they may complement a direct sales-force, calling on the larger accounts, with agents, covering the smaller customers and prospects. In addition, online retailing or e-commerce is leading to disintermediation. Retailing via smart phone or m-commerce is also a growing area.

The firm's marketing department needs to design the most suitable channels for the firm's products, then select appropriate channel members or intermediaries. The firm needs to train staff of intermediaries and motivate the intermediary to sell the firm's products. The firm should monitor the channel's performance over time and modify the channel to enhance performance.

1. 2 Agency

In political science and economics, the principal-agent problem or agency dilemma concerns the difficulties in motivating one party (the "agent"), to act in the best interests of another (the "principal") rather than in his or her own interests.

Common examples of this relationship include corporate management (agent) and shareholders (principal). In fact the problem potentially arises in almost any context where one party is being paid by another to do something, whether in formal employment or a negotiated deal such as paying for household jobs or car repairs.

The problem arises where the two parties have different interests and asymmetric information (the agent having more information), such that the principal cannot directly ensure that the agent is always acting in its (the principal's) best interests, particularly when activities that are useful to the principal are costly to the agent, and where elements of what the agent does are costly for the principal to observe. Moral hazard and conflict of interest may arise. Indeed, the principal may be sufficiently concerned at the possibility of being exploited by the agent that he chooses not to enter into a transaction at all, when that deal would have actually been in both parties' best interests: a sub-optimal outcome that lowers welfare overall. The deviation from the principal's interest by the agent is called agency costs.

Various mechanisms may be used to align the interests of the agent with those of the principal. In employment, employers (principal) may use piece rates/commissions, profit sharing, efficiency wages, performance measurement (including financial statements), the agent posting a bond, or the threat of termination of employment.

A supposition that explains the relationship between principals and agents in business. Agency theory is concerned with resolving problems that can exist in agency relationships; that is, between principals (such as shareholders) and agents of the principals. The two problems that agency theory addresses are: (1) the problems that arise when the desires or goals of the principal and agent are in conflict, and the principal is unable to verify (because it difficult and/or expensive to do so) what the agent is actually doing; and (2) the problems that arise when the principal and agent have different attitudes towards risk. Because of different risk tolerances, the principal and agent may each be inclined to take different actions.

An agency, in general terms, is the relationship between two parties, where one is a principal and the other is an agent who represents the principal in transactions with a third party. Agency relationships occur when the principals hire the agent to perform a service on the principals' behalf. Principals commonly delegate decision-making authority to the agents. Agency problems can arise because of inefficiencies and incomplete information. In finance, two important agency relationships are those between stockholders and managers, and stockholders and creditors.

2. Tender and Auction

It is important for traders to know the main content and procedure of tend and auction since both forms are quite often during international trade activities.

2. 1 Tender

A request for tenders (RFT) is a formal, structured invitation to suppliers to bid to supply products or services. In the public sector, such a process may be required and determined in detail by law to ensure that such competition for the use of public money is open, fair and free from bribery and nepotism. For example, a government may put a building project "out to tender"; that is, publish an invitation for other parties to make a proposal for the building's construction, on the understanding that any competition for the relevant government contract must be conducted in response to the tender, no parties having the unfair advantage of separate, prior, closed-door negotiations for the contract. An evaluation team will go through the tenders and decide who will get the contract.

As a consequence of the scale of the tender process the majority of RFTs are published by the government sector, but companies in the infrastructure and utilities sectors may also publish RFTs.

RFTs may be distributed to potential bidders through a tender service, allowing businesses to receive and search live tenders from a range of public and private sources. These alerts are most commonly sent daily and can be filtered down by geographical area, or by business sector. Some tendering services even divide types of business very finely in their own way, by CPV (Common Procurement Vocabulary) codes. This enables a business to find RFTs specific to what that business can supply.

The closest equivalent to an RFT in the mainstream private sector is a request for proposal (RFP), which, since public money is not involved, typically has a less rigid structure.

An RFT is usually an open invitation for suppliers to respond to a defined need as opposed to a request being sent to selected potential suppliers. The RFT often requests information following on from other information gathered previously from responses to a Request for Information (RFI). This will usually not only cover product and service requirements, but will also ask for information about the suitability of the business.

An RFT is usually expected to conform to some legally standardized structure designed to ensure impartiality.

The procedure of international tendering is as follows: invitation for application for pre-qualifications, purchase of pre-qualification documents and preparation of the pre-qualification documents by the tenderers, submission of pre-qualification documents, pre-qualification on the tenderers by the owner, preparation of tendering documents, invitation to tenders, purchase of tendering documents by the tenderers, completion of the tendering documents and quotation of the tendering price by the tenderers, submission of tendering documents, tender opening, evaluation of tenders, award of contract and signing of contract.

2. 2 Auction

An auction is a process of buying and selling goods or services by offering them up for bid, taking bids, and then selling the item to the highest bidder. In economic theory, an auction may refer to any mechanism or set of trading rules for exchange.

Each type of auction has its specific qualities such as pricing accuracy and time required for preparing and conducting the auction. The number of simultaneous bidders is of critical importance. Open bidding during an extended period of time with many bidders will result in a final bid that is very close to the true market value. Where there are few bidders and each bidder is allowed only one bid, time is saved, but the winning bid may not reflect the true market value with any degree of accuracy. Of special interest and importance during the actual auction is the time elapsed from the moment that the first bid is revealed to the moment that the final (winning) bid has become a binding agreement.

Auctions can differ in the number of participants: In a supply auction, the sellers offer a good that a buyer requests. On the other hand, in a demand auction, the buyers bid for a good being sold.

In a double auction the buyers bid to buy goods from the sellers. Prices are bid by buyers and asked (or offered) by sellers. Auctions may also differ by the procedure for bidding (or asking, as the case may be):

In an open auction participants may repeatedly bid and are aware of mutual sides' previous bids.

In a closed auction buyers and/or sellers submit sealed bids. Auctions may differ as to the price at which the item is sold, whether the first (best) price, the second price, the first unique price or some other. Auctions may set a reservation price which is the least/maximum acceptable price for which a good may be sold/bought.

Without modification, auction generally refers to an open, demand auction, with or without a reservation price (or reserve), with the item sold to the highest bidder.

Although less publicly visible, the most economically important auctions are the commodities auctions in which the bidders are businesses even up to corporation level. Examples of this type of auction include: sales of businesses and spectrum auctions, in which companies purchase licenses to use portions of the electromagnetic spectrum for communications (e. g. , mobile phone networks).

3. Counter-trade

Counter-trade means exchanging goods or services which are paid for, in whole or part, with other goods or services, rather than with money. A monetary valuation can however be used in counter-trade for accounting purposes. In dealings between sovereign states, the term bilateral trade is used. Or "Any transaction involving exchange of goods or service for something of equal value."

There are five main variants of counter-trade:

3. 1　Barter

It is the exchange of goods and services for goods and services without any use of money. Like the trade relationship between China and Thailand where fruit has been traded by Thailand for buses made by China.

Barter is the direct exchange of goods between two parties in a transaction. The principal exports are paid for with goods or services supplied from the importing market. A single contract covers both flows, in its simplest form involves no cash. In practice, supply of the principal exports is often held up until sufficient revenues have been earned from the sale of bartered goods. One of the largest barter deals to date involved Occidental Petroleum Corporation's Agreement to ship sulphuric acid to the former Soviet Union for ammonia urea and potash under a 2-year deal which was worth 18 billion Euros. Furthermore, during negotiation stage of a barter deal, the seller must know the market price for items offered in trade. Bartered goods can range from hams to iron pellets, mineral water, furniture or olive-oil all somewhat more difficult to price and market when potential customers must be sought.

3. 2　Switch Trading

In this method one company trades products and services or, in some cases, builds infrastructure like roads, railway lines, hospitals with another nation and, in turn, are obligated to make a purchase from that nation. One such example is a deal proposed by the Philippine Government where they offer to trade Philippine coffee for essential products.

3. 3　Counter Purchase

A foreign company, or country, trades with a nation with the promise that in the future they will make purchase of a specific product from the nation. A recent example of this is the ongoing trade between Congo and China where infrastructure is being traded for a supply of metals.

3. 4   Buyback

In this type of counter trade, a company builds a plant, supplies technology, training, etc. In exchange they take a part of output of the plant. For example, a company based in the USA sets up a lets say an automobile factory in X country. They take a part of the total produce as their own but they have setup the industry, provided the technology and the training to X country.

3. 5   Offset

This is an agreement by one nation to buy a product from a company in another. The terms of contract are subject to the purchase of some or all of the components and raw materials from the buyer of the finished product, or the assembly of such product in the buyer nation. This is more common in terms of defense equipment or space craft, etc.

3. 6   Compensation Trade

Compensation trade is a form of barter in which one of the flows is partly in goods and partly in hard currency.

A significant chunk of international commerce, possibly as much as 25%, involves the barter of products for other products rather than for hard currency. Counter-trade may range from a simple barter between two countries to a complex web of exchanges that end up meeting the needs of all countries involved.

It should be noted that US economist Paul Samuelson was skeptical about the viability of counter-trade as a marketing tool, claiming that "Unless a hungry tailor happens to find an undraped farmer, who has both food and a desire for a pair of pants, neither can make a trade". (This is called "double coincidence of wants".) But this is arguably a too simplistic interpretation of how markets operate in the real world. In any real economy, bartering occurs all the time, even if it is not the main means to acquire goods and services.

The volume of counter-trade is growing. In 1972, it was estimated that counter-trade was used by business and governments in 15 countries; in 1979, 27 countries; by the start of 1990s, around 100 countries. A large part of counter-trade has involved sales of military equipment.

More than 80 countries nowadays regularly use or require counter-trade exchanges. Officials of the General Agreement on Tariffs and Trade(GATT) organization claimed that counter-trade accounts for around 5% of the world trade. The British Department of Trade and Industry has suggested 15%, while some scholars believe it to be closer to 30%, with east-west trade having been as high as 50% in some trading sectors of Eastern European and Third World Countries for some years. A consensus of expert opinions has put the percentage of the value of world trade volumes linked to counter-trade transactions at between 20% to 25%.

According to an official U. S. statement, "The U. S. Government generally views counter-trade, including barter, as contrary to an open, free trading system and, in the long run, not in the interest of the U. S. business community. However, as a matter of policy the U. S. Government will not oppose U. S. companies' participation in counter-trade arrangements unless such action could have a negative impact on national security."

3. 7 Futures

In finance, a futures contract (more colloquially, futures) is a standardized contract between two parties to buy or sell a specified asset of standardized quantity and quality for a price agreed upon today (the *futures price* or strike price) with delivery and payment occurring at a specified future date, the *delivery date*. The contracts are negotiated at a futures exchange, which acts as an intermediary between the two parties. The party agreeing to buy the underlying asset in the future, the "buyer" of the contract, is said to be "long", and the party agreeing to sell the asset in the future, the "seller" of the contract, is said to be "short". The terminology reflects the expectations of the parties—the buyer hopes or expects that the asset price is going to increase, while the seller hopes or expects that it will decrease in near future.

In many cases, the underlying asset to a futures contract may not be traditional commodities at all—that is, for financial futures the underlying item can be any financial instrument (also including currency, bonds, and stocks); they can be also based on intangible assets or referenced items, such as stock indexes and interest rates.

While the futures contract specifies a trade taking place in the future, the purpose of the futures exchange institution is to act as intermediary and minimize the risk of default by either party. Thus the exchange requires both parties to put up an initial amount of cash, the margin. Additionally, since the futures price will generally change daily, the difference in the prior agreed-upon price and the daily futures price is settled daily also (variation margin). The exchange will draw money out of one party's margin account and put it into the other's so that each party has the appropriate daily loss or profit. If the margin account goes below a certain value, then a margin call is made and the account owner must replenish the margin account. This process is known as *marking to market*. Thus on the delivery date, the amount exchanged is not the specified price on the contract but the spot value (since any gain or loss has already been previously settled by marking to market).

A closely related contract is a forward contract. A forward is like a futures in that it specifies the exchange of goods for a specified price at a specified future date. However, a forward is not traded on an exchange and thus does not have the interim partial payments due to marking to market. Nor is the contract standardized, as on the exchange.

Unlike an option, both parties of a futures contract must fulfill the contract on the delivery date. The seller delivers the underlying asset to the buyer, or, if it is a cash-settled futures contract, then cash is transferred from the futures trader who sustained a loss to the one who made a profit. To exit the commitment prior to the settlement date, the holder of a futures position can close out its contract obligations by taking the opposite position on another futures contract on the same asset and settlement date. The difference in futures prices is then a profit or loss.

4. Outsourcing

4. 1　Overview of Outsourcing

Outsourcing is the contracting out of an internal business process to a third-party organization. The term "outsourcing" became popular in the United States near the turn of the 21st century. Outsourcing sometimes involves transferring employees and assets from one firm to another, but not always. Outsourcing is a practice that should not be considered without considering the impact on the organization.

The definition of outsourcing includes both foreign and domestic contracting, and sometimes includes offshoring, which means relocating a business function to another country. Financial savings from lower international labor rates is a big motivation for outsourcing offshoring.

The opposite of outsourcing is called insourcing, which entails bringing processes handled by third-party firms in-house, and is sometimes accomplished via vertical integration. However, a business can provide a contract service to another business without necessarily insourcing that business process.

Outsourcing can offer greater budget flexibility and control. Outsourcing lets organizations pay for only the services they need, when they need them. It also reduces the need to hire and train specialized staff, brings in fresh engineering expertise, and reduces capital and operating expenses.

4. 2　Reasons for Outsourcing

Companies outsource can avoid certain types of costs. They outsource the non core activities. Among the reasons companies elect to outsource include avoidance of burdensome regulations, high taxes, high energy costs, and unreasonable costs that may be associated with defined benefits in labor-union contracts and taxes for government-mandated benefits. Perceived or actual gross margin in the short run incentivizes a company to outsource. With reduced short-run costs, executive management sees the opportunity for short-run profits, while the income growth of the consumer base is strained. This motivates companies to outsource for lower labor costs. However, the company may or may not incur unexpected costs to train these overseas workers. Lower regulatory costs are an addition to companies saving money when outsourcing. On comparative costs, a U. S. employer typically incurs higher defined benefit costs associated with taxes to account for social security, medicare, and safety protection etc. than in other countries. On comparative CEO pay, executive pay in the United States in 2007 was more than 400 times more than average workers—a gap 20 times bigger than it was in 1965. In 2011, twenty-six of the largest U. S. corporations paid more to CEO's than they paid in federal taxes. However, it appears companies do not outsource to reduce executive or managerial costs.

Companies may seek internal savings to focus money and resources towards core business. A company may outsource its landscaping functions irrelevant to the core business. Companies and public entities may outsource certain specialized functions, such as payroll, to ADP or Ceridian. Companies may find the same level of consumer satisfaction.

Import marketers may make short-run profits from cheaper overseas labor and currency mainly in wealth-consuming sectors at the long-run expense of an economy's wealth-producing sectors, thus straining the home country's tax base, income growth, and increasing the debt burden. When companies offshore products and services, those jobs may leave the home country for foreign countries, at the expense of the wealth-producing sectors. Outsourcing may increase the risk of leakage and reduce confidentiality, as well as introduce additional privacy and security concerns.

📖 Words & Expressions

1.product distribution 产品分销
2.marketing mix 营销组合
3.channels 渠道
4.merchants 商人
5.intermediaries 中介
6.agents 代理
7.brokers 经纪人
8.direct sales-force 直接销售动力
9.calling on 要求
10.the larger accounts 更大账户
11.online retailing 网络零售

12. e-commerce 电子商务

13. disintermediation 非中介化

14. smart phone 智能电话

15. m-commerce 移动电子商务

16. marketing department 营销部

17. principal-agent problem 委托与代理问题

18. agency dilemma 代理困境

19. corporate management（agent）企业管理（代理）

20. shareholders（principal）投资者（委托人）

21. household jobs 家务活

22. car repairs 汽车修理

23. asymmetric information 不对称信息

24. moral hazard 道德风险

25. conflict of interest 利益冲突

26. suboptimal outcome 次优结果

27. welfare overall 总体福利

28. deviation 偏离

29. agency costs 代理成本

30. commissions 佣金

31. profit sharing 利润分成

32. efficiency wages 绩效工资

33. performance measurement 绩效衡量

34. financial statements 财务报表

35. agent posting a bond 代理发布债券

36. threat of termination of employment 终止雇佣关系威胁

37. supposition 假定；推测；想象；见解

38. agency theory 代理理论

39. risk tolerances 风险承受能力

40. on the principals' behalf 代理委托人

41. decision-making authority 决策权威

42. agency problems 代理机构问题

43. inefficiencies and incomplete information 信息不足和信息不完整

44. Finance 金融学

45. stockholders 股东；投资人

46. creditors 债权人

47. request for tenders（RFT）邀请投标

48. public sector 公共经济部门

49. bribery 贿赂

50. nepotism 裙带关系
51. tender 投标
52. evaluation team 评估团队
53. infrastructure 基础设施
54. utilities sectors 公用事业部门
55. live tenders 现场直播投标
56. CPV（Common Procurement Vocabulary）codes 常用采购词汇代码
57. equivalent 等值；等同
58. private sector 私营部门
59. request for proposal（RFP）要求投标
60. Request for Information（RFI）信息征询
61. suitability of the business 业务适度性
62. impartiality 公正性
63. auction 拍卖
64. bid 招标
65. taking bids 接标
66. bidder 投标
67. pricing accuracy 定价精度
68. open bidding 开标
69. winning bid 中标
70. binding agreement 招标协议
71. pre-qualification documents 资格预审文件
72. supply auction 供给拍卖
73. demand auction 需求拍卖
74. double auction 双向拍卖
75. open auction 开放式拍卖
76. closed auction 封闭式拍卖
77. commodities auctions 商品拍卖
78. Spectrum auctions 频谱拍卖
79. licenses 许可证
80. electromagnetic spectrum 电磁频谱
81. mobile phone networks 移动电话网络
82. countertrade 对销贸易
83. monetary valuation 货币估价
84. sovereign states 主权国家
85. bilateral trade 双边贸易
86. variants 变异
87. barter 易货贸易

88.sulphuric acid 硫酸

89.the former Soviet Union 前苏联

90.ammonia urea 尿素

91.potash 钾肥

92.Euros 欧元

93.hams 汉堡包

94.iron pellets 铁矿

95.mineral water 矿泉水

96.furniture 家具

97.olive-oil 橄榄油

98.switch trading 转手贸易;转口贸易

99.counter purchase 互购贸易

100.buyback 回购贸易

101.offset 抵消贸易

102.compensation trade 补偿贸易

103.hard currency 硬通货

104.chunk 数据块;大块

105.skeptical 怀疑的

106.viability 可行性

107.double coincidence of wants 双重需求偶合

108.General Agreement on Tariffs and Trade(GATT) 关贸总协定

109.British Department of Trade and Industry 英国工贸部

110.trading sectors 贸易部门

111.Eastern European 东欧

112.Third World Countries 第三世界国家

113.consensus 一致;共识

114.business community 商界;工商业界

115.negative impact 负面影响

116.national security 国家安全

117.futures contract 期货合同

118.specified asset 约定资产

119.standardized quantity and quality 标准质量和数量

120.futures exchange 期货交易所;远期外汇

121.intermediary 中介机构;中介

122.terminology 术语

123.financial instrument 金融票据

124.bonds 债券

125.stocks 股票

126. intangible assets 有形资产
127. referenced items 参照物
128. stock indexes 股票指数
129. interest rates 利率
130. futures exchange institution 期货交易所
131. default 过失
132. variation margin 价格变动押金；盈亏保证金
133. margin account 保证金账户
134. margin call 追加保证金；征收保证金的要求
135. marking to market 逐日盯市制度
136. forward contract 期货合同
137. interim partial payments 过渡部分支付
138. option 期权
139. delivery date 交货期
140. cash-settled futures contract 现金结算期货合同
141. exit the commitment 退出承诺
142. holder 持票人
143. outsourcing 外包
144. third-party organization 第三方机构
145. turn of the 21st century 21 世纪初
146. transferring employees and assets 转移员工和资产
146. financial savings 金融储蓄
148. international labor rates 国际劳工利率
149. in-house 内部的；自身的
150. vertical integration 纵向一体化
151. hire and train specialized staff 雇用和培训专业人员
152. fresh engineering expertise 新的工程专业知识
153. operating expenses 运营费用
154. non core activities 非核心活动
155. avoidance of burdensome regulations 避免繁琐的法规
156. high taxes 高税收
157. high energy costs 高能源成本
158. comparative costs 比较成本
159. social security 社会保障
160. Medicare 医疗保险
161. safety protection 安全保护
162. CEO pay 高层管理人员（首席执行官）薪酬
163. executive pay 高管薪酬

164.federal taxes 联邦税收

165.managerial costs 管理成本

166.core business 核心业务

167.landscaping functions 景观功能

168.public entities 公共部门实体;政府公共部门实体

169.payroll 工资册

170.ADP (Automatic Data Processing) 自动数据处理公司

171.Ceridian 赛瑞迪安指数

172.wealth-consuming sectors 财富消耗领域

173.economy's wealth-producing sectors 经济财富创造行业

174.home country's tax base 母国的税基

175.wealth-producing sectors 财富创造行业

176.risk of leakage 毒物泄漏危险性;渗漏风险

177.confidentiality 保密性;机密性

178.privacy and security concerns 隐私与安全顾虑

179.debt burden 债务负担

⋙　Exercises

I. True or False

1. RFTs may be distributed to potential bidders through a tender service, allowing businesses to receive and search live tenders from a range of public and private sources.

2. Each type of auction has its specific qualities such as pricing accuracy and time required for preparing and conducting the auction.

3. Barter means the exchange of goods or services indirectly for other goods or services without the use of money as means of purchase or payment.

4. Offset is an agreement that a company will offset a soft currency purchase of an unspecified product from that nation in the future. Agreement by one nation to buy a product from another, subject to the purchase of some or all of the components and raw materials from the buyer of the finished product, or the assembly of such product in the buyer nation.

5. Switch trading means the practice in which one company sells to another its obligation to make a purchase in a given country.

6. Compensation trade is a form of barter in which one of the flows is partly in goods and partly in soft currency.

7. It should be noted that U. S. economist Paul Samuelson was skeptical about the viability of counter-trade as a marketing tool, claiming that "Unless a hungry tailor happens to find an undraped farmer, who has both food and a desire for a pair of pants, neither can make a

trade".

8. While the futures contract specifies a trade taking place in the future, the purpose of the futures exchange institution is to act as intermediary and maximize the risk of default by either party.

9. A company may outsource its landscaping functions irrelevant to the core business. Companies and public entities may outsource certain specialized functions, such as payroll, to ADP or Ceridian.

10. Import marketers may make short-run profits from cheaper overseas labor and currency mainly in wealth-consuming sectors at the long-run expense of an economy's wealth-producing sectors, thus straining the home country's tax base, income growth, and increasing the debt burden.

II. Multiple Choice

1. Indeed, the _____ may be sufficiently concerned at the possibility of being exploited by the agent that he chooses not to enter into a transaction at all, when that deal would have actually been in both parties' best interests: a suboptimal outcome that lowers welfare overall.
   A. principal   B. agent   C. agency   D. representative

2. Auctions can differ in the number of participants: In a _____, the sellers offer a good that a buyer requests.
   A. demand auction   B. double auction   C. open auction   D. supply auction

3. An _____ is usually an open invitation for suppliers to respond to a defined need as opposed to a request being sent to selected potential suppliers.
   A. RFI   B. REP   C. RFT   D. CEO

4. _____ occurs when a firm builds a plant in a country or supplies technology, equipment, training, or other services to the country and agrees to take a certain percentage of the plant's output as partial payment for the contract.
   A. Buyback   B. Offset   C. Counter purchase D. Barter

5. The opposite of outsourcing is called _____, which entails bringing processes handled by third-party firms in-house, and is sometimes accomplished via vertical integration.
   A. offshoring   B. insourcing   C. compensation   D. bartering

Chapter 10

E-commerce

In this chapter, the main description is involved in introducing the concepts and main functions of E-commerce. Therefore, after learning, the student should get to know the knowledge of E-commerce. On the other hand, they may need to familiarize with how E-commerce to be used in international trade. Finally, they need to grasp the major procedure of E-commerce.

1. Development of E-commerce

In 2016, the United Kingdom had the biggest e-commerce market in the world when measured by the amount spent per capital. The Czech Republic is the European country where E-commerce delivers the biggest contribution to the enterprises' total revenue. Almost a quarter (24%) of the country's total turnover is generated via the online channel.

Among emerging economies, China's E-commerce presence continues to expand. With 384 million internet users, China's online shopping sales rose to $ 36. 6 billion in 2009 and one of the reasons behind the huge growth has been the improved trust level for shoppers. China's E-commerce trade was worth 8. 1 trillion yuan (US $ 1. 29 trillion) in 2016, up 31. 7 percent from 2015, with a growth rate about 4. 1 times larger than China's gross domestic product last year, according to a report released by the Ministry of Commerce (MOC), at the 2016 China (Beijing) E-commerce Conference.

The Chinese retailers have been able to help consumers feel more comfortable shopping online. E-commerce is also expanding across the Middle East. Having recorded the world's fastest growth in internet usage between 2000 and 2009, the region is now home to more than 60 million internet users. Retail, travel and gaming are the region's top E-commerce segments, in spite of difficulties such as the lack of region-wide legal frameworks and logistical problems in cross-border transportation. E-commerce has become an important tool for small and large businesses worldwide, not only to sell to customers, but also to engage them.

In 2016, E-commerce sales topped $ 1 trillion for the first time in history.

1. 1　Definition of E-commerce

Electronic commerce, commonly known as E-commerce, is a type of industry where buying and selling of product or service is conducted over electronic systems such as the Internet and other computer networks. Electronic commerce draws on technologies such as mobile commerce, electronic funds transfer, supply chain management, Internet marketing, online transaction processing, electronic data interchange (EDI), inventory management systems, and automated data collectionsystems. Modern electronic commerce typically uses the World Wide Web at least at one point in the transaction's life-cycle, although it may encompass a wider range of technologies such as e-mail, mobile devices social media, and telephones as well.

Electronic commerce is generally considered to be the sales aspect of E-business. It also consists of the exchange of data to facilitate the financing and payment aspects of business transactions. This is an effective and efficient way of communicating within an organization and one of the most effective and useful ways of conducting business.

E-commerce can be divided into:

E-tailing or "virtual storefronts" on websites with online catalogs, sometimes gathered into a "virtual mall";

The gathering and use of demographic data through Web contacts and social media;

Electronic Data Interchange (EDI), the business-to-business exchange of data;

E-mail and fax and their use as media for reaching prospective and established customers (for example, with newsletters);

Business-to-business buying and selling;

The security of business transactions.

1. 2　Governmental Regulation

In the United States, some electronic commerce activities are regulated by the Federal Trade Commission (FTC). These activities include the use of commercial E-mails, online advertising and consumer privacy. The CAN-SPAM Act of 2003 establishes national standards for direct marketing over E-mail. The Federal Trade Commission Act regulates all forms of advertising, including online advertising, and states that advertising must be truthful and non-deceptive. Using its authority under Section 5 of the FTC Act, which prohibits unfair or deceptive practices, the FTC has brought a number of cases to enforce the promises in corporate privacy statements, including promises about the security of consumers' personal information. As result, any corporate privacy policy related to E-commerce activity may be subject to enforcement by the FTC.

The Ryan Haight Online Pharmacy Consumer Protection Act of 2008, which came into law in 2008, amends the Controlled Substances Act to address online pharmacies.

Internationally, there is the International Consumer Protection and Enforcement Network (ICPEN), which was formed in 1991 from an informal network of government customer fair trade organizations. The purpose was stated as being to find ways of cooperating on tackling consumer problems connected with cross-border transactions in both goods and services, and to help ensure exchanges of information among the participants for mutual benefit and understanding.

There is also Asia Pacific Economic Cooperation (APEC) which was established in 1989 with the vision of achieving stability, security and prosperity for the region through free and open trade and investment. APEC has an Electronic Commerce Steering Group as well as working on common privacy regulations throughout the APEC region.

In Australia, trade is covered under Australian Treasury Guidelines for Electronic Commerce, and the Australian Competition and Consumer Commission regulates and offers advice on how to deal with businesses online, and offers specific advice on what happens if things go wrong. Also Australian government E-commerce website provides information on E-commerce in Australia.

In the United Kingdom, the FSA (Financial Services Authority) is the competent authority for most aspects of the Payment Services Directive (PSD). The UK implemented the PSD through the Payment Services Regulations 2009 (PSRs), which came into effect on 1 November 2009. The PSR affects firms providing payment services and their customers. These firms include banks, non-bank credit card issuers and non-bank merchant acquirers, E-money issuers, etc. The PSRs created a new class of regulated firms known as payment institutions (PIs), who are subject to prudential requirements.

1.3 E-commerce Procedures

1.3.1 Implementing an E-commerce Solution Using QuikPAY

The customer completes the online e-commerce service request form. Pressing the submit button emails the form to the E-commerce support team.

The E-commerce support team reviews the request and contacts the customer. The E-commerce team schedules a phone call with you. The University's payment processing solution, QuikPAY, introduced from Nelnet Business Solutions (NBS).

If you want to use a vendor-purchased front-end application, the system E-commerce team arranges contact between the vendor and Nelnet Business Solutions. NBS requires you to sign a nondisclosure agreement before you can receive NBS documentation.

If you want to use a payment processing solution other than QuikPAY, provide the Treasurer's Office with vendor contact information, proof of vendor PCI compliance, and application documentation. The Treasurer's Office, Commerce Bank, Information Security & Access Management (ISAM) and the E-commerce team evaluate the vendor product for compliance with the University's E-commerce security guidelines. The Treasurer's Office contacts you within two weeks as to whether the vendor product meets University of Missouri E-commerce requirements.

1. 3. 2　Final Approval for E-commerce Activity from the Treasurer's Office

The E-commerce support team sends information to the customer such as pricing information, E-commerce security guide, Nelnet Business Solutions technical documentation to interface with QuikPAY, pass-through authentication from customer's application to QuikPAY, receipt redirect from QuikPAY to customer's application, code examples of the pass-through authentication and receipt redirect, QuikPAY generic test site URL and nondisclosure agreement (sent to customers using a vendor front-end application), etc.

The E-commerce team schedules the application in a future QuikPAY implementation phase and notifies the customer of the tentative project time frame. The formal implementation typically lasts from six to eight weeks, including testing. You should begin development of the front-end application one or two months prior to the QuikPAY project kick-off. The E-commerce team works with Nelnet Business Solutions schedules the project kick-off meeting and notifies you. Prior to the project kick-off meeting, The E-commerce team sends you the following documents: business requirements checklist, merchant ID request form, and project plan. Then, it requests you to provide a PeopleSoft item type for feeds to PeopleSoft student financials. After that, the customer completes and returns the business requirements checklist and merchant ID request form. During the formal implementation, The E-commerce team works with the Nelnet Business Solutions project manager to complete the project tasks and meet objectives defined in the project time line. Similarly, he needs to submit a request to the Treasurer's Office for a merchant ID and your pay account requests ISAM schedule an audit during the project acceptance testing phase notifies the help desk about the project scope. He also needs to provide accounting information for Nelnet Business Solutions invoice recharge processing downloads a PEM file from YourPay and registers it with QuikPAY. The customer provides QuikPAY API technical support to customers and campus e-commerce contacts and provides QuikPAY API support to their campus customers. Later, he participates in the project status calls.

Normally, the customer modifies the front-end application to transfer data to and receive data from QuikPAY according to the QuikPAY API specifications. He should meet all project deadlines as outlined in the Nelnet Business Solutions project plan. Then, he may require to complete the security documents when requested by ISAM and work with ISAM to meet audit requirements as outlined in the e-commerce security guidelines. Finally, the customer should participate in the project status calls and develops reconciliation procedures.

1. 3. 3   How an E-commerce Credit Card Payment Works

This is an example of how a credit card payment is processed from an E-commerce web application using QuikPAY. The web application could be designed for a variety of business needs, including a shopping cart, conference registration, or to accept donations.

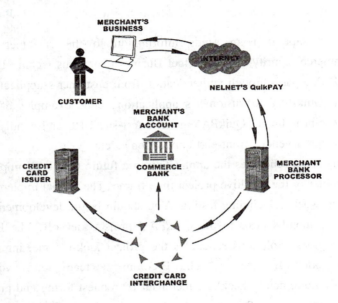

(1) The customer uses a web application to select goods or services for purchase. The customer clicks a "pay now" button to initiate payment.

(2) The customer is transferred to QuikPAY. The customer enters the credit card account number and expiration date. The customer presses the "confirm" button to submit the payment.

(3) QuikPAY passes the transaction to the merchant bank's processor, YourPay.

(4) YourPay submits the transaction to the credit card interchange.

(5) The credit card interchange submits the transaction to the issuer for authorization.

(6) The credit card issuer approves or declines the transaction and passes the results back through the credit card interchange.

(7) The credit card interchange passes the authorization results to YourPay.

(8) YourPay passes the transaction results to QuikPAY.

(9) QuikPAY stores the transaction results and sends them to the web application.

(10) The web application presents a transaction successful or declined message to the customer.

Then, the credit card interchange passes the funds to the University's commerce bank account.

Next, successful transaction information is sent to the University through QuikPAY real-time notification and end-of-day files. The data is stored in the University's oracle databases.

After that, a University process creates feeder files to the general ledger for all QuikPAY transactions and, optionally, to CSAR or PeopleSoft student financials.

By now, QuikPAY transactions are posted to PeopleSoft general ledger.

Finally, when applicable, QuikPAY transactions are posted to PeopleSoft student financial recordings.

2. Application of E-commerce in International Trade

The United Nations Commission on International Trade Law (UNCITRAL) Convention on the Use of Electronic Communications in International Contracts (CUECIC) was adopted on 23 November 2005.

Its essential objective is to establish uniform rules intended to "remove obstacles to the use of electronic communications in international contracts, including obstacles that might result from the operation of existing international trade law instruments, with a view to enhancing legal certainty and commercial predictability." Some common applications related to electronic commerce are the following:

2.1　Document Automation in Supply Chain and Logistics

Document automation is the design of systems and workflows that assist in the creation of electronic documents. These include logic based systems that use segments of pre-existing text and/or data to assemble a new document. This process is increasingly used within certain industries to assemble legal documents, contracts and letters. Document automation systems can also be used to automate all conditional text, variable text, and data contained within a set of documents.

A supply chain is a system of organizations, people, activities, information, and resources involved in moving a product or service from supplier to customer. Supply chain activities transform natural resources, raw materials, and components into a finished product that is delivered to the end customer. In sophisticated supply chain systems, used products may re-enter the supply chain at any point where residual value is recyclable. Supply chains link value chains.

Automation systems allow companies to minimize data entry, reduce the time spent proof-reading, and reduce the risks associated with human error during the documentation process of international settlement. Additional benefits include: savings due to decreased paper handling, document loading, storage, distribution, postage/shipping, faxes, telephone, labor and waste.

2. 2 Electronic Payment

Electronic payment is the term used for any kind of payment processed without using cash or paper checks. An E-commerce payment system facilitates the acceptance of electronic payment for online transactions. Also known as a sample of Electronic Data Interchange (EDI) , E-commerce payment systems have become increasingly popular due to the widespread use of the internet-based shopping and banking. There are numerous different payments systems available for online merchants. These include the traditional credit, debit and charge card but also new technologies such as digital wallets, E-cash, mobile payment and E-checks. Another form of payment system is allowing a third part to complete the online transaction for you. These companies are called Payment Service Providers (PSP) .

When it comes to payment options in E-commerce, nothing is more convenient than electronic payment. You don't have to write a check, swipe a credit or handle any paper money; all you have to do is enter some information into your Web browser and click your mouse. It's no wonder that more and more people are turning to electronic payment—or E-payment—as an alternative to sending checks through the Internet.

Electronic Funds Transfer (EFT) is a system of transferring money from one bank account directly to another without any paper money changing hands. One of the most widely-used EFT programs is Direct Deposit, in which payroll is deposited straight into an employee's bank account, although EFT refers to any transfer of funds initiated through an electronic terminal, including credit card, ATM and point-of-sale (POS) transactions. It is used for both credit transfers, such as payroll payments, and for debit transfers, such as mortgage payments. The growing popularity of EFT for online bill payment is paving the way for a paperless universe where checks, stamps, envelopes, and paper bills are obsolete. The benefit of EFT include reduced administrative costs, increased efficiency, simplified bookkeeping, and greater security. However, the number of companies who send and receive bills through the Internet is still relatively small.

2. 3 Group Buying

Group buying, also known as collective buying, offers products and services at significantly reduced prices on the condition that a minimum number of buyers would make the purchase. Origins of group buying can be traced to China where team buying was executed to get discount prices from retailer when a large group of people were willing to buy the same item. In recent time, group buying websites have emerged as a major player in online shopping business. Typically, these websites feature a "deal of the day", with the deal kicking in once a set number of people agree to buy the product or service. Buyers then print off a voucher to claim their discount at the retailer. Many of the group-buying sites work by negotiating deals with local merchants and promising to deliver crowds in exchange for discounts.

2. 4　Internet Buying and Transactions

Today, the Internet is reshaping the way business transactions are conducted. It is empowering both consumers and businesses by providing expanding markets and choices to not only national, but also int'l communities. It enriches competition in products and prices, and it drives change and improvement, given its ability to provide information and comparative choices.

Buyers looking for the best deals may purchase goods from Singapore, Hong Kong area; China; Argentina or South Africa. With the Internet, the globalization of commerce has arrived, and both consumers and corporations have more choices to address their personal and corporate purchasing requirements. It raises global trade and global economic growth.

The Internet is a vast new frontier of consumer-to-business and business-to-business commerce. For consumers, Internet-based shopping holds an attraction because of its breadth of coverage and ease to use. For corporations, Internet-based commerce represents an as-yet largely untapped medium for expanding and growing of their business.

Putting up a Web site to promote and display products, and then luring online shoppers in to look around at the offerings, however, is only one dimension of conducting business via the Internet. To realize the true potential of electronic commerce, an effective method of receiving payment for products sold or delivered through the Internet is a necessity. Developing and implementing effective and simple "cyber-payment" methods is a major focus of current Internet-related research. While it is currently possible to make purchases over the internet, this form of commerce has not yet gained sufficient popularity to deem it a significant factor in foreign trade. Still, it does have potential.

The ability to order and pay for products over the Internet can revolutionize int'l trade. It can provide purchasers in one country with access to goods and services from another of which they might otherwise not even be aware.

Since many governments restrict imports of certain products and regulate advertising and other marketing tools within their national borders, purchaser are often forced to choose from a limited—or even monopolistic—supply of a desired product. With Internet access, purchasers can scour the world in minutes to find the right product at the best price.

Until recently, however, suppliers used the Internet primarily for advertising purposes. All others were taken either over the telephone or by mail. While this certainly opened the door and paved the way for Internet commerce. It still required that business be conducted through traditional methods. Shopping at these days is easy and convenient with home shopping networks and mail order catalogs. What has been added is Internet shopping. As you surf in the Internet and come across to some vendor's home page you'll be able to purchase commodities.

2. 5　Online Shopping

Online shopping or online retailing is a form of electronic commerce which allows consumers to directly buy goods or services from a seller over the Internet using a web browser. Alternative names are: e-web-store, e-shop, e-store, Internet shop, web-shop, web-store, online store, and virtual store. An online shop evokes the physical analogy of buying products or services at a bricks-and-mortar retailer or shopping center; the process is called business-to-consumer (B2C) online shopping. In the case where a business buys from another business, the process is called business-to-business (B2B) online shopping. The largest of these online retailing corporations are eBay and Amazon.com, both based in the United States. Retail success is no longer all about physical stores, this is evident because of the increase in retailers now offering online store interfaces for consumers. With the growth of online shopping, comes a wealth of new market footprint coverage opportunities for stores that can appropriately cater to offshore market demands and service requirements.

2. 6　Teleconference

A teleconference or teleseminar is the live exchange and mass articulation of information among several persons and machines remote from one another but linked by a telecommunications system. Terms such as audio conferencing, telephone conferencing and phone conferencing are also sometimes used to refer to teleconferencing.

The telecommunications system may support the teleconference by providing one or more of the following: audio, video, and/or data services by one or more means, such as telephone, computer, telegraph, teletypewriter, radio, and television.

In international activities, some negotiation activities may be conducted through teleconference. Therefore, a lot of expenditures can be saved for both parties.

📖 **Words & Expressions**
1. inventory management systems 库存管理系统
2. automated data collection systems 自动化数据采集系统
3. amount spent per capita 人均消费金额
4. Ministry of Commerce 商务部
5. CAN-SPAM Act 反垃圾电子邮件法案
6. FTC Act 联邦贸易委员会法
7. Online Pharmacy Consumer Protection Act 瑞安海特网上药店消费者保护法
8. International Consumer Protection and Enforcement Network (ICPEN) 国际消费者保护

和执法部门网络

9. Electronic Commerce Steering Group 电子商务指导小组

10. Asia Pacific Economic Cooperation（APEC）亚太经合组织

11. privacy regulations 隐私规则

12. Australian Competition and Consumer Commission 澳洲竞争与消费者公署

13. Payment Services Directive（PSD）支付服务指令

14. Financial Services Authority 英国金融业管理局

15. Treasurer's Office 财务科

16. Commerce Bank 商业银行

17. Information Security & Access Management（ISAM）信息安全与访问管理

18. logistics 物流

19. document automation 文档自动化

20. United Nations Commission on International Trade Law（UNCITRAL）联合国国际贸易法律委员会

21. Convention on the Use of Electronic Communications in International Contracts（CUECIC）联合国国际合同使用电子通信公约

22. supply chain 供应链

23. residual value 残值

24. recyclable 可循环的

25. value chains 价值链

26. electronic payment 电子支付

27. Electronic Data Interchange（EDI）电子数据交换

28. Payment Service Providers（PSP）支付服务提供商

29. payment institutions（PIs）支付机构

30. swipe a credit 刷卡

31. Electronic Funds Transfer（EFT）电子资金转移支付

32. payroll 工资单

33. debit transfers 借记划拨

34. mortgage 抵押贷款,按揭

35. stamps 印章

36. paper bills 票据

37. obsolete 废弃

38. bookkeeping,记账

39. group buying 团购

40. voucher 优惠凭证,购物优待券

41. discount 折扣

42. online shopping 网购

43. web browser 网络浏览器

44. virtual store 虚拟商典
45. bricks-and-mortar retailer 实体零售商
46. business-to-consumer（B2C）企业对消费者经营模式
47. business-to-business（B2B）企业对企业经营模式
48. offshore market demands 离岸市场需求
49. teleconference 远程会议
50. teleseminar 远程研讨会
51. audio 音频
52. video 视频
53. data services 数据服务
54. breadth of coverage 种类繁多
55. as-yet 迄今为止
56. untapped medium 未开发的媒介

Exercises

I. True or False

1. In 2010, the United Kingdom had the biggest E-commerce market in the world when measured by the amount spent per capital.
2. In 2012, E-commerce sales topped ＄1 trillion for the first time in history.
3. Electronic commerce, commonly known as E-commerce, is a type of industry where buying and selling of product or service is conducted over electronic systems such as the Internet and other computer networks.
4. The PSRs created a new class of regulated firms known as payment institutions（PIs）, who are not subject to prudential requirements.
5. A supply chain is a system of organizations, people, activities, information, and resources involved in moving a product or service from supplier to customer.
6. Document automation is the design of systems and work-flow that assist in the creation of electronic documents.
7. When it comes to payment options in E-commerce, nothing is less convenient than electronic payment.
8. Collective buying offers products and services at significantly reduced prices on the condition that a minimum number of buyers would make the purchase.
9. Online shopping or online retailing is a form of electronic commerce which allows consumers to directly buy goods or services from a seller over the Internet using a website.
10. Actually, the telecommunications system may not fully support the teleconference by providing one or more of the following: audio, video, and/or data services by one or more

means, such as telephone, computer, telegraph, teletypewriter, radio, and television.

II. Multiple Choice

1. The Czech Republic is the European country where E-commerce delivers the biggest _____ to the enterprises' total revenue.

   A. contribution   B. country   C. target   D. distribution

2. Electronic commerce, commonly known as E-commerce, is a type of industry where buying and selling of product or service is conducted over electronic systems such as the _____ and other computer networks.

   A. channel   B. Internet   C. outlet   D. pipeline

3. APEC has an Electronic Commerce Steering Group as well as working on common _____ regulations throughout the APEC region.

   A. scandal   B. secret   C. privacy   D. information

4. When it comes to _____ in E-commerce, nothing is more convenient than electronic payment.

   A. payment terms   B. remittance   C. clean collection   D. payment options

5. An online shop evokes the physical analogy of buying products or services at a bricks-and-mortar retailer or shopping center; the process is called _____ online shopping.

   A. B2C   B. B2B   C. B2G   D. face-to-face

III. Answer Questions

1. What are the main advantages of document automation?
2. How to define Electronic Fund Transfer?
3. When you are going to do online shopping, what things should you do?

Key to the Exercises

Unit 1
I. 1-5 FTTTT 6-10 TTFTT
II. 1-5 ADCBC 6-10 DADBA

Unit 2
I. 1-5 FTFFT 6-10 FFFFT
II. 1-5 DABCD

Unit 3
I. 1-5 TTFFT 6-10 FTFTF
II. 1-5 DBAAD 6-10 CAADD

Unit 4
I. 1-5 FTTTF 6-10 FTTTT
II. 1-5 DCACA 6-10 DABAA

Unit 5
I. 1-5 TFTTT 6-10 TFTTT
II. 1-5 ABDCA 6-10 ABBBD

Unit 6
I. 1-5 FTFTT 6-10 TTFTT
II. 1-5 ADDAB 6-10 CDADA

Unit 7
I. 1-5 TTFFT 6-10 FTFFT
II. 1-5 BCBCA 6-10 BDBDD

Unit 8
I. 1-5 FFFTT 6-10 FTFTT

II. 1-5   ACABB   6-10   BBACD

Unit 9
I. 1-5   TTFFT   6-10   FFTFF
II. 1-5   ADCAB

Unit 10
I. 1-5   TTTFT   6-10   TFTFF
II. 1-5   ABCDA

Uniform Customs and Practice for Documentary Credits (ICC Publication No. 600)

A. General Provisions and Definitions

Article 1

Application of UCP

The Uniform Customs and Practice for Documentary Credits, 1993 Revision, ICC Publication No. 500, shall apply to all Documentary Credits (including to the extend to which they may be applicable, Standby Letter(s) of Credit where they are incorporated into the text of the Credit. They are binding on all parties thereto, unless otherwise expressly stipulated in the credit.

Article 2

Meaning of Credit

For the purposes of these Articles, the expressions "Documentary Credit(s)" and "Standby Letter(s) of Credit" (hereinafter referred to as Credit(s)), mean any arrangement, however named or described, whereby a bank (the "Issuing Bank") acting at the request and on the instructions of a customer (the "Applicant") or on its own behalf.

i. is to make to payment to or to the order of a third party (the "Beneficiary"), or is to accept and pay bills of exchange (Draft(s)) drawn by the Beneficiary.

or

ii. authorizes another bank to effect such payment, or to accept and pay such bills of exchange (Draft(s)).

iii. authorizes another bank to negotiate, against stipulated documents(s), provided that the terms and conditions of the Credit are complied with.

For the purposes of these Articles, branches of a bank in different countries are considered another bank.

Article 3

Credits v. Contracts

a.Credits, by their nature, are separate transactions from the sales or other contracts(s) on which they may be based and banks are in no way concerned with or bound by such contract(s), even if any reference whatsoever to such contract(s) is included in the Credit. Consequently, the undertaking of a bank to pay, accept and pay Draft(s) or negotiate and/or to fulfill any other obligation under the Credit, is not subject to claims or defences by the Applicant resulting from his relationships with the Issuing Bank or the Beneficiary.

b. A Beneficiary can in no case avail himself of the contractual relationships existing between the banks or between the Applicant and the Issuing Bank.

Article 4

Documents v. Goods/Services/Performances

In credit operations all parties concerned deal with documents, and not with goods, services and/or other performances to which the documents may relate.

Article 5

Instructions to Issue/Amend Credits

a.Instructions for the issuance of a Credit, the Credit itself, instructions for an amendment thereto, and the amendment itself must be complete and precise.

In order to guard against confusion and misunderstanding, banks should discourage any attempt:

i. to include excessive detail in the Credit or in any amendment thereto,

ii. to give instructions to issue, advise or confirm a Credit by reference to a Credit previously issued (similar Credit) where such previous Credit has been subject to accepted amendment(s), and /or unaccepted amendment(s).

b.All instructions for the issuance of a Credit and the Credit itself and, where applicable, all instructions for an amendment thereto and the amendment itself, must state precisely the document(s) against which payment, acceptance or negotiation is to be made.

B. Form and Notification of Credits

Article 6

Revocable v. Irrevocable Credits

a.A Credit may be either

i. revocable,

or

ii. irrevocable

b.The Credit, therefore, should clearly indicate whether it is revocable or irrevocable.

c. In the absence of such indication the Credit shall be deemed to be irrevocable.

Article 7

Advising Bank's Liability

a. A Credit may be advised to a Beneficiary through another bank (the "Advising Bank") Without engagement on the part of the Advising Bank, but that bank, if it elects to advise the Credit, shall take reasonable care to check the apparent authenticity of the Credit which it advises. If the bank elects not to advise the Credit, it must so inform the Issuing Bank without delay.

b. If the Advising Bank cannot establish such apparent authenticity it must inform, without delay, the bank from which the instructions appear to have been received that it has been unable to establish the authenticity of the Credit and if it elects nonetheless to advise the Credit it must inform the Beneficiary that it has not been able to establish the authenticity of the Credit.

Article 8

Revocation of a Credit

a. A Revocable Credit may be amended or canceled by the Issuing Bank at any moment and without prior notice to the Beneficiary.

b. However, the Issuing Bank must:

i. reimburse another bank with which a revocable Credit has been made available for sight payment, acceptance or negotiation for any payment, acceptance or negotiation made by such bank prior to receipt by it of notice of amendment or cancellation, against documents which appear on their face to be in compliance with the terms and conditions of the Credit.

ii. reimburse another bank with which a Revocable Credit has been made available for deferred payment, if such a bank has, prior to receipt by it of notice of amendment or Cancellation, taken up documents which appear on their face to be in compliance with the terms and conditions of the Credit.

Article 9

Liability of Issuing and Confirming Banks

a. An Irrevocable Credit constitutes a definite undertaking of the Issuing Bank, provided that the stipulated documents are presented to the Nominated Bank or to the Issuing Bank and that the terms and conditions of the Credit are complied with:

i. if the Credit provides for sight payment to pay at sight;

ii. if the Credit provides for deferred payment to pay on the maturity date(s) determinable in accordance with the stipulations of the Credit.

iii. if the Credit provides for acceptance:

a. by the Issuing Bank to accept Draft(s) drawn by the Beneficiary on the Issuing Bank and pay them at maturity, or

b. by another drawee bank to accept and pay at maturity Draft(s) drawn by the Beneficiary on the Issuing Bank in the event the drawee bank stipulated in the Credit does not accept Draft(s) drawn on it, or to pay Draft(s) accepted but not paid by such drawee bank at maturity;

iv. if the Credit provides for negotiation to pay without recourse to drawers and/or bona fide holders, Draft(s) drawn by the Beneficiary and/or document(s) presented under the Credit. A Credit should not be issued available by Draft(s) on the Applicant. If the Credit nevertheless calls for Draft(s) on the Applicant, banks will consider such Draft(s) as an additional documents(s).

A confirmation of an Irrevocable Credit by another bank (the "Confirming Bank") upon the authorization or request of the Issuing Bank, constitutes a definite undertaking of the Confirming Bank, in addition to that of the Issuing Bank, provided that the stipulated documents are presented to the Confirming Bank or to any other Nominated Bank and that the terms and condition of the Credit are complied with:

i. if the Credit provides for sight payment to pay at sight;

ii. if the Credit provides for deferred payment to pay on the maturity date(s) determinable in accordance with the stipulations of the Credit;

iii. if the Credit provides for acceptance:

a. by the Confirming Bank to accept Draft(s) drawn by the Beneficiary on the Confirming Bank and pay them at maturity. or

b. by another drawee bank to accept and pay at maturity Draft(s) drawn by the Beneficiary on the Confirming Bank, in the event the drawee bank stipulated in the Credit does not accept Draft(s) drawn on it, or to pay Draft(s) accepted but not paid by such drawee bank at maturity;

c. if the Credit provides for negotiation to negotiate without recourse to drawers and/or bona fide holders, Draft(s) drawn by the Beneficiary and/or document(s) presented under the Credit. A Credit should not be issued available by Draft(s) on the Applicant. If the Credit nevertheless calls for Draft(s) on the Applicant, banks will consider such Draft(s) as an additional document(s).

i if another: bank is authorized or requested by the Issuing Bank to add its confirmation to Credit but is not prepared to do so, it must so inform the Issuing Bank without delay.

ii. unless the Issuing Bank specifies otherwise in its authorization or request to add confirmation, the Advising Bank may advise the Credit to the Beneficiary without adding its confirmation.

d. i.The Issuing Bank shall be irrevocably bound by an amendment(s) issued by it from the time of the issuance of such amendment(s). A Confirming Bank may, extend its confirmation to an amendment and shall be irrevocably bound as of the time of its advice of the amendment. A Confirming Bank may, however, choose to advise an amendment to the Beneficiary without extending its confirmation and if so, must inform the Issuing Bank and the Beneficiary without delay.

ii. The terms of the original Credit (or a Credit incorporating previously accepted amendment(s)) will remain in force for the Beneficiary until the Beneficiary communicates his acceptance of the amendment to the bank that advise such amendment. The Beneficiary should give notification of acceptance or refection of amendment(s). If the Beneficiary fails to give such notification, the tender of documents to the Nominated Bank or Issuing Bank, that conform to the Credit and to not yet accepted amendment(s), will be deemed to be notification of acceptance by the Beneficiary of such amendment(s) and as of that moment the Credit will be amended.

iii. Partial acceptance of amendments contained in one and the same advice of amendment is not allowed and consequently will not be given any effect.

Article 10

Types of Credit

a. All credits must clearly indicate whether they are available, by sight payment, by deferred payment, by acceptance or by negotiation.

b. i. Unless the Credit stipulates that it is available only with the Issuing Bank, all Credits must nominate the bank (the "Nominated Bank") which is authorized to pay, to incur a deferred payment undertaking, to accept Draft(s) or to negotiate. In a freely negotiable Credit, any bank is a Nominated Bank.

ii. Negotiation means the giving of value for Draft(s) and/or document(s) by the bank authorized to negotiate. Mere examination of the documents without giving of value does not constitute a negotiation.

c. Unless the Nominated Bank is the Confirming Bank, nomination by the Issuing Bank does not constitute any undertaking by the Nominated Bank to pay, to incur a deferred payment undertaking, to accept Draft(s), or to negotiate. Except where expressly agreed to by the Nominated Bank's receipt of and/or examination and/or forwarding of the documents does not make that bank liable to pay, to incur a deferred payment undertaking, to accept Draft(s), or to negotiate.

d. By nominating another bank, or by allowing for negotiation by any bank, or by authorizing or requesting another bank to add its confirmation, the Issuing Bank authorizes such bank to pay, accept Draft(s) or negotiate as the case may be, against documents which appear on their face to be in compliance with the terms and conditions of the Credit and undertakes to reimburse such bank in accordance with the provisions of these Articles.

Article 11

Teletransmitted and Pre-advised Credits

a. i. When an Issuing Bank instructs and Advising Bank by an authenticated teletransmission to advise a Credit or an amendment to a Credit, the teletransmission will be deemed to be the operative Credit instrument or the operative amendment, and no mail confirmation should be sent. Should a mail confirmation nevertheless be sent, it will have no effect and the Advising Bank will have no obligation to check such mail confirmation against the operative Credit instrument or the operative amendment received by teletransmission.

ii. If the teletransmission states "full details to follow" (or words of similar effect) or states that the mail confirmation is to be the operative Credit instrument or the operative amendment, then the teletransmission will not be deemed to be the operative Credit instrument or the operative amendment. The Issuing Bank must forward the operative Credit instrument or the operative amendment to such Advising Bank without delay.

a. If a bank uses the service of an Advising Bank to have the Credit advised to the Beneficiary, it must also the services of the same bank for advising and amendment(s).

b. A preliminary advice of the issuance or amendment of an irrevocable Credit (pre-advice), shall only be given by an Issuing Bank if such bank is prepared to issue the operative credit instrument or the operative amendment thereto. Unless otherwise stated in such preliminary advice by the Issuing Bank, an Issuing Bank having given such pre-advice shall be irrevocably committed to issue or amend the Credit, in terms not inconsistent with the pre-advice, without delay.

Article 12

Incomplete or Unclear Instructions

If incomplete or unclear instructions are received to advise, confirm or amend a Credit, the bank requested to act on such instructions may give preliminary notification to the Beneficiary for information only and without responsibility. This preliminary notification should state clearly that the notification is provided for information event, the Advising Bank must inform the Issuing Bank of the action taken and request it to provide the necessary information.

The Issuing Bank must provide the necessary information without delay. The Credit will be advised, confirmed or amended, only when complete and clear instructions have been received and if the Advising Bank is then prepared to act on the instructions.

C. Liabilities and Responsibilities

Article 13

Standard for Examination of Documents

Banks must examine all documents stipulated in the Credit with reasonable care, to ascertain whether or not they appear, on their face, to be in compliance with the terms and conditions of the Credit. Compliance of the stipulated documents on their face with the terms and conditions of the Credit, shall be determined by international standard banking practice as reflected in these Articles. Documents which appear on their face to be inconsistent with one another will be considered as not appearing on their face to be in compliance with the terms and conditions of the Credit.

Documents not stipulated in the Credit will not be examined by banks. If they receive such documents, they shall return them to presenter or pass them on without responsibility.

a. The Issuing Bank, the Confirming Bank, if any, or a Nominated Bank acting on their behalf, shall each have a reasonable time, not to exceed seven banking days following the day of receipt of the documents to examine the documents and determine whether to take up or refuse the documents and to inform the party from which it received the documents accordingly.

b. If a Credit contains conditions without stating the document(s) to be presented in compliance therewith, banks will deem such conditions as not stated and will disregard them.

Article 14

Discrepant Documents and Notice

a. When the Issuing Bank authorities another bank to pay, incur a deferred payment undertaking, accept Draft(s), or negotiate against documents which appear on their face to be in compliance with the terms and conditions of the Credit, the Issuing Bank and the Confirming Bank, if any, are bound:

i. to reimburse the Nominated Bank which has paid, incurred a deferred payment.

a. Upon receipt of the documents the Issuing Bank and/or Confirming Bank, if any, or a Nominated Bank acting on their behalf, must determine on the basis of the documents alone whether or not they appear on their face to be in compliance with the terms and conditions of the Credit. If the documents appear on their face not to be in compliance with the terms and conditions of the Credit, such banks may refuse to take up the documents.

b. If the Issuing Bank determines that the documents appear on their face not to be in compliance with the terms and conditions of the Credit, it may in its sole judgment approach the Applicant for a waiver of the discrepancy(ies). This does not, however, extend the period mentioned in sub-Article 13 (b).

a. i. If the Issuing Bank and/or Confirming Bank, if any, or a Nominated Bank acting on their behalf, decides to refuse the documents, it must give notice to that effect by telecommunication or, if that is not possible, by other expeditions means, without delay but on later than the close of the seventh banking day following the day of receipt of the documents. Such notice shall be given to the bank from which it received the documents, or to the Beneficiary, if it received the documents directly from him.

ii. Such notice must state all discrepancies in respect of which the bank refuses the documents and must also state whether it is holding the documents at the disposal of, or is returning them to the presenter.

iii. The Issuing Bank and/or Confirming Bank, if any, shall then be entitled to claim from the remitting bank refund, with interest, of any reimbursement which has been made to that bank.

a. If the Issuing Bank and/or Confirming Bank, if any, fails to act in accordance with the provisions of this Article and/or fails to hold the documents at the disposal of, or return them to the presenter, the Issuing Bank and/or Confirming Bank, if any, shall be preclude from claiming that the documents are not in compliance with the terms and conditions of the Credit.

b. If the Remitting Bank draws the attention of the Issuing Bank and/or Confirming Bank, if any, to any discrepancy(ies) in the document(s) or advises such banks that it has paid, incurred a deferred payment undertaking, accepted Draft(s) or negotiated under reserve or against an indemnity in respect of such discrepancy(ies), the Issuing Bank and/or Confirming Bank, if any, shall not be thereby relieved from any of their obligations under any provision of the Article. Such reserve or indemnity concerns only the relations between the remitting bank and the party towards whom the reserve was made, or from whom, or on whose behalf, the indemnity was obtained.

Article 15

Disclaimer on Effectiveness of Documents

Banks assume no liability or responsibility for the form, sufficiency, accuracy genuineness, falsification or legal effect of any document(s), or for the general and/or particular conditions stipulated in the document(s) or superimposed thereon; nor do they assume any liability or responsibility for the description, quantity, weight, quality, condition, packing, delivery, value of existence of the goods represented by any document(s), or for the good faith or acts and/or omissions, solvency, performance or standing of the consignors, the carriers the forwarders, the consignees or the insurers of the goods, or any other person whomsoever.

Article 16

Disclaimer on the Transmission of Messages

Banks assume no liability or responsibility for the consequences arising out of delay and/or loss in transit of any message(s), letter(s) or document(s), or for delay, mutilation or other error(s) arising in the transmission of any telecommunication. Banks assume no liability or responsibility for errors in translation and/or interpretation of technical terms, and reserve the right to transmit Credit terms without translating them.

Article 17

Force Majeure

Banks assume no liability or responsibility for the consequences arising out of the interruption of their business by Acts of Good, riots civil commotions, insurrections, wars or any other causes beyond their control, or by any strikes or lockouts. Unless specifically authorized, banks will not, upon resumption of their business, pay, incur a deferred payment undertaking, accept Draft(s) or negotiate under Credits which expired during such interruption of their business.

Article 18

Disclaimer for Acts of an Instructed Party

a. Banks utilizing the services of another bank or other banks for the purpose of giving effect to the instructions of the applicant do so for the account and at the risk of such Applicant.

b. Banks assume no liability or responsibility should the instructions they transmit not be carried out, even if they have themselves taken the initiative in the choice of such other bank (s).

c. i. A party instructing another party to perform services is liable for any charges, including commissions, fees, costs or expenses incurred by the instructed party in connection with its instructions.

ii. Where a Credit stipulates that such charges are for the account of a party other than the instructing party, and charges cannot be collected, the instructing party remains ultimately liable for the payment thereof.

d. The Applicant shall be bound by and liable to indemnify the banks against all obligations and responsibilities imposed by foreign laws and usages.

Article 19

Bank-to-Bank Reimbursement Arrangements

a. If an Issuing Bank intends that the reimbursement to which a paying, accepting or negotiating bank is entitled, shall be obtained by such bank (the "Claiming Bank"), claiming on another party (the "Reimbursing Bank"), it shall provide such Reimbursing Bank in good time with the proper Instructions or authorization to honor such reimbursement claims.

b. Issuing Banks shall not require a Claiming Bank to supply a certificate of compliance with the terms and conditions of the Credit to the Reimbursing Bank.

c. An Issuing Bank shall not be relieved from any obligations when reimbursement is not received by the Claiming Bank from the Reimbursing Bank,

d. The Issuing Bank shall be responsible to the Claiming Bank for any loss to interest If reimbursement is not provided by the Reimbursing Bank on first demand, or as otherwise specified in the Credit, or mutually agreed, as the case may be.

e. The Reimbursing Bank's charges should be for the account of the Issuing Bank. However, in cases where the charges are for the account of another party, it is the responsibility of the Issuing Bank to so indicate in the original Credit and in the reimbursement authorization. In cases where the Reimbursing Bank's charges are for the account of another party they shall be collected from the Claiming Bank when the Credit is drawn under. In cases where the Credit is not drawn under, the Reimbursing Bank's charges remain the obligation of the Issuing Bank.

D. Documents

Article 20

Ambiguity as to the Issuers of Documents

a. Terms such as "first class", "well-known", "qualified", "independent", "official"." competent", "local" and the like, shall not be used to describe the issuers of any document(s) to be presented under a Credit. If such terms are incorporated in the Credit banks will accept the relative document(s) as presented, provided that it appears on its face to be in compliance with the other terms and conditions of the Credit and not to have been issued by the Beneficiary.

b. Unless otherwise stipulated in the Credit, banks will also accept as an original document (s), a document(s) produced or appearing to have been produced:

a. By reprographic, automated or computerized systems;

b. As carbon copies;

Provided that it is marked as original and, where necessary, appears to be signed. A document may be signed by handwriting, by facsimile signature, by perforated signature, by stamp, by symbol, or by any other mechanical or electronic method of authentication.

i. Unless otherwise stipulated in the Credit, banks will accept as a copy(ies), a document (s) either labeled copy or not marked as an original a copy(ies) need not be signed.

ii. Credits that require multiple document(s) such as "duplicate", "two fold", "two copies" and the like, will be satisfied by the presentation of one original and the remaining number in copies except where the document itself indicates otherwise.

c. Unless otherwise stipulated in the Credit, a condition under a Credit calling for a document to be authenticated, validated, legalized, visaed, certified or indicating a similar requirement, will be satisfied by any signature, mark, stamp or label on such document that on its face appears to satisfy the above condition.

Article 21

Unspecified Issuers or Contents of Documents

When documents other than transport documents, insurance documents and commercial invoices are called for, the Credit should stipulate by whom such documents are to be issued and their wording or data content. If the Credit does not so stipulate, banks will accept such documents as presented, provided that their data content is not inconsistent with any other stipulated document presented.

Article 22

Issuance Date of Documents v. Credit Date

Unless otherwise stipulated in the Credit, banks will accept a document bearing a date of issuance prior to that of the Credit, subject to such document being presented within the time limits set out in the Credit and in these Articles.

Article 23

Marine/Ocean Bill of Lading

If a Credit calls for a bill of lading covering a port-to-port shipment, banks will, unless otherwise stipulated in the Credit, accept a document , however named, which :

i. appears on its face to indicate the name of the carrier and to have been signed or otherwise authenticated by :

—the carrier of a named agent for or on behalf of the carrier, or

—the master of a named agent for or on behalf of the master,

Any signature or authentication of the carrier or master must be identified as carrier of master, as the case may be. An agent signing or authenticating for the carrier or master must also indicate the name and the capacity of the party, i. e. carrier or master, on whose behalf that agent is acting;

And

ii. indicates that the goods have been loaded on board, or shipped on a named vessel. Loading on board or shipment on a named vessel may be indicated by preprinted wording on the bill of lading that the goods have been loaded on board a named vessel or shipped on a named vessel. In which case the date of issuance of the bill of lading will be deemed to be the date of loading on board and the date of shipment.

In all other cases loading on board a named vessel must be evidenced by a notation on the bill of lading which gives the date on which the goods have been loaded on board, in which case the date of the on board notation will be deemed to be the date of shipment.

If the bill of lading contains the indication "intended vessel" , or similar qualification in relation to the vessel, loading on board a named vessel must be evidenced by an on board notation on the bill of lading which, in addition to the date on which the goods have been loaded on board, also includes the name of the vessel on which the goods have been loaded, even if they have been loaded on the vessel named as the "intended vessel".

If the bill of lading indicates a place of receipt or taking in charge different from the port of loading, the on board notation must also include the pout of loading stipulated in the Credit and the name of the vessel on which the goods have been loaded, even if they have been loaded on the vessel named in the bill of lading. This provision also applies whenever loading on board the vessel is indicated by pre printed wording on the bill of lading.

iii. indicates the port of loading and the port of discharge stipulated in the Credit, notwithstanding that it:

a. indicates a place of taking in charge different from the port of loading, and/or a port of destination different from the port of discharge, and/or

b. contains the indication "intended" or similar qualification in relation to the port of loading and/or port of discharge, as long as the document also states the ports of loading and/or discharge stipulated in the document also states the ports of loading and /or discharge stipulated in the Credit, and

iv. consists of a sole original bill of lading or, if issued in more than on original, the full set as so issued, and

v. appears to contain all of the terms and conditions of carriage, or some of such terms and conditions by reference to a source or document other than the bill of lading (short form/blank back bill of lading); banks will not examine the contents of such terms and conditions, and

vi. contains no indication that it is subject to a charter party and/or no indication hat he carrying vessel is propelled by sail only, and

vii. in all other respects meets the stipulations of the Credit.

b. For the purpose of this Article, transshipment means unloading and reloading from one vessel to another vessel during the courses of ocean carriage from the port of loading to the port of discharge stipulated in the Credit.

c. Unless transshipment is prohibited by the terms or the Credit, banks will accept a bill of lading which indicates that he goods will be transshipped, provided that the entire ocean carriage is covered by one and the same bill of lading.

d. Even if the Credit prohibits transshipment, banks will accept a bill of lading which:

i. indicates that transshipment will take place as long as the relevant cargo is shipped in Container(s), Trailer(s) and/or "LASTH" barge(s) as evidenced by the bill of lading, provide that the entire ocean carriages covered by one and the same bill of lading, provided that the entire ocean carriages covered by one and the same bill of lading, and/or

ii. incorporates clauses stating that the carrier reserves the right to transship.

Article 24

Non-negotiable Sea Waybill

a. If a Credit calls for a non-negotiable sea waybill covering a port-to-port shipment, banks will, unless otherwise stipulated in the Credit, accept a document, however named, which:

i. appears on its face to indicate the name of the carrier and to have been signed or otherwise authenticated by:

—the carrier or a named agent for of on behalf of the carrier, or

—the master or a named agent for of on behalf of the master.

Any signature or authentication of the carrier or maser must be identified as carrier or master, as the case may be. An agent signing or authenticating for the carrier or master must also indicate the name and the capacity of the party, i. e. carrier or master, on whose behalf that agent is acting, and

ii. indicates that the goods have been loaded on board, or shipped on a named vessel.

Loading on board or shipment on a named vessel may be indicated by pre-printed wording on the non-negotiable sea way bill that the goods have been loaded on board a named vessel or shipped on a named vessel, in which case the date of loading on board and the date of shipment.

In all other cases loading on board a named vessel must be evidenced by a notation on the non-negotiable sea way bill which gives the date on which the goods have been loaded on board, in which case the date of the on board notation will be deemed to be the date of shipment.

If the non-negotiable sea waybill contains the indication "intended vessel", or similar qualification in relation to the vessel, loading on board a named vessel must be evidenced by an on board notation on the non-negotiable sea waybill which, in addition to the date on which the goods have been loaded on board, includes the name of the vessel on which the goods have been loaded, even if they have been loaded on the vessel named as the "intended vessel".

If the non-negotiable sea waybill indicates a place of receipt or taking in charge different from the port of loading, the on board notation must also include the port of loading stipulated in the Credit and the name of the vessel on which the goods have been loaded, even if they have been loaded on a vessel named in the non-negotiable sea waybill. This provision also applies whenever loading on board the vessel is indicated by pre-printed wording on the non-negotiable sea waybill, and

iii. indicates the port of loading and the port of discharge stipulated in the Credit, notwithstanding that it:

a. indicates a place of taking in charge different from the port of loading, and/or a place of final destination different from the port of discharge, and/or

b. contains the indication "intended" or similar qualification in relation to the port of loading and/or port of discharge, as long as the document also states the ports of loading and/or discharge stipulated in the Credit, and

iv. consists of a sole original non-negotiable sea waybill, or if issued in more than one original, the full set as so issued, and

v. appears to contain all of the terms and conditions of carriage, or some of such terms and condition by reference to a source of document other than the non-negotiable sea waybill (short form/blank back non-negotiable sea waybill); banks will not examine the contents of such terms and conditions, and

vi. contains no indication that it is subject to a charter party and/or no indication that the carrying vessel is propelled by sail only, and

vii. in all other respects meets the stipulations of the Credit.

a. For the purpose of this Article, transshipment means unloading and reloading from one vessel to another vessel during the course of ocean carriage from the port of loading to the port of discharge stipulated in the Credit.

b. Unless transshipment is prohibited by the terms of the Credit, banks will accept a non-negotiable sea waybill which indicates that the goods will be transshipped, provided that the entire ocean carriage is covered by one and the same non-negotiable sea waybill.

c. Even if the Credit prohibits transshipment, banks will accept a non-negotiable sea waybill which:

i. indicates that transshipment will take place as long as the relevant cargo is shipped in Container(s), Trailer(s) and/or "LASH" barge(s) as evidenced by the non-negotiable sea waybill, provided that the entire ocean carriage is covered by one and the same non-negotiable sea waybill, and/or

ii. incorporates clauses stating that the carrier reserves the right to tranship.

Article 25

Charter Party Bill of Lading

a. If a Credit calls for or permits a charter party bill of lading banks will, unless otherwise stipulated in the Credit, accept a document, however named, which:

i. contains any indication that it is subject to a charter party, and

ii. appears on its face to have been signed or otherwise authenticated by:

—the master or a named agent for or on behalf of the master, or

—the owner or a named agent for or on behalf of the owner.

Any signature or authentication of the master or owner must be identified as master or owner as the case may be. An agent signing or authenticating for the master or owner must also indicate the name and the capacity of the party, i. e. master or owner, on whose behalf that agent is acting, and

i. does or does not indicate the name of the carrier, and

ii. indicates that the goods have been loaded on board or shipped on a named vessel. Loading on board or shipment on a named vessel may be indicated by pre-printed wording on the bill of lading that the goods have been loaded on board a named vessel or shipped on a named vessel, in which case the date of issuance of the bill of lading will be deemed to be the date of loading on board and the date of shipment.

In all other cases loading on board a named vessel must be evidenced by a notation on the bill of lading which gives the date on which the goods have been loaded on board, in which case the date of the on board notation will be deemed to be the date of shipment, and

i. indicates the port of loading and the port of discharge stipulated in the Credit, and

ii. consists of a sole original bill of lading or, if issued in more than one original, the full set as so issued, and

iii. contains no indication that the carrying vessel is propelled by sail only, and

iv. in all other respects meets the stipulations of the Credit.

Even if the Credit requires the presentation of a charter party contract in connection with a charter party bill of lading, banks will not examine such charter party contract, but will pass it on without responsibility on their part.

Article 26

Multimodal Transport Document

a. If a Credit calls for a transport document covering at least two different modes of transport (multimodal transport), banks will, unless otherwise stipulated in the Credit, accept a document, however named, which:

i. appears on its face to indicate the name of the carrier or multimodal transport operator and to have been signed or otherwise authenticated by:

—the carrier or multimodal transport operator or a named agent for or on behalf of the carrier or multimodal transport operator, or

—the master or a named agent for or on behalf of the master.

Any signature or authentication of the carrier, multimodal transport operator or master must be identified as carrier, multimodal transport operator or master, as the case may be. An agent signing of authenticating for the carrier, multimodal transport operator or master must also indicate the name and the capacity of the party, i. e. carrier, multimodal transport operator or master, on whose behalf that the agent is acting, and

i. indicates that the goods have been dispatched, taken in charge or loaded on board.

Dispatch, taking in charge or loading on board may be indicated by wording to that effect on the multimodal transport document and the date of issuance will be deemed to be the date of dispatch, taking in charge or loading on board and the date of shipment. However, if the document indicates, by stamp or otherwise, a date of dispatch, taking in charge or loading on board, such date will be deemed to be the date of shipment, and

ii. (a) indicates the place of taking in charge stipulated in the Credit which may be different from the port, airport or place of loading, and the place of final destination stipulated in the Credit which may be different from the port, airport or place of discharge, and/or

(b) contains the indication "intended" or similar qualification in relation to the vessel and/or port of loading and/or port of discharge, and

iii. consists of a sole original multimodal transport document or, in issued in more than one original, the full set as so issued, and

iv. appears to contain all of the terms and conditions of carriage, or some of such terms and conditions by reference to a source or document other than the multimodal transport document (short form/blank back multimodal transport document); banks will not examine the contents of such terms and conditions, and

v. contains no indication that it is subject to a charter party and/or no indication that the carrying vessel is propelled by sail only, and

vi. in all other respects meets the stipulations of the Credit.

vii. even if the Credit prohibits transshipment, banks will accept a multimodal transport document which indicates that transshipment will or may take place, provided that the entire carriage is covered by one and the same multimodal transport document.

Article 27

Air Transport Document

a. If a Credit calls for an air transport document, banks will, unless otherwise stipulated in the Credit, accept a document, however named, which:

i. appears on its face to indicate the name of the carrier and to have been signed or otherwise authenticated by:

—the carrier, or

—a named agent for or on behalf of the carrier.

Any signature or authentication of the carrier must be identified as carrier. An agent signing or authenticating for the carrier must also indicate the name and the capacity of the party, i. e. carrier, on whose behalf that agent is acting, and

ii. indicates that the goods have been accepted fro carriage. and

iii. where the Credit calls for and actual date of dispatch, indicates a specific notation of such date, the date of dispatch so indicated on the air transport document will be deemed to be the date of shipment.

For the purpose of this Article, the information appearing in the box on the air transport document (marked "For Carrier Use Only" or similar expression) relative to the flight number and date will not be considered as a specific notation of such date of dispatch.

In all other cases, the date of issuance of the air transport document will be deemed to be the date of shipment, and

iv. indicates the airport of departure and the airport of destination stipulated in the Credit, and

v. appears to be the original for consignor/shipper even if the Credit stipulates an full set of originals, or similar expressions, and

vi. appears to contain all of the terms and conditions of carriage, or some of such terms and conditions, by reference to a source or document other than the air transport document; banks will not examine the contents of such terms and conditions, and

vii. in all other respects meets the stipulations of the Credit.

a. for the purpose of this Article, transshipment means unloading and reloading from one air reloading from one aircraft to another aircraft during the course of carriage form the airport of departure to the airport of destination stipulated in the Credit.

b. even if the Credit prohibits transshipment, banks will accept an air transport document which indicates that transshipment will or may take place, provided that the entire carriage is covered by one and the same air transport document.

Article 28

Road, Rail or Inland Waterway Transport Documents

a. If a Credit calls for a road, rail, or inland waterway transport document, banks will, unless otherwise stipulated in the Credit, accept a document of the type called for, however named, which:

i. appears on its face to indicate the name of the carrier and to have been signed or otherwise authenticated by the carrier or a named agent for or on behalf of the carrier and/or to bear a reception stamp or other indication of receipt by the carrier or a named agent for or on behalf of the carrier.

Any signature, authentication, reception stamp or other indication of receipt of the carrier, must be identified on its face as that of the carrier. An agent signing or authenticating for the carrier, must also indicate the name and the capacity of the party, i. e. carrier, on whose behalf that agent is acting, and

ii. indicates that the goods have been received for shipment, dispatch or carriage or wording to this effect. The date of issuance will be deemed to be the date of shipment unless the transport document contains a reception stamp, in which case the date of the reception stamp will be deemed to be the date of shipment, and

iii. indicates the place of shipment and the place of destination stipulated in the Credit, and

iv. in all other respects meets the stipulations of the Credit.

b. in the absence of any indication on the transport document as to the numbers issued, banks will accept the transport document(s) presented as constituting a full set. Banks will accept as original(s) the transport document(s) whether marked as original(s) or not.

c. for the purpose of this Article, transshipment means unloading and reloading from one means of conveyance to another means of conveyance, in different modes of transport, during the course of carriage from the place of shipment to the place of destination stipulated in the Credit.

d. even if the Credit prohibits transshipment, banks will accept a road, rail, or inland waterway transport document which indicates that transshipment will or may take place, provided that the entire carriage is covered by one and the same transport document and within the same mode of transport.

Article 29
Courier and Post Receipts
a. If a Credit calls for a post receipt or certificate of posting, banks will, unless otherwise stipulated in the Credit, accept a post receipt or certificate of posting which:

i. appears on its face to have been stamped or otherwise authenticated and dated in the place from which the Credit stipulates the goods are to be shipped or dispatched and such date will be deemed to be the date of shipment or dispatch, and

ii. in all other respects meets the stipulations of the Credit.

b. If a Credit calls for a document issued by a courier or expedited delivery service evidencing receipt of the goods for delivery, banks will, unless otherwise stipulated in the Credit, accept a document, however named, which:

i. appears on its face to indicate the name of the courier/service, and to have been stamped, signed or otherwise authenticated by such named courier/service (unless the Credit specifically calls for a document issued by a named Courier/Service, banks will accept a document issued by any Courier/Service), and

ii. indicates a date of pick-up or of receipt or wording to this effect, such date being deemed to be the date of shipment or dispatch, and

iii. in all other respects meets the stipulations of the Credit.

Article 30
Transport Documents Issued by Freight Forwarders
Unless otherwise authorized in the Credit, banks will only accept a transport document issued by a freight forwarder if it appears on its face to indicate:

i. the name of the freight forwarder as a carrier or multimodal transport operator and to have been signed or otherwise authenticated by the freight forwarder as carrier or multimodal transport operator, or

ii. the name of the carrier or multimodal transport operator and to have been singed or otherwise authenticated by the freight forwarder as a named agent for or on behalf of the carrier or multimodal transport operator.

Article 31
"On Deck", "Shipper's Load and Count", Name of Consignor
Unless otherwise stipulated in the Credit, banks will accept a transport document which:

i. does not indicate, in the case of carriage by sea or by more than one means of conveyance including carriage by sea, that the goods are or will be loaded on deck. Nevertheless, banks will accept a transport document which contains a provision that the goods may be carried on deck, provided that it does not specifically state that they are or will be loaded on deck, and/or

    ii. bears a clause on the face thereof such as "shipper's load and count" or "said by shipper to contain" or words of similar effect, or

    iii. indicates as the consignor of the goods a party other than the Beneficiary of the Credit.

Article 32

Clean Transport Documents

    a. A clean transport document is one which bears no clause or notation which expressly declares a defective condition of the goods and/or the packaging.

    b. Banks will not accept transport documents bearing such clauses or notations unless the Credit expressly stipulates the clauses or notations which may be accepted.

    c. Banks will regard a requirement in a Credit for a transport document to bear the clause "clean on board" as complied with if such transport document meets the requirements of this Article and of Articles 23, 24, 25, 26, 27, 28 or 30.

Article 33

Freight Payable/Prepaid Transport Documents

    a. Unless otherwise stipulated in the Credit, or inconsistent with any of the documents presented under the Credit, banks will accept transport documents stating that freight or transportation charges (hereafter referred to as "freight") have still to be paid.

    b. If a Credit stipulates that the transport document has to indicate that freight has been paid or prepaid, banks will accept a transport document on which words clearly indicating payment or prepayment of freight appear by stamp or otherwise or on which payment or prepayment of freight is indicated by other means. If the Credit requires courier charges to be paid or prepaid banks will also accept a transport document issued by a courier or expedited delivery service evidencing that courier charges are for the account of a party other than the consignee.

    c. The words "freight prepayable" or "freight to be prepaid" or words of similar effect, if appearing on transport documents, will not be accepted as constitution evidence of the payment of freight.

    d. Banks will accept transport documents bearing reference by stamp or otherwise to costs additional to the freight, such as coasts of, or disbursements incurred in connection with, loading, unloading or similar operations, unless the conditions of the Credit specifically prohibit such reference.

Article 34

Insurance Documents

a. Insurance documents must appear on their face to be issued and signed by insurance signed by insurance companies or underwriters or their agents.

b. If the insurance document indicates that it has been issued in more than one original, all the originals must be presented unless otherwise authorized in the Credit,

c. Cover notes issued by brokers will not be accepted, unless specifically authorized in the Credit.

d. Unless otherwise stipulated in the Credit, banks will accept an insurance certificate or a declaration under an open cover presigned by insurance companies or underwriters or their agents. If a Credit specifically calls for an insurance certificate or a declaration under an open cover, banks will accept, in lieu thereof, an insurance policy.

e. Unless otherwise stipulated in the Credit, or unless it appears from the insurance document that the cover is effective at the latest from the date of loading on board or dispatch or taking in charge of the goods, banks will not accept an insurance document which bears a date of issuance later than the date of loading on board or dispatch or taking in charge as indicated in such transport document.

f. i. unless otherwise stipulated in the Credit, the insurance document must be expressed in the same currency as the Credit.

ii. unless otherwise stipulated in the Credit, the minimum amount for which the insurance document must indicate the insurance cover to have been effected is the CIF (cost, issuance and freight(… "named port of destination")) or CIP (carriage and insurance paid to (… "named place of destination")) value of the goods, as the case may be, plus 10%, but only when the CIF or CIP value can be determined from the documents on their face. Otherwise, banks will accept as such minimum amount 110% of the amount for which payment, acceptance or negotiation is requested under the Credit, or 110% of the gross amount of the invoice, whichever is the greater.

Article 35

Type of Insurance Cover

a. Credits should stipulate the type of insurance required and, if any, the additional risks which are to be covered. Imprecise terms such as "usual risks" or "customary risks" shall not be used; if they are used, banks will accept insurance documents as presented, without responsibility for any risks not being covered.

b. Failing specific stipulations in the Credit, banks will accept insurance documents as presented, without responsibility for any risks not being covered.

c. Unless otherwise stipulated in the Credit, banks will accept an insurance document which indicates that the cover is subject to a franchise or an excess (deductible).

Article 36

All Risks Insurance Cover

Where a Credit stipulates "insurance against all risks", banks will accept an insurance document which contains any "all risks" notation or clause, whether or not bearing the heading "all risks", even if the insurance document indicates that certain risks are excluded, without responsibility for any risk(s) not being covered.

Article 37

Commercial Invoices

a. Unless otherwise stipulated in the Credit, commercial invoices:

i. must appear on their face to be issued by the Beneficiary named in the Credit (except as provided in Article 48),

and

ii. must be made out in the name of the Applicant (except as provided in sub-Article 48(h)), and

iii. need not be signed

b. Unless otherwise stipulated in the Credit, banks may refuse commercial invoices issued fro amounts in excess of the amount permitted by the Credit. Nevertheless, if a bank authorized to pay, incur a deferred payment undertaking, accept Draft(s), or negotiate under a Credit accepts such invoices, its decision will be binding upon all parties, provided that such bank ahs not paid, incurred a deferred payment undertaking, accepted Draft(s) or negotiated for an amount in excess of that permitted by the Credit.

c. The description of the goods in the commercial invoice must correspond with the description in the Credit. In all other documents, the goods may be described in general terms not inconsistent with the description of the goods in the Credit.

Article 38

Other Documents

If a credit calls fro an attestation or certification of weight in the case of transport other than by sea, banks will accept a weight stamp or declaration of weight which appears to have been superimposed on the transport document by the carrier or his agent unless the Credit specifically stipulated that the attestation or certification of weight must be by means of a separate document.

E. Miscellaneous Provisions

Article 39

Allowances in Credit Amount, Quantity and Unit Price

a. The words " about ", " approximately ", " circa " or similar expressions used in connection with the amount of the Credit or the quantity or the unit price stated in the Credit are to be constructed as allowing a difference not to exceed 10% more or 10% less than the amount or the quantity or the unit price to which they refer.

b. Unless a Credit stipulates that the quantity of the goods specified must not exceeded or reduced, a tolerance of 5% more or 5% drawings does not exceed the amount of the Credit. This tolerance does not apply when the Credit stipulates the quantity in terms of a stated number of packing units or individual items.

c. Unless a Credit which prohibits partial shipments stipulates otherwise, or unless sub-Article (b) above is applicable, a tolerance of 5% less in the amount of the drawing will be permissible, provided that if the Credit stipulates the quantity of the goods, such quantity of goods in shipped in full, and if the Credit stipulates a unit price, such price is not reduced. This provision does not apply when expression referred to in sub-Article (a) above are used in the Credit.

Article 40

Partial Shipments/Drawings

a. Partial drawing and/or shipments are allowed, unless the Credit stipulates otherwise.

b. Transport documents which appear on their face to indicate that shipment has been made on the same means of conveyance and for the same journey, provided they indicate the same destination, will not be regarded as covering partial shipments, even if the transport documents indicate different dates of shipment and/or different ports of loading, places of taking in charge, or dispatch.

c. Shipments made by post or by courier will not be regarded as partial shipments if the post receipts or certificates of posting or courier's receipts or dispatch notes appear to have been stamped, signed or otherwise authenticated in the place from which the Credit stipulates the goods are to be dispatched, and on the same date.

Article 41

Installment Shipments/Drawings

If drawing and/or shipments by installments within given periods are stipulated in the Credit and any installment is not drawn and/or shipped within the period allowed for that installment, the Credit ceases to be available for that and any subsequent instalments, unless otherwise stipulated in the Credit.

Article 42

Expiry Date and Place for Presentation of Documents

a. All Credits must stipulate an expiry date and a place for presentation of documents for payment, acceptance, or with the exception of freely negotiable Credits, a place for presentation of documents for negotiation. An expiry date stipulated for payment, acceptance or negotiation will be constructed to express and expiry date for presentation of documents.

b. Except as provided in sub-Article 44(a), documents must be presented on or before such expiry date.

c. If an Issuing Bank states that the Credit is to be available "for one month", "for six months", or the like, but does not specify the date from which the time is to run, the date of issuance of the Credit by the Issuing Bank will be deemed to be the first day from which such time is to run, Banks should discourage indication of the expiry date of the Credit in this manner.

Article 43

Limitation on the Expiry Date

a. In addition to stipulating an expiry date for presentation of documents, every Credit which calls for a transport document(s) should also stipulate a specified period of time after the date of shipment during which presentation must be made in compliance with the terms and conditions of the Credit. If no such period of time is stipulated, banks will not accept documents presented to them later than 21 days after the date of shipment. In any event, documents must be presented not later than the expiry date of the Credit.

b. In cases in which sub-Article 40(b) applies, the date of shipment will be considered to be the latest shipment date on any of the transport documents presented.

Article 44

Extension of Expiry Date

a. If the expiry date of the Credit and/or the last day of the period of time for presentation of documents stipulated by the Credit or applicable by virtue of Article 43 falls on a day on which the bank to which presentation has to be made is closed for reasons other than those referred to in Article 17, the stipulated expiry date and/or the last day of the period of time after the date of shipment for presentation of documents, as the case may be, shall be extended to the first following day on which such bank is open.

b. The latest date for shipment shall not be extended by reason of the extension of the expiry date and/or the period of time after the date of shipment for presentation of documents in accordance with sub-Article (a) above. In no such latest date for shipment is stipulated in the Credit or amendments thereto, banks will not accept transport documents indicating a date of shipment later than the expiry date stipulated in the Credit or amendments thereto.

c. The bank to which presentation is made on such first following business day must provide a statement that the documents were presented within the time limits extended in accordance with sub-Article 44 (a) of the Uniform Customs and Practice for Documentary Credits, 1993 Revision, ICC Publication No. 500.

Article 45

Hours of Presentation

Banks are under no obligation to accept presentation of documents outside their banking hours.

Article 46

General Expressions as to Dates for Shipment.

a. Unless otherwise stipulated in the Credit, the expression "shipment" used in stipulating an earliest and/or a latest date for shipment will be understood to include expressions such as, "loading on board", "dispatch", "accepted for carriage", "date of post receipt", "date of pick up", and the like, and in the case of a Credit calling for a multimodal transport document the expression "taking in charge".

b. Expressions such as "prompt", "immediately", "as soon as possible", and the like should not be used. If they are used banks will disregard them.

c. If the expression "on or about" or similar expressions are used, banks will interpret them as a stipulation that shipment is to be made during the period from five days before to five days after the specified date, both end days included.

Article 47

Date Terminology for Periods of Shipment

a. The words "to", "until", "till", "from" and words of similar import applying to any date or period in the Credit referring to shipment will be understood to include the date mentioned.

b. The word "after" will be understood to exclude the date mentioned.

c. The terms "first half", "second half" of a month shall be construed respectively as the 1st to the 15th, and the 16th to the last day of such month, all dates inclusive.

d. The terms "beginning", "middle", or "end" of a month shall be construed respectively as the 1st to the 10th, the 11th to the 20th, and the 21st to the last day of such month, all dates inclusive.

F. Transferable Credit

Article 48

Transferable Credit

a. A transferable Credit is a Credit under which the Beneficiary (First Beneficiary) may request the bank authorized to pay, incur a deferred payment undertaking, accept or negotiate (the "Transferring Bank"), or in the case of a freely negotiable Credit, the bank specifically authorized in the Credit as a Transferring Bank, to make the Credit available in whole or in part to one or more other Beneficiary(ies) (Second Beneficiary(ies)).

b. A Credit can be transferred only if it is expressly designated as "transferable" by the Issuing Bank. Terms such as "divisible", "fractionable", "assignable", and "transmissible" do not render the Credit transferable. If such terms are used they shall be disregarded.

c. The Transferring Bank shall be under no obligation to effect such transfer except to the extent and in the manner expressly consented to by such bank.

d. At he time of making a request for transfer and prior to transfer of the Credit, the First Beneficiary must irrevocably instruct the Transferring Bank whether or not be retains the right to refuse to allow the Transferring Bank to advise amendments ot the Second Beneficiary(ies). If the Transferring Bank consents to the transfer under these conditions, it must, at the time of transfer, advise the Second Beneficiary(ies) of the First Beneficiary's instructions regarding amendments.

e. If a Credit is transferred to more than on Second Beneficiary(ies), refusal of an amendment by one or more Second Beneficiary(ies) does not invalidate the acceptance(s) by the other Second Beneficiary(ies) with respect to whom the credit will be amended accordingly. With respect to the Second Beneficiary(ies) who rejected the amendment, the Credit will remain unamended.

f. Transferring Bank charges in respect of transfers including commissions, fees, costs or expenses are payable by the First Beneficiary, unless otherwise agreed. If the Transferring Bank agrees to transfer the Credit it shall be under no obligation to effect the transfer until such charges are paid.

g. Unless otherwise stated in the Credit, a transferable Credit can be transferred once only. Consequently, the Credit cannot be transferred at the request of the Second Beneficiary to any subsequent Third Beneficiary. For the purpose of this Article, a retransfer to the First Beneficiary does not constitute a prohibited transfer.

Fractions of a transferable Credit (not exceeding in the aggregate the amount of the Credit) can be transferred separately, provided partial shipments/drawings are not prohibited, and the aggregate of such transfers will be considered as constituting only one transfer of the Credit.

h. The Credit can be transferred only on the terms and conditions specified in the original Credit, with the exception of:

—the amount of the Credit

—any unit price stated therein

—the expiry date

—the last date for presentation of documents in accordance with Article 43

—the period for shipment, any or all of which may be reduced or curtailed.

The percentage for which insurance cover must effected may be increased in such a way as to these provide the amount of cover stipulated in the original Credit, or Articles.

In addition, the name of the first Beneficiary can be substituted for that of the Applicant, but if the name of the Applicant is specifically required by the original Credit to appear in any document(s) other than the invoice, such requirement must be fulfilled.

i. The First Beneficiary has the right to substitute his own Invoice(s) (and Draft(s)) for those of the Second Beneficiary(ies), for amounts not in excess of the original amount stipulated in the Credit and for the original unit prices if stipulated in the Credit and upon such substitution of Invoice(s) (and Draft(s)) the First Beneficiary can draw under the Credit for the difference, if any, between his Invoice(s) and the Second Beneficiary's(ies) Invoice(s).

When a Credit has been transferred and the First Beneficiary is to supply his own Invoice (s) (and Draft(s)) in exchange for the Second Beneficiary's(ies) Invoice(s) (and Draft(s)) but fails to do so on first demand, the Transforeign Bank has the right to deliver to the Issuing Bank the documents received under the transferred Credit, including the Second Beneficiary's (ies') Invoice(s) (and Draft(s)) without further responsibility to the First Beneficiary.

j. The First Beneficiary may request that payment or negotiation be effected to the Second Beneficiary(ies) at the place to which the Credit has been transferred up to and including the expiry date of the Credit, unless the original Credit expressly states that it may not be made available for payment or negotiation at a place other than that stipulated in the Credit. This is without prejudice to the First Beneficiary's right to substitute subsequently his own Invoice(s) (and Draft(s)) for those of the Second Beneficiary(ies) and to claim any difference due to him.

G. Assignment of Proceeds

Article 49

Assignment of Proceeds

The fact that a Credit is not stated to be transferable shall not affect the Beneficiary's right to assign any proceeds to which he may be, or may become, entitled under such Credit, in accordance with the provisions of the applicable law. This Article relates only to the assignment of proceeds and not to the assignment of the right to perform under the Credit itself.

Uniform Rules for Collections
(ICC Publication No. 522)

A. General Provisions and Definition

Article 1

Application of URC 522

a. The Uniform Rules for Collections, 1995 Revision, ICC Publication No. 522, shall apply to all collections as defined in Article 2 where such rules are incorporated into the text of the 《Collection Instruction》referred to in Article 4 and are binding on all parties thereto unless otherwise expressly agreed or contrary to the provisions of a national, state or local law and/or regulation which cannot be departed from.

b. Bank shall have no obligation to handle either a collection or any collection instruction or subsequent related instructions.

c. If a bank elects, for any reason, not to handle a collection or any related instructions received by it, it must advise the party from whom it received the collection or the instructions by telecommunication or, if that is not possible, by other expeditious means, without delay.

Article 2

Definition of Collection

For the purposes of these Articles:

a. "Collection" means the handling by banks of documents as defined in sub-Article 2 (b), in accordance with instructions received, in order to:

i. obtain payment and/or acceptance.

or

iii. deliver documents against payment and/or against acceptance,

or

iii. deliver documents on other terms and conditions.

b. "Documents" financial documents and/or commercial documents :

i. "Financial Documents" means bills of exchange, promissory notes, cheques, or other similar instruments used for obtaining the payment of money ;

ii. "Commercial Documents" means invoices, transport documents, documents of title of other similar documents, or any other documents whatsoever, not being financial documents.

c. "Clean Collection" means collection of financial documents not accompanied by commercial documents.

d. "Documentary Collection" means collection of:

i. financial documents accompanied by commercial documents;

ii. commercial documents not accompanied by financial documents.

Article 3

Parties to a Collection

a. For the purposes of these Articles the "Parties Thereto" are:

i. the "Principal" who is the party entrusting the handling of a collection to a bank;

ii. the "Remitting Bank" which is the bank to which the principal has entrusted the handling of a collection ;

iii. the "Collecting Bank" which is any bank, other than the remitting bank, involved in processing the collection ;

iv. the "Presenting Bank" which is the collecting bank making presentation to the drawee.

b. The "Drawee" is the one to whom presentation is to be made in accordance with the collection instruction.

B.Form and Structure of Collections

Article 4

Collection Instruction

a. i. All documents sent for collection must the accompanied by a collection instruction indicating that the collection is subject to URC 522 and giving complete and precise instructions. Bank are only permitted to act upon the instructions given in such collection instruction, and in accordance with these Rules.

ii. Banks will not examine documents in order to obtain instructions.

iii. Unless otherwise authorized in the collection instruction, banks will disregard any instructions from any party/bank other than the party/bank—from whom they received the collection

b. A collection instruction should contain the following items of information, as appropriate.

i. Details of the bank from which the collection was received including full name. postal and SWIFT addresses, telex, telephone, facsimile numbers and reference.

ii. Details of the principal including full name, postal address, and if applicable telex, telephone and facsimile numbers.

iii. Details of drawee including full name, postal address, or the domicile at which presentation is to be made and if applicable telex, telephone, and facsimile numbers.

iv. Details of the presenting bank, if any, including full name, postal address and if applicable telex, telephone and facsimile numbers

v. Amount(s) and currency(ies) to be collected.

vi. List of documents enclosed and the numerical count of each document

vii. a. Terms and conditions upon which payment and/or acceptance is to obtained

b. Terms of delivery of documents against :

1) payment and/or acceptance

2) other terms and conditions

It is the responsibility of the Party preparing the collection instruction to ensure that the terms for the delivery documents are clearly and unambiguously stated, otherwise banks will not be responsible for any consequences arising therefrom.

viii Charges to be collected, indicating whether they may be waived or not

ix. Interest to be collected if applicable, indicating whether it may be waived or not including:

a. rate of interest

b. interest period

c. basis of calculation(for example 360 or 365 days in a year) as applicable

x. Method of payment and form of payment advice

xi. Instructions in case of non-payment, non-acceptance and/or non-compliance with other instructions

c i. Collection instructions should bear the complete address of the drawee or of the domicile at which the presentation is to be made, if the address is incomplete or incorrect, the collecting bank may, without any liability and responsibility on its part, endeavor to ascertain the proper address.

ii. The collecting bank will not be liable or responsible for any ensuing delay as a result of incomplete/incorrect address being provided.

C. Form of Presentation

Article 5

Presentation

a. For the purposes of these Articles, presentation is the procedure whereby the presenting bank makes the documents available to the drawee as instructed.

b. The collection instruction should state the exact period of time within which any action is to be taken by the drawee.

Expressions such as " first", "prompt", "immediate", and the like should not be used in connection with presentation or with reference to any period of time within which documents have to be taken up or for any other action that is to be taken by the drawee. If such terms are used banks will disregard them.

c. Documents are to be presented to the drawee in the form in which they are received, except that banks are authorized to affix any necessary stamps, at the expense of the party from whom they received the collection unless otherwise instructed, and to make any necessary endorsements or place any rubber stamps or other identifying marks or symbols customary to or required for the collection operation.

d. For the purpose of giving effect to the instructions of the principal, the remitting bank will utilize the bank nominated by the principal as the collecting bank. In the absence of such nomination, the remitting bank will utilize any bank of its own, or another bank's choice in the country of payment or acceptance or in.-the country where other terms and conditions have to be complied with.

e. The documents and collection instruction may be sent directly by the remitting bank to the collecting bank or through another bank as intermediary.

f. If the remitting bank does not nominate a specific presenting bank, the collecting bank may utilize a presenting bank of its choice.

Article 6

Sight/Acceptance

In the case of documents payable at sight the presenting bank must make presentation for payment without delay. In the case of documents payable at a tenor other than sight the presenting bank must, where acceptance is called for, make presentation for payment not later than the appropriate maturity date.

Article 7

Release of Commercial Documents

Documents Against Acceptance (D/A) vs.Documents Against Payment (D /P)

a. Collections should not contain bills of exchange payable at a future date with instructions that commercial documents are to be delivered against payment.

b. If a collection contains a bill of exchange payable at a future date, the collection instruction should state whether the commercial documents are to be released to the drawee against acceptance (D/A) or against payment (D/P)

In the absence of such statement commercial documents will be released only against payment and the collecting bank will not be responsible for any consequences arising out of any delay in the delivery of documents.

c. If a collection contains a bill of exchange payable at a future date and the collection instruction indicates that commercial documents are to be released against payment, documents will be released only against such payment and the collecting bank will not be responsible for any consequences arising out of any delay in the delivery of documents.

Article 8

Creation of Documents

Where the remitting bank instructs that either the collecting bank or the drawee is to create documents (bills of exchange, promissory notes, trust receipts, letters of undertaking or other documents) that were not included in the collection, the form and wording of such documents shall be provided by the remitting bank, otherwise the collecting bank shall not be liable or responsible for the form and wording of any such document provided by the collecting bank and/ or the drawee.

D. Liabilities and Responsibilities

Article 9

Good Faith and Reasonable Care

Banks will act in good faith and exercise reasonable care.

Article 10

Documents vs. Goods/Services/ Performances

a. Goods should not be despatched directly to the address of a Bank or consigned to or to the order of a bank without prior agreement on the part of that bank.

Nevertheless, in the event that goods are dispatched directly to the address of a bank or consigned to or to the order of a bank for release to a drawee against payment or acceptance or upon other terms and conditions without prior agreement on the part of that bank, such bank shall have no obligation to take delivery of the goods, which remain at the risk and responsibility of the party despatching the goods.

b. Banks have no obligation to take any action in respect of the goods to which a documentary collection relates, including storage and insurance of the goods even when specific instructions are given to do so. Banks will only take such action if, when, and to the extentthat they agree to do so in each case. Not withstanding the provisions of sub-Article 1 (c), this rule applies even in the absence of any specific advice to this effect by the collecting bank.

c. Nevertheless, in the case that banks take action for the protection of the goods, whether instructed or not, they assume no liability or responsibility with regard to the fate and/or condition of the goods and/or for any acts and/or omissions on the part of any third parties entrusted with the custody and/or protection of the goods. However, the collecting bank must advice without delay the bank from which the collection instruction was received of any such action taken.

d. Any charges and/or expenses incurred by banks in connection with any action taken to protect the goods will be for the account of the party from whom they received the collection.

e. i. Notwithstanding the provisions of sub-Article 10 (a), where the goods are consigned to or to the order of the collection bank and the drawee has honored the collection by payment, acceptance or other terms and conditions, and the collection bank arranges for the release of the goods, the remitting bank shall be deemed to have authorized the collecting bank to do so.

ii. Where a collecting bank on the instructions of the remitting bank or in terms of sub-Article 10 (e) i, arranges for the release of the goods, the remitting bank shall indemnify such collecting bank for all damages and expenses incurred.

Article 11

Disclaimer for Acts of an Instructed Party

a. Banks utilizing the services of another bank or other banks for the purpose of giving effect to the instructions of the principal do so for the account and at the risk of such principal.

b. Banks assume no liability or responsibility should the in structions they transmit not be carried out, even if they have themselves taken the initiative in the choice of such other bank(s).

c. A party instructing another party to perform services shall be bound by and liable to indemnify the instructed party against all obligations and responsibilities imposed by foreign laws and usages.

Article 12

Disclaimer on Documents Received

a. Banks must determine that the documents received appear to be as listed in the collection instruction and must advise by telecommunication or, if that is not possible, by other expeditious means, without delay, the party from whom the collection instruction was received of any documents missing, or found to be other than listed.

Banks have no further obligation in this respect.

b. If the documents do not appear to be listed, the remitting bank shall be precluded from disputing the type and number of documents received by the collecting bank.

c. Subject to sub-Article 5(c) and sub-Articles 12(a) and 12 (b) above, banks without present documents as received without further examination.

Article 13

Disclaimer on Effectiveness of Documents

Banks assume no liability or responsibility for the form, Sufficiency, accuracy, genuineness, falsification or legal effect of any document(s), or for the general and/or particular conditions stipulated in the document(s) or superimposed thereon; nor do they assume any liability or responsibility for the description, quantity, weight, quality, condition, packing, delivery, value or existence of the goods represented by any document(s), or for the good faith or acts and/or omissions, solvency, performance or standing of the consignors, the carriers, the forwarders, the consignees or the insurers of the goods, or any other person whomsoever.

Article 14

Disclaimer on Delays, Loss in Transit and Translation

a. Banks assume no liability or responsibility for the consequences arising out of delay and/or loss in transit of any message(s), letter(s) or document(s), or for delay, mutilation or other error(s) arising in transmission of any Telecommunication or for error(s) in translation and/or interpretation of technical terms.

b. Banks will not be liable or responsible for any delays resulting from the need to obtain clarification of any instructions received.

Article 15

Force Major

Banks assume no liability or responsibility for consequences arising out of the interruption of their business by Acts of God, riots, civil commotions, insurrections, wars, or any other causes beyond their control or by strikes or lockouts.

E. Payment

Article 16

Payment Without Delay

a. Amounts collected (less charges and/or disbursements and/ or expenses where applicable) must be made available without delay to the party from whom the collection instruction was received in accordance with the terms and conditions of the collection instruction.

b. Notwithstanding the provisions of sub-Article 1 (c) and unless otherwise agreed, the collecting bank will effect payment of the amount collected in favour of the remitting bank only.

Article 17

Payment in Local Currency

In the case of documents payable in the currency of the country of payment (local currency), the presenting bank must, unless otherwise instructed in the collection instruction, release the documents to the drawee against payment in local currency only if such currency is immediately available for disposal in the manner specified in the collection instruction.

Article 18

Payment in Foreign Currency

In the case of documents payable in a currency other than that of the country of payment (foreign currency), the presenting bank must, unless otherwise instructed in the collection instruction, release the documents to the drawee against payment in the designated foreign currency only if such foreign currency can immediately be remitted in accordance with the instructions given in the collection instruction.

Article 19

Partial Payments

a. In respect of clean collections, partial payments may be accepted if and to the extent to which and on the conditions on which partial payments are authorised by the law in force in the place of payment. The financial document(s) will be released to the drawee only when full payment thereof has been received.

b. In respect of documentary collections, partial payments will only be accepted if specifically authorised in the collection instruction. However, unless otherwise instructed, the presenting bank will release the documents to the drawee only after full payment has been received, and the presenting bank will not be responsible for any consequences arising out of any delay in the delivery of documents.

c. In all cases partial payments will be accepted only subject to compliance with the provisions of either Article 17 or Article 18 as appropriate.

Partial payment, if accepted, will be dealt with in accordance with the provisions of Article 16.

F. Interest, Charges and Expenses

Article 20

Interest

a. If the collection instruction specifies that interest is to be collected and the drawee refuses to pay such interest, the presenting bank may deliver the document(s) against payment or acceptance or on other terms and conditions as the case may be, without collecting such interest, unless sub-Article 20(c) applies.

b. Where such interest is to be collected, the collection instruction must specify the rate of interest, interest period and basis of calculation.

c. Where the collection instruction expressly states that interest may not be waived and the drawee refuses to pay such interest the presenting bank will not deliver documents and will not be responsible for any consequences arising out of any delay in the delivery of document(s). When payment of interest has been refused, the presenting bank must inform by telecommunication or, if that is not possible, by other expeditious means without delay the bank from which the collection instruction was received.

Article 21

Charges and Expenses

a. If the collection instruction specifies that collection charges and/or expenses are to be for account of the drawee and the drawee refuses to pay them, the presenting bank may deliver the document(s) against payment or acceptance or on other terms and conditions as the case may be, without collecting charges and/or expenses, unless sub-Article 21 (b) applies.

Whenever collection charges and/or expenses are so waived they will be for the account of the party from whom the collection was received and may be deducted from the proceeds.

b. Where the collection instruction expressly states that charges and/or expenses may not be waived and the drawee refuses to pay such charges and/or expenses, the presenting bank will not deliver documents and will not be responsible for any consequences arising out of any delay in the delivery of the document(s). When payment of collection charges and/or expenses has been refused the presenting bank must inform by telecommunication or, if that is not possible, by other expeditious means without delay the bank from which the collection instruction was received.

c. In all cases where in the express terms of a collection instruction or under these Rules, disbursements and/or expenses and/or collection charges are to be borne by the principal, the collecting bank(s) shall be entitled to recover promptly outlays in respect of disbursements, expenses and charges from the bank from which the collection instruction was received, and the remitting bank shall be entitled to recover promptly from the principal any amount so paid out by it, together with it's own disbursements, expenses and charges, regardless of the fate 0f the collection.

d. Banks reserve the right to demand payment of charges and/or expenses in advance from the party from whom the collection instruction was received, to cover costs in attempting to carry out any instruction& and pending receipt of such payment also reserve the right not to carry out such instructions.

G. Other Provisions

Article 22

Acceptance

The presenting bank is responsible for seeing that the form of the acceptance of a bill of exchange appears to be complete and correct, but is not responsible for the genuineness of any signature or for the authority of any signatory to sign the acceptance.

Article 23

Promissory Notes and Other Instruments

The presenting bank is not responsible for the genuineness of any signature or for the authority of any signatory to sign a promissory note, receipt, or other instruments.

Article 24

Protest

The collection instruction should give specific instructions regarding protest (or other legal process in lieu thereof), in the event of non-payment or non-acceptance.

In the absence of such specific instructions, the banks concerned with the collection have no obligation to have the document(s) protested (or subjected to other legal process in lieu thereof) for nonpayment or non-acceptance.

Any charges and/or expenses incurred by banks in connection with such protest, or other legal process, will be for the account of the party from whom the collection instruction was received.

Article 25

Case-of-Need

If the principal nominates a representative to act as case-of-need in the event of non-payment and/or non-acceptance the collection instruction should clearly and full indicate the powers of such case-of-need. In the absence of such indication banks will not accept any instructions from the case-of-need.

Article 26

Advices

Collecting banks are to advise fate in accordance with the following rules:

a. Form of Advice

All advices or information from the collecting bank to the bank from which the collection instruction was received, must beer appropriate details including, in all cases, the latter bank's reference as stated in the collection instruction.

b. Method of Advice

It shall tae the responsibility of the remitting bank to instruct the collecting bank regarding the method by which the advices detailed in (c) i, (c) ii and (c) iii are to be given. In the absence of such instructions, the collecting bank will send the relative advices by the method of its choice at the expense of the bank from which the collection instruction was received.

c. i. Advice of Payment

The collecting bank must send without delay advice of payment to, the bank from which the collection instruction was received, detailing the amount or amounts collected, charges and/or disbursements and/or expenses deducted, where appropriate, and method of disposal of the funds.

ii. Advice of Acceptance

The collecting bank must send without delay advice of acceptance to the bank from which the collection instruction was received.

iii. Advice of Non-payment and/or Non-acceptance

The presenting bank should endeavor to ascertain the reasons for non-payment and/or non-acceptance and advise accordingly, without delay, the bank from which it received the collection instruction.

The presenting bank must send without delay advice of nonpayment and/or advice of non-acceptance to the bank from which it received the collection instruction.

On receipt of such advice the remitting bank must give appropriate instructions as to the further handling of the documents. If such instructions are not received by the presenting bank within 60 days after its advice of non-payment and/or non-acceptance, the documents may be returned to the bank from which the collection instruction was received without any further responsibility on the part of the presenting bank.

References

1. 朱意秋. 国际贸易结算新编(英汉对照). 青岛：青岛海洋大学出版社，2001.
2. Edward G. Hinkelman. *International Payments*. 上海：上海外语教育出版社，2000.
3. 刘启萍等. 外贸英文制单. 北京：对外贸易大学出版社，1999.
4. 贺瑛. 金融专业英语证书考试指南——国际结算. 上海：上海财经大学出版社，1996.
5. 周振邦. 实用国际贸易. 青岛：青岛海洋大学出版社，1998.
6. 贺瑛，漆腊应主编. 国际结算. 北京：中国金融出版社，1997.
7. 庞红、尹继红、沈瑞年. 国际结算(第四版). 北京：中国人民大学出版社，2012.
8. 蒋琴儿，秦定. 国际结算：理论·实务·案例(双语教材). 北京：清华大学出版社，2007.
9. 许南，张雅. 国际结算(英文版). 北京：中国人民大学出版社，2013.
10. 岳华，杨来科. 国际结算双语教程. 上海：立信会计出版社，2007.
11. 纪洪天. 外贸财务会计及国际结算(英汉双语教材). 上海：立信会计出版社，2011.
12. 杨娟. 国际经济与贸易精品教材：国际结算(双语教材). 北京：北京师范大学出版社，2012.